Urban Sanctuaries

With special thanks to our advisors:
Chad
Dinesha
Felicia
Izzy
Johnny
Manuel
Marvin
Peggie

Urban

Neighborhood Organizations in the

Sanctuaries

Lives and Futures of Inner-City Youth

Milbrey W. McLaughlin,
Merita A. Irby, Juliet Langman

FOREWORD BY JOHN W. GARDNER

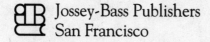 Jossey-Bass Publishers
San Francisco

Substantial discounts on bulk quantities of Jossey-Bass books are available to corporations, professional associations, and other organizations. For details and discount information, contact the special sales department at Jossey-Bass Inc., Publishers. (415) 433–1740; Fax (415) 433–0499.

Manufactured in the United States of America on Lyons Falls Pathfinder Tradebook. This paper is acid-free and 100 percent totally chlorine-free.

Library of Congress Cataloging-in-Publication Data

McLaughlin, Milbrey W.
    Urban sanctuaries : neighborhood organizations in the lives and futures of inner-city youth / Milbrey W. McLaughlin, Merita A. Irby, Juliet Langman. — 1st ed.
    p. cm. — (Jossey-Bass social and behavioral science series)
    Includes bibliographical references and index.
    ISBN 1-55542-599-2
    1. Urban youth—United States.   2. Youth centers—United States.
3. Inner cities—United States.   4. Self-esteem in adolescence—
United States.   5. Social work with youth—United States.
I. Irby, Merita A.   II. Langman, Juliet.   III. Title.   IV. Series.
HQ796.M385   1994
305.23′5—dc20
                              93-40706
                              CIP

FIRST EDITION
HB Printing   10 9 8 7 6 5 4 3 2   Code 9406

Contents

Foreword

This book is a beam of light in the dark world of inner-city youth, and as beams of light often do, it shows the way. Discouraged observers of our troubled times may sigh with relief to discover that *somewhere, someone* is doing *something* right. More experienced observers know that such good things do happen and will be glad to see them publicized.

The disintegration of community and of the sense of community that is so evident throughout U.S. society (and the world) is an even more spectacular reality in the inner city. Too many young persons go from families that are not families to schools that are not communities to streets that offer a deadly mix of drugs and violence.

Like everyone else, young people need community. If they cannot find it in conventional settings, gangs offer a grim alternative.

The authors of *Urban Sanctuaries* introduce us to community builders who address themselves to precisely that need. They create environments in which people care and in which worth is assumed and individuals valued; environments in which the young person has an identity, a role, and pride in membership; and family-like environments in which youth find the protection and security we all need. The youthful members of the communities established by these builders share a sense of responsibility and purpose. They support one another. They have trust.

One could easily make the mistake of thinking that meeting young people's need for a community is a fairly common occurrence, but it is all too rare. There are large numbers of people whose task it is to serve the needs of youth, but most are delivering specialized services. Delivery of services is not enough.

Someone has to build community, and as everyone knows, community is built on shared values.

Absence of instruction in values is the least of our problems. What is a problem is that the values taught may be destructive. The young person is bombarded by value instruction, for good or evil, every waking hour—at home and in school, in Sunday school and at the movies. The playground teaches. The street corner teaches. Television teaches.

The instruction is vivid, disorderly, and incessant, teaching good lessons and bad, by precept and example, through children's games and unlawful transactions, in an all-out assault on mind and heart. No one escapes. Banish from your thoughts any picture of value instruction that shows an older mentor quietly educating a child in the rules of behavior. The environment teaches—insistently and in many voices. Where family and community have disintegrated, the likelihood of good lessons is minimal.

And therein lies the problem. Both family and community have suffered devastating blows in modern society, and to be blunt about it, neither will ever be wholly reinstated in its old form. Those of us concerned for youth have focused heavily on the schools and have paid all too little attention to what happens after school. Yet that is a time of particular danger. That is when much of the trouble occurs.

In describing the work of a handful of particularly gifted community builders, the authors of *Urban Sanctuaries* underscore some basic realities. One such reality is the importance and vitality of youth activities that are firmly rooted in the local community and shaped by local knowledge. The community builders know their locality—the streets, the neighborhood, the threats, and the opportunities. They do not apply a formula written in some distant planning office. What they achieve grows organically out of local soil.

Another reality is that young people (like all the rest of us!) become more deeply involved in and committed to the activities in which they have a shaping role. It is not just that these activities serve *youth's* needs rather than some outside planner's perceptions, but that the young people who are allowed to shape their own activities are no longer being put in the position of "problems" to be "dealt with." Instead, they are drawn in and celebrated as participants and contributors.

The sense of personal control engendered in youth by their participation is another reality and an important ingredient in the discipline and respect for rules that are evident in the endeavors described in this book. Indeed, these endeavors cast discipline in a wholly new light; discipline becomes something young people impose on themselves in the interest of their shared purposes. It grows out of their respect for one another, their commitment to shared norms, their sense of responsibility to the group. It is the healthy discipline of a vital community.

The young people described in this book *want* to work hard in some challenging and worthwhile activity. They *want* to be seen as respected and trusted contributors to the common venture. They *want* to be valued members of society.

It is all very encouraging, but these programs and others like them need additional funding. Spreading them to other settings also calls for funding. Governments—federal, state, and local—and private philanthropy are the normal funding sources, but these sources operate in the climate created by public attitudes. And these attitudes leave much to be desired. In many subtle ways, more fortunate citizens distance themselves from the besieged young people of the inner city, viewing them as instances of social pathology, as problems to be treated.

One of the triumphs of this book is that it puts inner-city youth back into human form and demonstrates that, though they live with incomparably greater risks, they are remarkably like us. They need a sense of community, and they are willing to do their share of community building. They want to be respected, and they are willing to work for it. They are glad to live by the rules if there is fairness and trust. They want a haven of security in a violent world—as do all of us.

Make no mistake about it; we have before us the task of healing a deeply troubled society. We shall never make it unless we reinstate our sense of responsibility for one another. We cannot write off the inner city. It will fester and the consequences, already violent, will become more so. These young people are our responsibility.

The programs described in this book are not exceptionally expensive. Yet they can supply priceless resources, the things money cannot buy—hope, spirit, and a commitment to worthy social goals. We should be eager supporters.

Stanford, California   John W. Gardner
January 1994   Former Secretary of
U.S. Department of Health,
Education, and Welfare
and Founder of Common Cause

Preface

"Just to live, to duck the bullet," in the words of one youth worker, is the daily goal of numerous youth in U.S. inner cities. For many of these youth the seemingly simple task of making it through adolescence is a challenge. For them success comes from surviving the everyday urban threats—the figurative and literal bullets of drugs, violence, crime, pregnancy, abuse, and neglect. In the inner-city environment of pain and despair, what future will these young people find? How can they duck the bullets that are aimed at them daily?

Motivated by our observation that some young people from the turbulent and violent neighborhoods—or 'hoods as the youth call them—of U.S. inner cities do move through adolescence to become contributing community members, responsible parents, and productive participants in mainstream institutions, we undertook the research on which this book is based. We hoped to understand what it was that made a vast difference in the lives of certain inner-city youth whom we came to call the hopefuls. These young people were exceptions to the grim statistical descriptions of urban youth, portraits sketched in terms of escalating rates of teen pregnancy, school failure, adolescent violence, and substance abuse. The hopefuls' experiences and sense that a positive future was possible made us ask: What do these young people have in common? What is the source of their hope? Who helps them to find that hope? As expressed in the title of this book, Where can they, and we, find urban sanctuaries?

Background of the Book

The five-year research project of which *Urban Sanctuaries* is one result involved many people. In 1987, Shirley Brice Heath and Milbrey W. McLaughlin, supported by a grant from the Spencer Foundation, set about trying to identify the role of neighborhood organizations in the lives of urban youth, relying greatly upon the direct contributions to the research of numerous inner-city youth who participated in neighborhood organizations. Merita A. Irby and Juliet Langman, coauthors of this book, joined the project as senior research associates and assumed major responsibility for carrying out the field research. McLaughlin, Irby, and Langman collaborated fully in the preparation of this book, sharing responsibilities for conceptualizing, writing, rewriting, and reviewing.

What the young hopefuls whom we met had in common was involvement in some kind of neighborhood organization—a youth group, sports team, arts program, or other activity—that engaged their time, attention, and commitment. These neighborhood-based organizations were especially important in the lives of the hopefuls because they provided not only more but different resources to inner-city youngsters whose needs far exceeded the meager resources or opportunities of their families or schools.

We selected three urban areas in which to pursue our questions about the value of neighborhood-based organizations for inner-city youth—cities that are referred to by pseudonyms in this book: River City in the Northeast, Lakeside in the Midwest, and Big Valley in the Southwest. These cities, with their different demographics, economies, and social histories, offered us an opportunity to explore the significance of ethnicity for neighborhood organizations and other community youth resources. We also had reason to believe that we would find effective neighborhood-based organizations and activities in these communities since each had a reputation for community spirit, social concern, collaboration among diverse policy groups, and philanthropic involvement.

Our research relies on ethnographic methods of interview, observation, and situated perspective or view located in the everyday realities of the individuals and organizations participating in the study. We focused on organizations judged successful by local youth themselves, not necessarily by criteria defined and imposed by outsiders. We took youth and youth advocates to be the experts about the types of organizations, activities, and programs that "worked" and about the features that made a neighborhood organization successful.

Langman lived in River City for more than two years, getting to know the diverse neighborhoods that make up the city, "mapping" the myriad organizations and resources available to youth, participating in and observing many River City neighborhood organizations, interviewing adults and youth, and training and supervising local young people—our "junior ethnographers"—who collected data for the project. Irby split her time over a three-year period between Lakeside and Big Valley and spent that time in much the same way—getting to know the communities, finding her way around youth policies and politics, and spending extended periods of time "hanging out" in organizations youth found successful. Irby also managed the activities of junior ethnographers in both sites.

The junior ethnographers, young people from each of the neighborhood organizations we wanted to understand, were key to our research. They interviewed other youth to gather their views about the community, the organization, their involvement in the activity, and their sense of a future. They interviewed adults about the neighborhood's positive and negative aspects, the ways in which things had changed since the adults first moved there, and the adults' perspectives on young people growing up in the area today. The junior ethnographers taped their interviews, and provided us with written abstracts of the key issues raised by each interview. These young people gave us access to youth perspectives, to activities, and to neighborhood respondents that otherwise would have been closed to us. The junior ethnographers also recorded planning sessions, peer discussions, and other conversations to which they alone had access, and they negotiated entrance for us with youth and adults suspicious of European Americans, especially middle-aged university professors.

In the five years of field work undertaken for this project, we spent extended time in more than sixty neighborhood-based organizations, which together counted more than 24,000 youth as members. Irby and Langman, together with Heath and McLaughlin when possible, attended performances and meetings, observed daily activities, and generally hung around the organizations and activities that engaged youth. We also interviewed members of the community—social, religious, and political leaders; philanthropists; and officials of agencies such as local United Ways and city parks and recreation departments to ask about policies and priorities for youth and the resources allocated to youth. In the course of our research, we collected volumes of record information from the communities and organizations with which we were involved. These newspaper accounts, project evaluations, planning materials, published histories, agency background documents, organizational mission statements, program materials, and the like fill more than five filing drawers and provide important background for this book.

To honor the confidentiality promised respondents and organizations, we use pseudonyms not only for the names of cities but also for the organizations and individuals who participated in our research. We use actual names when we draw from published material or general information for general analytical points. In some instances we have modified details of identity to protect sites and individuals. Photographs used throughout the book are from across the nation and are not necessarily related to our research sites.

The young people we feature in this book are composite portraits based on youth we met and got to know in the course of our research. We constructed these composites to be typical of an organization and a neighborhood. Our descriptions and representations of the adults who lead the six successful youth organizations on which we focus, however, are based on these adults' actual life histories and experience. The leader of each organization described here has reviewed our manuscript, provided comment, and concurred with our representations of him or her, the community context, the organization, and the participating youth.

Overview of the Contents

Urban Sanctuaries is about the ways in which environments that nurture and engage inner-city youth are imagined, created, and sustained. It attempts to describe what makes certain neighborhood organizations places of hope, resources that enable inner-city youth to survive and supersede the harsh realities of everyday urban America.

Chapter One introduces the problem and a challenge to society that is nothing less than to change despair into hope. This chapter contrasts the grim views and accepted predictions about young people who live in violent and troubled inner cities with the sense of hopeful future expressed by youth who have found their way to neighborhood organizations that engage their interest, time, and commitment.

Chapter Two introduces the hopefuls, six young people who are representative of the youth involved with urban sanctuaries and their neighborhoods. The hopefuls describe what it is like to grow up in their neighborhoods; each tells how and why a local organization has made a positive difference in his or her life.

In Chapters Three, Four, and Five, we introduce the adults who lead the organizations that attract and enable the hopefuls, and we examine these leaders' missions, ideas, and motivations. We call these individuals wizards, because they have succeeded where so many have not. They have created environments that draw adolescents, that demand and receive the commitment, energy, and hard work of youth. They reach, motivate, and promote young people, sometimes including gang members, whom many dismiss as unreachable, irredeemable, or hopeless.

We distinguish two breeds of wizards: insiders, who can usefully trade on their local connections and knowledge, and outsiders, who can usefully profit from connections and resources external to the inner-city neighborhood. Chapter Three examines the three insiders, Chapter Four the three outsiders, and Chapter Five considers what all these wizards, leaders of quite different programs or organizations, share in common. What makes them wizards? Why are they successful? What we found in each of the six was a love for youth, a commitment to serve them, a strong sense of mission, and a passion for some particular set of activities. In short, the genius and success of these leaders lies less in *what* they do than in *how* they do it.

Chapters Six and Seven consider the wizards' assistants, the professional and junior staff that leaders must rely on to translate mission into practice and to create and sustain these sanctuaries on a daily basis. Chapter Six looks specifically at the role of staff in organizations successful in guiding inner-city youth to better futures and healthy adulthood. Chapter Seven treats one of the two problems wizards rate as most challenging to them and the effectiveness of their organizations: recruiting and retaining staff who can work successfully with inner-city youth and the kinds of organizations they need.

Meeting the needs of youth in urban sanctuaries demands more resources, hearts, and hands than even talented wizards and staff can muster. Successful youth leaders look to volunteers for extra resources, time, and talent. Chapter Eight describes both the critical role of volunteered assets and the considerable costs often associated with them. Attracting and managing volunteers are critical pieces of wizardry.

Finding and sustaining resources to support youth organizations is the second of the two greatest problems leaders say they face in achieving their visions. Chapters Nine and Ten describe the different challenges and opportunities youth organization wizards confront in Big Valley, River City, and Lakeside. Each city differs in terms of available resources, competing demands for those resources, and traditions of support for urban youth and youth organizations. Further, youth leaders drawn from inside a neighborhood have different channels of access and knowledge than do leaders from the outside. Each wizard has defined his or her own strategy for negotiating local political, social, and economic resources. Moreover, even highly successful youth organizations are fragile and dependent on support from outside as well. Managing the complex setting outside the youth organization is a never-finished and often frustrating job, one that can threaten a leader's ability to craft a program that genuinely fits the needs of neighborhood youth. The wizards invest as much time and energy in negotiating with the external environment upon which they depend as they do in creating sanctuaries for youth. As these chapters show, energy invested in the larger community ultimately enables the wizards to carry out their organizational visions for inner-city youth and to moderate these youth's isolation.

Chapter Eleven presents myths and realities about inner-city youth and describes our conclusions about these young people and the organizations that provide them hope. We challenge the myths about inner-city youth with our evidence from the hopefuls themselves and the sanctuaries in their communities.

Audience

This book is intended for policymakers, educators, foundation officers, and anyone else who wants to learn what makes an effective youth organization and what that organization can contribute to the development and hope of inner-city youth. We aim to show what it takes to turn despair into hope and to create environments that treat inner-city youth as resources to be encouraged instead of problems to be managed. *Urban Sanctuaries* is about this nation's social compact with its youth; it is also a broad-based call to action based on that compact.

Acknowledgments

The Spencer Foundation provided resources to support our project, "Language, Socialization, and Neighborhood-Based Organizations: Moving Beyond Dependency on School and Family," through a grant to Shirley Brice Heath and Milbrey W. McLaughlin. Individuals at the Spencer Foundation provided moral support and encouragement as well. Marian Valdet and Linda Fitzgerald enabled us to do what we needed to do, as our research needs shifted and plans changed. The late Lawrence Cremin was an early and enthusiastic supporter of our interest in neighborhood youth organizations, believing as we did that many important educational experiences take place outside school in community organizations. The Rockefeller Foundation provided McLaughlin a rare occasion for reflection and uninterrupted writing at the idyllic Villa Serbelloni in Bellagio, Italy.

Many individuals have been important to the conceptualization, conduct, and understanding of this project. John W. Gardner listened with close interest to our stories of neighborhood-based organizations, asked hard questions about them, and encouraged us to communicate the lessons of the youth and organizations we had studied to policymakers, foundation officials, and others responsible for shaping the environment in which youth grow up and move. Michael Kirst enabled Heath and McLaughlin to take a close look at collaborative services for youth and at innovative policy arrangements, and introduced us to the myriad policy frames that touch the lives of young people. Jane Quinn and members of the Carnegie Corporation Task Force on Youth Development and Community Programs, through McLaughlin's membership on the task force, were an ongoing source of ideas, fugitive resources, and challenging insight. Elizabeth M. Davis read and commented on a draft of this manuscript, making untold numbers of suggestions that clarified prose, sharpened ideas, or generally made for more readable text. Her good sense, care for the topic, and editorial intelligence are reflected throughout. Elspeth MacHattie, developmental editor for Jossey-Bass, further improved our text, providing missing transitions, rearranging narrative, and transforming manuscript into a book. Our colleague Shirley Brice Heath has read many drafts of this manuscript and participated actively in countless discussions about what to tell and how to tell it. She has made critical contributions to this project at every step.

Ali Calicoatte and Steven Balt assisted in the collection of data and immersed themselves for stretches of time in several of the youth organizations. Transcribing field notes and cataloguing audio tapes, record data, and other project artifacts was an immense undertaking; we owe an enormous debt to Melissa Groo and Carol Smith for managing all of these details and for contributing important insights gained from their hundreds of hours of listening to the voices of young people and adults describing their thoughts and feelings about their organizations and communities. Jeffrey Lox developed a computer program to manage the language data and provided other computerized organizational assistance. Julie Cummer, administrative assistant for the project, helped us tally and explain expenditures odd in the Stanford University context, such as pizzas, cartons of soda, cake, and ice cream, and kept her eye on the bottom line as we moved among cities, organizations, constituencies, and forms of transportation. We are also grateful to Ben McLaughlin for his continuing insight and comment on the lives of youth.

None of this would have been possible, of course, without the cooperation, interest, and candor of the youth and adults who spent days and weeks with us over the years of this research project. In particular, the generosity of the organizational leaders who participated in our research is impossible to capture. They invited us into their organizations, their homes, and their neighborhood events, and involved us in their visions. Their investment in our project reflects their commitment to inner-city youth as valued resources and their mission to create places of hope for more than just a few of these youth. Our debt, and society's debt, to these talented individuals is enormous.

Stanford, California   Milbrey W. McLaughlin
January 1994   Merita A. Irby
                                               Juliet Langman

The Authors

Milbrey W. McLaughlin is professor of education and public policy and director of the Center for Research on the Contexts of Teaching at Stanford University. She received her B.A. degree (1963) from Connecticut College in philosophy and her M.Ed. and Ed.D. degrees (1973) from Harvard University in education and social policy. McLaughlin's primary research activities have been in the areas of policy implementation, educational change, school contexts, and community-based organizations for youth. Her books include *The Contexts of Teaching in Secondary Schools* (1990, with J. Talbert and N. Bascia), *Steady Work* (1989, with R. Elmore), and *Teacher Evaluation: Improvement, Accountability, and Effective Learning* (1989, with R. S. Pfeifer). She is an editor of other recent publications, including *Teaching for Understanding* (1993, with D. K. Cohen and J. E. Talbert), *Teachers' Work* (1993, with J. W. Little), and *Identity and Inner-City Youth* (1993, with S. B. Heath). Prior to joining the Stanford faculty, McLaughlin was a policy analyst with the Rand Corporation. At Rand, she conducted, with Paul Berman, the Change Agent study and coauthored the multivolume *Federal Programs Affecting Educational Change* (1974–1978).

Merita A. Irby received her B.A. degree from Wheaton College in English literature and her M.P.P. degree (1993) from the John F. Kennedy School of Government at Harvard University in urban social policy. Her interests focus on institutional equity issues in the urban centers of the United States as well as in international contexts. Her special concern for youth policy developed while teaching in U.S. inner-city neighborhoods as well as in Central America.

Juliet Langman is a visiting assistant professor at the Linguistics Institute, National Academy of Sciences, Budapest, Hungary. She received her B.S. degree (1980) from Georgetown University in language and linguistics, her M.A. degree (1987) from Stanford University in linguistics, and her Ph.D. degree (1989) from Stanford University in language, literacy, and culture. Her research interests center on the role of ethnic and community organizations in the development of individual and group identity. Her work also explores the manner in which voluntary organizations affect social and educational policy for minority youth both in and out of school. She has studied Yugoslav guest workers in the Netherlands, as well as European American and African American minority groups in U.S. urban areas.

Urban Sanctuaries

Chapter One

Neighborhood Organizations: Places of Hope in the Inner City

What would it mean to live
in a city whose people were changing
each other's despair into hope?
What would it mean to stand on the first
page of the end of despair?

—*Adrienne Rich*

Americans looking at the young people who live in U.S. inner cities are often overwhelmed by feelings of futility, desperation, and anger. Educated primarily by newspapers' chronicles of inner-city desperation, television's snapshots of the fury and loneliness in urban ghettos, and Hollywood's movies of gangs and life in the "'hood," many Americans of all ethnic and economic groups have concluded that little can be done to alter the bleak future of inner-city adolescents.

A frightening number of inner-city youth share this hopeless view of their future, and their voices of despair embody the inner city for many who live both inside and outside its confines: "You don't plan your future; you just take it as it comes. Life's a constant struggle 'cuz you can't count on anything. You don't know for sure what's even gonna happen the next day. You could get shot walkin' down the street."

"You get more respect for carryin' a Uzi than for going to school. Ain't nobody gonna cheer you on with 'I hope you do well, go to college.'"

"Lyin' by, gettin' high, drinkin' beer, smokin' weed, lyin'! Yeah, boy, that's our future. The future be dead."[1]

These voices that despair of their futures, these signs of social and moral decay, no longer startle or surprise many Americans when they too have lost hope in inner-city youth. When they hear that, by some estimates, more than one-quarter of U.S. young people confront a "serious" risk of never reaching productive maturity, and another one-quarter are at "moderate" risk.[2] When they hear that between 60 percent and 80 percent of the young people judged "seriously at risk" live in this nation's inner cities and are unlikely to achieve healthy, constructive adulthood.[3]

Yet, despite all the somber evidence of despair, there are voices of hope—hope among some special adults working in organizations that support inner-city youth and, most importantly, hope among youth themselves: "[People in the organization] push me to stay in there and work harder. They know I can go all the way. I know I can go all the way. It's just a choice of me doin' it. I'm gonna get there."

"I've decided in my mind that I can match anybody. . . . If you're smart and everything, or you're tryin' to make somethin' out of yourself and you live in the projects, that's good. . . . Because then you can encourage other people who live in other bad neighborhoods."

"The [youth organization] is an opportunity to become something. The people here, they'll help you become what you wanna become. They trust me. It makes me feel good. People here care, and I can become something."

In many respects the youth who speak of hope are no different from their desperate peers. Inner-city youth who believe they can have a good future are also products of violent streets, poverty, turbulent families, subpar and impersonal schools, and communities that seem to care little for their young people. Hopeful adolescents move in the same hellish vortex of gangs and drugs. They often get the same inadequate response from such "helping institutions" as their families, schools, local police, and social agencies. These youth are not "invulnerable" children, so called because they survive the precarious corridors of their environment against all odds.[4] Instead they have built hope through their participation in neighborhood-based organizations that offer inner-city teenagers support, guidance, safety, companionship, and engagement in ways they can accept.

Success Is Ducking the Bullet

This book is about six organizations that have given hope to inner-city adolescents. Most of these organizations are not listed in any formal collation of youth programs. To find them we defined organizational success differently from many other researchers. We interviewed, observed, hung around, and spent time with youth and grass-roots youth advocates in more than sixty youth organizations in three large metropolitan areas (the research methods are described in more detail in the Preface). We asked, What good things are happening for youth in the neighborhood or community? Where do teens go? Who is doing good stuff with youth? In other words, we looked for neighborhood-based organizations and activities youth themselves elected to join. We call these organizations successful in large part because inner-city youth themselves judge *respect* them highly and eagerly participate in them.

What we found was both inspiring and very different from the common picture of inner-city youth and organizations intended for them. We discovered that even though many organizations have apparently similar programs, most have few teenage participants. Many self-described youth organizations are often more effective with children and have difficulty retaining members once they become teenagers. However, the six organizations described in this book have not only attracted adolescents but also retained them. The difference is that the successful organizations' programs, activities, and missions are carried out in ways attuned to their adolescent members' values and goals. As described by youth and imagined by youth leaders, successful inner-city youth organizations look remarkably like the successful settlement houses of the late nineteenth century in their commitment to neighborhood, focus on the positive ("wellness"), multigenerational services, and ethnic sensitivity.[5] Moreover, in each successful organization, it is the vision, drive, and commitment of a single adult that makes much of the difference.

In youth's view these six organizations succeed by providing strong support for the youth's transition to adulthood. They enable adolescents to navigate the turbulent and often brutal avenues of their adolescence safely, and to move on to responsible futures as parents, wage earners, and community members. Sometimes these futures include graduating from college or playing with a prestigious athletic team, but mostly they are more ordinary futures, honorable and productive.

The hopeful youth we met live in inner cities where more than half of each entering high school class never graduates; where drug dealing and violence are commonplace; where young men, especially African Americans, face greatly increased odds of going to jail or dying by their late teens; and where having a baby changes the lives of female adolescents and often results in curtailing their choices before they have had a chance to test them. In this setting a primary measure of success is making it through adolescence without joining a gang or committing a crime, without having a baby, and without accumulating a crushing burden of failures in family life, school, and early employment. As one youth advocate in a successful organization puts it, the most important outcome for inner-city youth is ducking the bullet: "If they can be a doctor, great. But [their first need is] just to live, [to] duck the bullet, not just out of the gun but verbiage from their peers, a girl pregnant by sixteen, a man incarcerated by eighteen—that's the bullet."

Youth programs and interventions, or "treatments," are typically studied as program models, in isolation from the features we found meaningful to youth. Even studies that go beyond the program model approach rarely examine interactions between participants and particular aspects of a program's setting.[6] Instead, these interactions are treated as background phenomena (when they are considered at all), on the assumption that the treatment or program matters most and that a "robust" program will be independent of both its setting and its target (the youth themselves).

The question for all researchers in this field is, Did it work? But most researchers have defined "it" as a program. Looking for and not finding this specific model of success, practitioners, policymakers, and analysts have agreed that little factual is known about what makes an inner-city program work and about the role of neighborhood-based organizations in youth's development.[7] We questioned the assumption that what works has to be a particular program. Our research shows that a variety of neighborhood-based programs work as long as there is an *interaction* between the program and its youth that results in those youth's treating the program as a personal resource and a bridge to a hopeful future. To illustrate how inner-city youth programs become inner-city youth resources we base this book's descriptions and analyses on the experiences and perspectives of inner-city adolescents themselves, and we let their voices tell of their interactions with the people and places that successfully shelter and support them.

We place youth at the center, whereas researchers typically look at programs independent of the inner-city youth they are meant to serve. Policymakers and the general public tend to view youth as outsiders, as the "youth problem." This perspective often casts youth as deviants who violate the boundaries of acceptable behaviors and society's rules. Our research turns this analysis on its head. We found that the programs and policies that typically disappoint were developed by people unfamiliar with the daily rhythms, pressures, and ferocity of the inner cities. The actual world in which inner-city youth struggle to survive and to grow up exceeds the imagination of most mainstream Americans, even those considered expert in issues of youth policy or urban environments. Even when the gritty facts of urban life are intellectually understood, it is impossible for an outsider to know what it *feels like* when siblings are murdered, abuse occurs daily, crime and violence are the norm, and messages of rejection are everywhere.

As we looked at what inner-city youth themselves said and thought, it became clear that the public's discouraging conclusions and myths about the interests, motivation, and capacities of inner-city youth are in urgent need of revision. Many adolescents *do* want to belong to organizations that help them escape inner-city despair, imagine and move toward positive, hope-filled futures. We hope to increase public knowledge and understanding of these organizations, the adults who have created them, and the youth they engage, so as to confront and dispel the myths that limit and misdirect public as well as private policies for inner-city youth.

Lack of Interest or Lack of Attractive Opportunity?

Youth of the inner city have a lot of time on their hands. For adolescents in school, some 40 percent of their waking hours are discretionary and uncommitted.[8] When school doors shut in the early afternoon, these adolescents are claimed by the streets. For those not in school, free time hangs even heavier. In neighborhoods where recreational facilities are run-down and ill-equipped, parks are urban battlegrounds, shops or other commercial hangouts have closed one by one, and jobs are practically nonexistent, the risk to youth during this empty time is immense. Idle time provides occasion for excessive use of alcohol or drugs and for sex, crime, violence, or gangbanging. (The term *gangbanging* is a term used by inner-city youth to describe any activity, legal or illegal, undertaken together by gang members—hanging out, cruising the neighborhood, protecting turf, or engaging in violent, criminal acts. Youth use the term *gangbanger* synonymously with *gang member*.) For most of inner-city youth, especially young men, the time from the early afternoon through late evening is spent in fierce communion with the streets. While some young women engage in this communion, others isolate themselves behind locked doors in efforts to stay out of harm's way. But their time, too, is filled with little worthwhile.

These are not the activities inner-city teenagers prefer but those they find available. Youth who find their way from the streets to the few effective youth organizations in their neighborhoods encounter different environments that transform their discretionary hours into resources and opportunities for growth and hope. Here, they take part in a "training ground for adulthood,"[9] and develop the values, self-confidence, competencies, and attitudes that engender hope and enable a positive future.[10]

If some organizations are effective in redeeming the lives of inner-city youth, why are there not more modeled after them? Few opportunities of any stripe exist for urban adolescents, in part because many policymakers and funders believe it is too late to intervene effectively in the lives of youth who have reached adolescence. In a kind of policy triage, scarce resources are focused almost exclusively on younger children.

In addition, decision makers in foundations, government, and social agencies often subscribe to the view that adolescents from the tough inner cities are not interested in organized activities, whatever their content, and so decision makers decline to support them. A superficial reading of the statistics on adolescent participation in nonschool organizations appears to support this view. Most major youth organizations report a significant drop-off in youth's participation after age twelve. For example, only 9 percent of the Girl Scouts in the United States are eleven years old or older, and only approximately 12 percent of YMCA members are between the ages of twelve and seventeen. In general the membership of national organizations that serve youth contains relatively small (and shrinking) percentages of adolescents.[11] Policymakers and concerned citizens look at these discouraging figures and conclude, wrongly, that youth lack interest in all organizations. Disheartening evaluations of various prevention or remediation efforts have also supported the conventional wisdom that little can be done to make a difference for urban adolescents already set on a harmful path through life. Another commonplace holds that these adolescents *prefer* to be involved only with gangs, drugs, crime, and other destructive activities.

Such negative judgments about the promise inherent in inner-city adolescents are constraining myths. The research we present here suggests another interpretation of the evidence. Adolescents vote with their feet. Youth from inner-city neighborhoods do not participate in organizations or programs, even those with noble charters and intent, when they are irrelevant or inhospitable to youth. Furthermore, youth experience many so-called prevention or remediation activities—substance abuse prevention, remedial education courses, boot camp for juvenile offenders—as downright demeaning and punitive. It should come as no surprise that initiatives based on a negative view of inner-city youth typically do not change these youth's paths. Yet the outcomes of such initiatives matter enormously, both to the young people themselves and to society. Without attractive opportunities to shape a productive future, these youth turn to the demands and the dangers of the streets, and "ain't no makin' it"[12] becomes their only reality.

Places of Hope: Effective Neighborhood-Based Organizations

The voices of hope heard at the beginning of this chapter belong to young men and women from the inner city who have succeeded in finding local activities and organizations that offer them support and optimism, fun and friendship. Terms of reference matter to inner-city adolescents. Organizations where youth prefer to congregate do not refer to themselves as providers of "after-school" or "out-of-school" programming because inner-city youth often view their schools as places that offer only discouragement or rejection. Successful inner-city organizations present themselves in relation to no social institution or social problem. They explain themselves simply as "for youth." We call them places of hope.

The universe of organizations offering programs for inner-city adolescents is extraordinarily diverse. Largest and best known are such national organizations as the YMCA, Boy Scouts of America, Girl Scouts of America, Boys and Girls Clubs, and Girls Inc. Affiliates in communities around the country tailor activities to local clientele but also use nationally developed materials and resources and abide by the national organizations' charter and rules. Church-affiliated youth groups offer programs with varying degrees of religious content and orientation. Local governments, through park and recreation departments or community centers, sponsor programs that encompass such varied activities as sports, performing arts, training programs, and camping. Most diverse of all are the unaffiliated, grass-roots organizations—the dance troupes, tutoring centers, theater groups, sports teams, and social clubs—that arise out of communities and draw their definition and energy from the neighborhoods they serve.[13]

We found effective youth organizations in all these categories. Programs that work are nationally affiliated, church related, municipally supported, and independent. They define themselves in terms of a range of activities and missions including sports, literacy, theater, scouting, music, and school achievement. We found no single focus, strategy, or organizational type associated with success—no cookie cutter for policy. For each success, we can point to an apparently identical activity that inner-city youth scorned to attend.

What places of hope do have in common are the pressures and ills of contemporary inner-city America—unstable and depressed economies; spiraling demands for social and educational services; escalating levels of street violence, criminal activity, school failure, adolescent pregnancy, and other distress signals. And places of hope also share an ability to give inner-city youth an unusual chance to duck the bullet and change their lives.

The people, objectives, and attitudes that make these organizations work, the resources they need, and the youth who are nurtured there are the subjects of the chapters that follow. We confront the conventional wisdom that says inner-city youth are unmotivated, beyond redemption, and uninterested in anything worthwhile. We aim to show what it would mean "to live in a city whose people were changing each other's despair into hope."

Chapter Two

The Hopefuls:
Six Teens with a Bright Future

We start our discussion as successful youth organizations do, with the young people themselves. From the stories of typical inner-city adolescents who have found neighborhood-based organizations that are places of hope, we have formed six composite pictures of young "hopefuls"—Keisha, Rosa, Tyrone, Buddy, Teri, and Tito—one from each of six successful organizations we got to know. These six teenagers are representative of their organizations and of their neighborhoods and families, coming out of the same social setting as youth who are not connected with such organizations.

We looked briefly at this setting in Chapter One. A closer look shows that in at least one state, California, arrests for robbery, assault, drugs, and arson are higher among juveniles than adults.[1] In this country's bloodiest era of youthful violence, 72 percent of young people living in urban America know someone who has been shot, 24 percent have witnessed murder, 25 percent have been shot at or threatened.[2] More than two million new cases of physical or sexual abuse are reported each year; millions more remain unreported.[3] Homicide is now the leading cause of death among inner-city youth.[4] In the social warfare of the inner city, youth are both the victims and perpetrators of violence. They are killed in revenge, for their shoes, for their jackets, by mistake, or for no reason at all.

Inner-city youth are undereducated. More than half do not graduate from high school; by age eighteen, more African American males are in jail than are in school.[5] Youth who stay the educational course are often little better off. In Chicago, for example, where 63 percent of the inner-city African American and Latino students enrolled in the public schools do not graduate, only 2,000 of the approximately 9,000 who do graduate can read at the level of the national average.[6]

The birth rate among unmarried girls, especially inner-city Latino and African American girls, is higher than ever before.[7] Unprotected sex, efforts to please, or to "have someone to love" have generated an epidemic of adolescent pregnancies and deadly increases in AIDS among teenagers. America's "new orphans" or "zero-parent families" are everyday inner-city realities and are increasing at exponential rates.[8]

The hopefuls presented in this book are not especially gifted or otherwise advantaged. They represent both the diversities and similarities of youth growing up in inner-cities across America. They are African American, European American, Latino. All are poor. Some are academically talented as conventionally conceived; most are not. Some are gifted athletes; most are not. None have the "normal" nuclear families of this country's idealized past. They live with mothers, with grandparents, in foster homes, with friends, or nowhere in particular. A few are effectively heads of households. Every one of the hopefuls has lost a sibling, a friend, or a relative to the brutality of the inner city. Their background statistics are typical of inner-city youth as profiled by demographers, economists, and sociologists.

Moreover, these six hopefuls are not special in the context of their youth organizations. The stories we tell in this chapter illustrate the typical realities and experiences of youth growing up in a particular inner-city neighborhood that has a place of hope for them. (The six hopefuls' specific activities at their different youth organizations are not described here but in Chapters Three, Four, and Six.) The questions we answer here are, What are hopefuls' cities and neighborhoods like? What are their most important experiences? What are their true needs? What benefits do they think they get from their youth organizations? They themselves tell us.

Keisha and the Arroyo Community Center Girl Scouts

The three cities in which we studied youth and their organizations reflect diverse aspects of urban America and of U.S. social history, and these differences have shaped the contexts in which the six hopefuls grew up. Keisha's home, the fast-growing Southwestern city we call Big Valley, takes its character from agriculture. Variously described as a frontier town, a place where everybody knows everybody, and an all-American city, Big Valley grew from a sleepy Southwestern town in the 1950s to a bustling metropolitan area with a population just under half a million in the 1990s. It is a community of deep and longstanding divisions between wealthy farmers, ranchers, and bankers and the Latinos and African Americans who traditionally worked for them. Over the past ten years, these divisions have become more visible owing to enforced school desegregation and a sharp economic downturn.

Keisha, a fourteen-year-old Girl Scout, volunteers at the city-sponsored community center in Arroyo, Big Valley's oldest African American community, a hilly twenty-block-long and twelve-block-wide tract of working-class homes largely cut off from the upscale surrounding neighborhoods. Most of Arroyo's small wooden homes house multiple generations in their five or six rooms. Through the twenty blocks of Franklin Street, Arroyo's main thoroughfare, nearly every intersection is marked by a church or a sign directing passersby to a nearby meeting house. Few businesses—a couple of liquor stores and quickmarts—dot Franklin Street although a fenced-off carwash and boarded-up laundromat recall a time when locally owned businesses flourished, before the development of a new business district just outside Arroyo.

The crest of the highest hill is marked by two notorious hangouts for neighborhood youth—the Agate Tavern and the Franklin Games Room, the latter known more for its drug dealers than its pinball players. At the bottom of the last hill is the Arroyo Community Center, more often called simply the center. These dual attractions stand at social as well as physical opposite ends of the community, combatants in a struggle for influence over the lives of community youth.

Like many teenagers in her neighborhood Keisha is actively involved in her church, with Bible study one night of the week, youth meeting another, and choir a third. But except for Sunday when she is at church all day she spends her summer days and after-school time at the center. On her way to the center from her home with her mother and stepfather, Keisha always stops by her grand-mother's to relieve her of a few of the fifteen grandchildren that daily roam the small house while their parents are at work. An open-air tent in the front yard is a cool and contained play area in the hot, humid climate.

On one typical day, Keisha heads toward the center with her own little brother, two nephews, and a niece in tow. They soon meet up with three other Girl Scouts who also work as volunteers in the center's summer day-camp program. With their sophisticated wave hairdos, freshly done for the Fourth of July celebration the day before, Keisha and her friends might pass for a moment as older than high school freshmen, but their cutoffs, tank tops, and tennis shoes, as well as their laughter in playing with the gaggle of chil-dren about their knees, betray their true age.

Before heading further down Arroyo's sloping blocks, the girls look up the street for a moment to the brightly painted facade of the Agate Tavern, recalling the trouble there just two nights before. July third in Arroyo is traditionally a night for family reunions and preparations for the Fourth of July parade, but in recent years it has garnered unwanted notoriety for the community. This time, as before, the Agate was the focal point. Its customary thirty or forty patrons had swelled to two hundred, spilling out of the small wooden structure and its parking lot and blocking Franklin Street. That's when the police came.

Luanna Williams, director of the Arroyo Community Center and leader of the Arroyo Girl Scout troop, remains angry about what happened that night. She says, "[The media] said it was a riot but it wasn't, not until [the police] got here. They had riot gear, billy clubs. They had twenty to twenty-five on horseback and about a hundred officers marching behind. It was horrible. About midnight a police car drove through the crowd. Somebody threw a bottle and broke his window. Then the next car told the crowd to disperse, and they didn't even give them time to do it. They marched like they were an army or something."

Keisha and her friends think it's not just the police who provoke a negative image of Arroyo in Big Valley but the media as well. Keisha gets angry when she reflects on the media hype that has come to surround July third in Arroyo and the false impressions outsiders have. She says, "When I go to school a lot of people joke about where I live and how scared they'd be if they had to live in Arroyo.... But I've never been really scared.... They don't really know. They just know what they hear on the news. [If I were a reporter] I would show them ... some of the good stuff that people be doin', instead of just showin' the riots and stuff.... I would tell them that if the police didn't come out there, that stuff wouldn't happen."

Keisha wishes that people in Big Valley could understand that the Arroyo community is much more than what happens on July third. Arroyo's close-knit insularity, extended family networks, and rich traditions provide "a nice place to live." She says, "It needs a lot of work, but it's just like a family out here to me. Everybody know everybody. Just about everybody I know, I'm kin to. People ... work as one, as I see it. Like if somebody needs help with something, somebody around will always be there to help."

Keisha acknowledges the incidents involving drugs and other negative influences in the community. Her most combative encounters in this area occur close to home with her uncle, an occasional drug dealer in his early forties. Keisha says her grandmother does "whatever she can to help him, but he try to run over her.... He'll take things, you know.... He steal from his own mother!... I don't know what he use, but he's usin' somethin'. That I know. His attitude changes.... He come in, throw somethin'. He don't care. And he don't have any respect for himself. And if you don't have respect for yourself then no one's gonna have respect for you."

Like all adolescents, Keisha wants respect. She gets it through her reputation as an athlete and her connection with the Arroyo Community Center. Whether playing basketball, performing community service with the Girl Scouts, or working as a summer day-camp volunteer, much of her life is entwined with center activities. Her close relationship with Luanna Williams also draws her to the center's programs. Like many girls at the center, she regards Luanna as a primary confidante. Whether dealing with the erratic and violent behavior of her uncle or with her "lazy" stepfather, whom she wishes she could "kick out of the house," she finds she "can talk to Luanna about *anything*."

The most important thing Keisha has learned in growing up at the center is a sense of personal responsibility and self-respect. She says, "Luanna, the Girl Scouts, and the center taught me to be a more independent person, to be more responsible for my actions. . . . You can't always depend on someone else to do something for you, you have to do it yourself."

Rosa and the Cougar Hollow Boys and Girls Club

"Hasta noche, Mama." Rosa, a seventeen-year-old second-generation Latina, calls goodbye to her mother as the screen door slams behind her and she bounds across the small wooden porch and over the cement block that serves as a step. "Voy al firehouse." Rosa spends essentially all of her free time with the Cougar Hollow Boys and Girls Club, housed in an old firehouse and an old church at the center of the neighborhood. While Keisha lives in a neighborhood that is predominantly one ethnic group, Rosa lives in a community that has been marked by continual changes in ethnic makeup. Once a predominantly European American community, Cougar Hollow is now an often uneasy mix of European Americans, African Americans, and Latinos.

For Rosa, the short three blocks from her home to the club are full of contrast. Her house is on the edge of one of the bustling business strips that radiate from the downtown high rises, and Cougar Hollow homes look shabby and rundown in comparison with the strip's new office buildings. Rosa, navigating her way around piles of uncollected trash and domestic discards, wishes "they'd clean it up around here." With boarded-up windows and weatherworn exterior the firehouse and church housing the club might appear abandoned were it not for more than one hundred children already lined up in the walkway waiting for the club's 9:00 A.M. opening. Rosa joins several of her friends and her boyfriend, Rafael, who have already taken up their positions on the big steps that lead up to what was once the firehouse garage, now a basketball court. Occasionally one of the "knee-highs," the younger club members, ventures onto this teenagers' domain to wrap her arms around Rosa's neck or Rafael's knees. The teenagers seem to relish the attention, but they never entirely lose their facade of cool—when the doors open and the younger kids eagerly line up for entrance, the teenagers continue to lounge on the steps, waiting their own time to enter the club.

Like other lower-income and working-class communities throughout Big Valley, Cougar Hollow has only one community-wide center to serve neighborhood youth. While some of Big Valley's centers are bursting at the seams, others stand practically empty, struggling and failing to appeal to the older adolescents, who often stop coming after they turn fifteen. However, the Cougar Hollow Club, an affiliate of the national Boys and Girls Clubs, draws adolescents from both its own neighborhood near downtown and neighborhoods farther out to the south and west. One challenge for John Peña, executive director of the seven Boys and Girls Clubs in Big Valley, is to make the clubs home for an increasingly varied teen population. A program he is finding helpful is TeenTalk, a Big Valley Boys and Girls Club public-service drama group to which Rosa belongs. Dramatizing issues of concern to all teens, TeenTalk's high school–age members from diverse ethnic and economic backgrounds have found a popular way to increase communication among Big Valley's ethnic groups. Rosa spends about half of her club time at the firehouse, writing scripts and practicing them with other troupe members, and the other half performing at youth centers, churches, and schools throughout the Big Valley region.

Although Cougar Hollow is a focal point for Big Valley's growing problems with gangs, street violence, and illegal drug use,

Rafael comes over to Cougar Hollow from his own south side neighborhood partly because he thinks the gang problem is greater on the south side: "Anytime you go over there, there's guys hangin' that ain't got nothing to do.... It's always shootings and stuff over there. Killings." The dangers Rosa faced growing up in the inner city existed primarily at home, where she and her siblings endured daily verbal abuse from her father, who was "into drugs," and also witnessed his physical abuse of their mother. Rosa describes her father as "a really bad person. He put it in [my mother's] mind that if she left, she would be nothing without him—that she could never get a job, she could never do anything with her life. So she believed it." Rosa, her brother, and her sister would retreat to one of the two bedrooms in the house and turn up the television to drown out the violence of their parents' quarrels. She remembers that her sister "hated it 'cuz she was in her senior year, and she would be having to study." Rosa's mother left her husband on the "spur of the moment," taking the children with her, when Rosa's brother both dropped out of high school and got his girl friend pregnant. Rosa says her father told her mother, "If you leave ... I'll find you and kill you." But she also says the threats didn't bother them too much "'cuz he's threatened us all our life." Her responsibility now is to "figure out how I'm gonna help my mom out."

Rosa does not see her experiences as unique. The harsh realities facing inner-city youth are "everywhere ... with everyone." Participation in the drama group is important to her not only because the group helps other adolescents to deal with experiences like hers but also because she has become aware of other issues and concerns that face youth and of her own ability to take action. "I guess I've really woken up and seen reality," she comments. "[I've seen what] is really happening here. So now I feel I can do something about that. I can change it. I wish I could tell everybody that this could happen to you. Don't be narrow-minded, educate yourself." Rosa observes that adolescents often think they are immortal. She says TeenTalk helps teenagers see what can happen to them. "I know a lot of people saying, 'You know, I never really thought about AIDS until I saw a TeenTalk performance. And then I [thought] maybe that can happen to me.'" About one-third of TeenTalk's performances are before parent and adult community groups who are trying to understand their children's lives. Through participating in TeenTalk, Rosa hopes she can change the attitudes of adults as well as youth. She says some adults look at inner-city youth and think, "You're just a little thug. You're never gonna do anything with your life."

TeenTalk is witness and support for Rosa, and the Cougar Hollow Boys and Girls Club is her refuge from the violence of her home and the dangers of her neighborhood. It is a place where she can imagine something different for herself.

Buddy and Cooper House

Buddy lives two thousand miles away from Keisha and Rosa, on the hillsides of the metropolis we call River City. A Northeastern city of approximately one-half million, River City is in many ways an archetypal U.S. industrial city, built up at the close of the nineteenth century largely through the development of heavy industry and settlement of large numbers of European immigrants hoping to fulfill dreams of economic opportunity or freedom from religious persecution. However, economic prosperity and social stability ended abruptly in River City in the late 1970s when the city's heavy-industry economic base collapsed, rapidly propelling the city into the painful social and economic conditions of late-twentieth-century urban America.

Buddy's neighborhood is the inner-city community of Oak Ridge. From the steep cliffs high atop Oak Ridge he has a clear view of the factories that line the near bank of the Susman River, the glittering downtown River City skyline on the far side, and the narrow three-story factory workers' houses lining the steep hills and dark valleys. The air is clean—the remaining factories run only one or at most two shifts. The inner-city streets are filled with young and middle-aged men as well as teens, all victims of the latest layoffs and unrelieved economic downturn. There is little opportunity on these streets lined with convenience stores, bars, X-rated movie theaters, diners, and pawn shops.

Buddy is European American, nineteen years old, six-feet-five-inches tall, and 210 pounds, with a close-cut head of dark hair save for one long lock at the nape of his neck. At first glance he is more likely to engender caution than respect. He is, however, one of the revered "seniors" at Cooper House, a Boys and Girls Club affiliate chartered at the turn of the century. In addition to sharing in the Senior Boys Club activities, he works at Cooper House regularly as a part-time receptionist and supervisor for the younger members. Today he is hurrying to be on time for an orientation for summer counselors. As a returning senior, one who grew up at Cooper House, he is to "show the younger guys the ropes."

The short trip from his home on Oakridge Road to Cooper House takes Buddy from the pressures of the street to the vibrant activity of a successful youth organization. He finds his two realities worlds apart. Oakridge Road is "terrible," he says, with drug dealers and "street hangers" on "every corner" while "Cooper House is a place you can go [to] be with people that are decent."

Street hangers on Oakridge Road fight over girls, over territory, and more recently, over drugs. Buddy was never a dealer but was for a time a fighter, sometimes even traveling out of his neighborhood in search of action. The pattern is familiar to urban youth. "We just started [fights]," Buddy says. "[We'd say to someone,] 'What's up? You looked at me that funny way.' Just to start something. It was so boring, you know? Didn't have nowhere to go.... Nothing to do.... So we just started fighting."

At age fourteen, after a few scrapes with the police for car theft and street fighting, Buddy turned away from the streets to the Cooper House's red-bricked refuge. He still has friends on the streets, an essential to safe passage in his neighborhood. He says, "I still talk to 'em, and we're still good buddies," but the house is his new hangout. Buddy explains that his mother had "lived in this area most of her life and she knew what [Cooper House] was like, so she made me go there." While initially pushed to go, Buddy found that "after just a little bit I really started to realize why I was goin' there and what it could offer me." While Buddy chose to stick with Cooper House, many of his street-hanging friends have no interest in joining the club. Buddy says, "They know about Cooper House. They know what it's all about, and it's their choice not to be part of that. I made a different choice." About his former crowd he adds, "You can't change somebody that doesn't want to be changed." But if they would just give Cooper House a chance, Buddy believes, these friends would be hooked as he was.

Buddy credits his association with Cooper House with making fundamental changes in his attitudes toward others and toward himself. The opportunity to make friends with African Americans within the context of Cooper House values and traditions has been especially important to him. Buddy ranks racism as the number one cause of problems among River City youth. In Oakridge High the races were so antagonistic that, in Buddy's last year of school, he and his African American friend Marcus had to leave the school building separately through doors segregated by race in an effort to reduce fights on school property. "When you're in school and you hear of a fight, the first thing people ask is, 'Was the kid black or white that he got into a fight with?'" Buddy explains. "Even if they're fighting over something that has nothing to do with color, a lot of the kids will make it . . . right into a racial thing."

Marcus and Buddy's friendship is unusual for River City even though African Americans and European Americans have lived there in close proximity for generations. Individual neighborhoods are still largely segregated, their borders jealously guarded by the extended families who traditionally pass their homes on exclusively to relatives. This insularity is a way of life to the older generation. Buddy and Marcus now believe that it leads to ignorance — the main cause of racism. They are concerned that the older generation's attitudes are passing to the next generation. "My dad is racist," Buddy says, "[and] up until I started meeting friends [at Cooper House], I was racist, till I started actually talking to 'em. . . . It's the same way for blacks too. Their friends that are racist won't let [them] talk to whites. It's stupid; it really is. I look back and I think, 'The things we did and for what? Because [someone's] black?'" Marcus, standing by, echoes Buddy's sentiments. "That's right. It's just stupid." Cooper House director Steve Patterson says that at the house "color is left at the door," and cooperation and consideration are strong house norms. That is a main reason why Buddy and the other teenage members spend most of their free time "down the house," and say, "We all just practically live here."

At Cooper House, Buddy feels secure and respected, scarce commodities at both home and school. At home, Buddy's working-class father, laid off ten years ago, has values and expectations Buddy has difficulty respecting. His father thinks the only honorable future for a man is the army or the factory, where one "earns honest pay for a hard day's work." Such work is now rarely available in River City, yet when Buddy considered further schooling for himself, his father's response was, "So you think you're better than me that you need to get an education." The disillusionment of belonging to a generation brought up to be workers then denied work has been hard for young men like Buddy to handle.

At school Buddy received another message—that "tough kids" and "poor, white trash" would never amount to anything. In Buddy's view the Oakridge High teachers "ain't too strict.... You can do just about anything and get away with it." Buddy attributes the teachers' low expectations to the fact that "they don't know what they're doing." The tragedy is that "it hurts the kids 'cuz ... if you can get away with things, you know most people are gonna do it."

Buddy missed having rules at school at the same time as he suffered from strict but inconsistent rules at home, such as curfews erratically enforced. He also missed compassion and caring. He feels that even his high school sports coaches had no interest in him as a person although he was a prize player. "They focus only on winning." At Cooper House, Buddy finds genuine caring and clear, consistent rules. Although Cooper House teams "want to win too," Buddy experiences a key difference between house and high school teams. Cooper House coaches know the youth as individuals. "Sometimes when I play basketball down there," Buddy points out, "I've had a bad day, [and] Paul [the coach] realizes that. He doesn't ride me that hard. But if he sees me slackin', he'll get on my butt.... He knows our limitations and he knows our personalities.... When we step on the floor it turns into business, but he still knows each individual for what they are and what they can do."

The personal contact he gets at Cooper House has changed Buddy's goals. Once interested in a professional sports career, he now sees a future of helping the kids in his community in the way that Cooper House has helped him. The real satisfaction he derives from helping kids is apparent in his description of his counseling activities at the Cooper House day camp: "My summer jobs have basically consisted of working with kids. I like being around them.... It makes me feel good to help them. And I can see them [and] say, 'Well, I helped him make that decision. I helped him be a better person.'... Makes you feel good when you can see yourself having an influence on some kids. Most of the time I can accomplish it, and they look up to me a little more for it." Buddy has taken a guiding value system, a positive sense of worth, and direction for the future from his involvement with Cooper House.

Tyrone and the Reggie Jones Gymnasts

Tyrone is a sixteen-year-old African American who lives in the Francis Homes Housing Development, a notorious public housing project in the city we call Lakeside, a major Midwestern center of more than one million people. It has a diverse industrial base, is an important transportation hub, and like River City, has been a home to many immigrants. It also has a long history of social divisiveness among ethnic and racial groups. Owing to a strong and often violent labor movement and a highly politicized city government, power in Lakeside has been in the hands of an exclusive few, despite the fact that it is one of the country's most racially diverse cities. Race rather than ethnicity is the salient marker in Lakeside, and it remains one of the most segregated cities in the United States. Until the 1960s Lakeside was prosperous, but over the last twenty years fiscal crises have affected virtually every aspect of public services, triggering a steady job loss. The sprawling metropolis is increasingly plagued by gangs and illegal drugs.

Known for its high gang activity, trash-strewn playgrounds, dangerous hallways, and thorough-going state of disrepair, Lakeside's Francis Homes is seen by many as a testament to the failed social experiment of providing low-cost high-rise housing for the urban poor. From the street an invisible line seems to split the development's seventeen-story buildings in two. In the lower halves of the buildings a patchwork of curtains hangs and faded graffiti color the brick walls. Different buildings are the territories of three different gangs, and teenage gang members stand on guard by the front steps of their respective buildings while a few children play in the doorways, rarely venturing into the designated play areas where the rusting skeletons of gym bars and swingless playsets lie unused. Too many children playing here have been caught in rival gangs' gunfire. From the tenth floors on up, broken windows and closed-off floors are a constant reminder to Tyrone and the other residents of the declining occupancy in Francis Homes and the ongoing debate over its future. "They're trying to force us out," laments one community member. "They want this property because it's so close to downtown. Prime real estate."

"Who do you fly with?" When Tyrone hears this challenge called from behind him, he freezes. Keeping his hands still at his sides he turns slowly, and the two gang members posted at the high rise repeat their demand, flashing gang signs. "I'm not into gangs. Look!" Tyrone says, signaling with his chin to his chest and the red and white T-shirt that proclaims him a Reggie Jones Gymnast. Tyrone's two challengers squint, confer, and wave him on his way. Tyrone has grown up in Francis Homes and knows that his choice of response to gang challenges is fraught with danger. Gang members who dare to cross rival territory can be seriously harmed, and often the same threat extends to youth who simply live in a gang-held building. Targets by association, many of them are afraid to cross gang boundaries just to get to school, much less to attend optional after-school activities.

Yet some young men, like Tyrone, are able to negotiate a safe passage by asserting their relationship and loyalty to a group other than a gang, the Reggie Jones Gymnasts. According to Tyrone his affiliation with this youth group that performs throughout the city and is known everywhere simply as the Gymnasts lets the gangs know that he is "into something positive." He says, "[Adolescents] have to belong to somethin' in Francis Homes. When we say we're Gymnasts, [gangbangers] don't mess with us.... They know we are not a threat. Over in my end of Francis Homes there's a lot of gang-bangin', and it's like, man, these guys give us the fullest respect. [They] look up to us." In some ways the projects are less dangerous than when Tyrone was younger, because the gangs are now less concerned with territory than with the lucrative drug business. Gang-banging is fading out in Tyrone's neighborhood because "now it's all about makin' money." But the drugs have also led to increased addiction throughout the neighborhood.

Tyrone is separated from the gangbangers by both his membership in the Gymnasts and his relationship with Reggie Jones, the man who founded and runs the gymnastic team. Tyrone says, "If it weren't for Mr. Jones, nine times out of ten I'd be out hangin' around here with these guys, probably a drug user, a gang member, a convict or ex-con, something that's normal for this environment. Mostly everybody that I grew up with is in a gang or sellin' drugs or something. I just found a different road."

But Tyrone doesn't think society should give up on the gang-bangers who haven't yet found a different road. He feels that "some kids you can change 'cuz basically they just want some attention. And their parents aren't givin' them enough so they go outside and act bad and wild, but ... if somebody comes along and wants to give them a chance then maybe some of 'em will change. Probably some of 'em won't 'cuz they been so used to it and don't know no discipline or right from wrong, but I say you can change 'em 'cuz ... most of 'em didn't want to go the wrong way.... They just wanted to be noticed." Tyrone believes "there's always something you can do for someone."

Although Tyrone doesn't have a father at home to help direct him, he asserts that Reggie Jones has been the best father he could have: "If you don't have no father, [Mr. Jones is] the guy to be with 'cuz he'll help you in any way he can. He just don't want you to be with no gang. No drugs.... That man brought me a long way."

The waiting list of young people who want to be Gymnasts numbers almost three thousand. Tyrone thinks more teenagers would leave the gangs if there were more men like Reggie Jones around "to do what Mr. Jones do with us. . . . Make us stay outta trouble [and] constantly be there [for us]." What Reggie Jones, does, says Tyrone, is to help youth "see another light. . . . [He] is the strength behind us. He's our backbone. . . . He's our ticket outta here."

Teri and Building Educational Strategies for Teens

Teri, an eighteen-year-old African American girl, also knows Francis Homes well. Although she now lives with her family in a small apartment building a few blocks to the north of the forbidding high rises, her mother and grandmother had lived in the projects when they were brand new, and Teri was born there. Teri often hears that the projects were "nice for a few years, before it started going down like it is now."

It is dusk, and a few gang members stand post outside the high rise Teri is approaching. When Teri visits Francis Homes these days, usually to pay a call on the parents of the youngsters she works with as a junior staffer at the local education center, Building Educational Strategies for Teens (BEST), her mother always reminds her to be careful and to "announce." "Lashandra! Lashandra! You up there?" Teri yells at an eighth-floor window. She glances over to a ten-year-old girl holding a baby: "Tasha, is your auntie up there?" Teri has learned how to navigate threatening inner-city buildings and streets. Her call to Lashandra is an understood signal that Lashandra's apartment door should be open, a lighted destination at the end of a dark hallway filled with the stench of urine and scuttling roaches. Broken light fixtures are seldom replaced in city-owned Francis Homes.

Entering the building, Teri jogs up seven flights of stairs because the elevator, on the rare occasions when it works, is too dangerous. According to Teri, women are especially at risk because "people sit on top and make the elevator stick between floors. Then they drop through the roof on top and will rob, rape, or beat up on you." Getting around in the neighborhood, says Teri, means "having common sense and street smarts. There's just certain things you don't do. And if you do [them and get hurt], people don't feel much sympathy for you."

Teri sees many differences between the challenges and dangers that face young men and those that concern young women in Francis Homes, and she is glad she did not have to grow up in this environment as a boy:

The boys just have so many things up against 'em.... Most teachers expect the girls to be smart and not the boys, and so they put a lot more attention into the girls' learning than the boys'. I can even remember my kindergarten teacher or my first-grade teacher [telling] the boys, "You're nothin' but a gangbanger," and stuff like that.... Even now when I see a bunch of teens that's what they act. Boys just hangin' out. No future. Most of 'em probably didn't graduate from high school. [A lot of them probably thought,] 'Why should I go to school when I can get what I need?' A lot of 'em don't have an expectancy of living that long anyway, so [they think], "Why not live it up while I have a chance?"

However, Teri feels the perils facing inner-city adolescent girls are on the rise. She defines these perils as pregnancy, sexually transmitted diseases, and rape—all of them often related to pressures for sexual precocity among adolescents. Teri finds that even though other people "always try to take the blame," thinking they "didn't hand out enough birth control," some teenage girls "just *really* want to have their own kid! I mean, you meet girls that say, 'Bobby wants me to have his baby so I'm havin' a baby.' They think if they have a baby, they [will] always have a connection to that boy." Other girls get pregnant because "they're havin' family problems, and they think that their kid is theirs. Maybe their kid would always love 'em." And finally, some girls are "stupid enough just to do it for welfare.... I've talked to people in Francis who get food stamps and might get a couple hundred dollars a month. I say, 'Don't you know you gotta buy stuff with that for your kid?'"

Teri believes that the teenage girls in Francis Homes don't know date rape exists. Their attitudes about sex just don't include this concept. She doubts that "if it happened they could recognize it. They would think they 'shoulda stopped before.'" Adopting a matter-of-fact tone of voice Teri mimics what she thinks the girls would say: "'I was saying no and he just did it, anyway.' They wouldn't even say, 'He raped me.' It wouldn't be rape to them."

Teri has also observed that many young women in Francis Homes are now initiating violence. Speaking of the rise in girl gangs in the 1990s, she says, "They just want control over people.... They want you to be afraid of them. Last year, girl gangs were mostly fighting each other over guys, but now it's like they fight *anybody*. They had been associated with a male gang, but now they want a *separate* gang.... They know guy gangbangers [who give them guns]. It's just bad."

Like Tyrone and the other Gymnasts, Teri underscores the fact that identification with something positive—in her case, BEST— is sufficient for a teenager to avoid active recruitment by the gangs. Although many of the friends she grew up with have joined gangs, she points out that these friends "show you respect, even if you don't do what they do." She says, "You know 'em. You don't get on their bad side.... I hung with 'em some at school, but I didn't do the looting and stuff or trying to start fights. It's like they say, 'She okay, but she weird. Don't bother her 'cause she hangs with us.'" Laughing, Teri says that getting good grades "makes you popular. They think ... 'This is my friend Teri. She's real smart.'"

The youth organization that has made a difference for Teri occupies two floors and the gymnasium of a brick building at the edge of Francis Homes that once served as an educational wing for a church. Built up from a small church-sponsored tutoring program by Michael Carroll, BEST offers academic support and counseling to neighborhood young people, with the goal of enabling them to finish high school and attend college. Adolescents who participate in BEST see its academic program as antidotal to the shrillness and impersonality of the local schools and as their best hope for an adulthood different from the dead-end lives they see around them everyday.

It is not that Francis Homes is bereft of community attention. Teri says, somewhat cynically, "community services is all we have" in Francis Homes. Apparently because of the development's high-profile proximity to downtown Lakeside and national reputation for violence and despair, it has more youth and community services than most public housing. But residents quickly note that nearness to downtown, and the media, has disadvantages too. It often appears as though Francis Homes receives a disproportionate share of negative news coverage.

For Teri, BEST provides the catalyst for her to belie these negative stereotypes and to develop and demonstrate her academic abilities. She works about fifteen hours a week tutoring small groups of students, and when she came to BEST, "it just started out as a job." Now, Teri believes BEST has been instrumental in the development of her future and the futures of numerous other youth. Her mother and her two sisters have also been helped by the program, and her mother now works in BEST's adult education program. Without BEST, Teri would have been "a totally different person." When she first started high school and went to work at BEST she got "sad grades," but to continue working at BEST she had to get A's and B's. She brought her grades up. She says, "Without BEST I probably wouldn't have graduated [let alone have gotten] on the honor roll." Teri also believes that "the majority of the people that attend [BEST] feel like maybe there's help, and they're trying to grasp it. Most of the kids there, they probably would've grown up like their [older] sisters and brothers on the streets. Now you have sisters and brothers who are looking toward [the adolescents at BEST and] saying, 'He's gonna be somebody and she's gonna be somebody because of BEST.'"

Tito and the Porter Crossing YMCA
Gang Alternatives and Intervention Program

Across the river from Francis Homes is Porter Crossing, often called Little Puerto Rico. Here the main thoroughfares are crowded, and behind grillwork and iron bars the storefront windows display huge signs heralding this week's sale in English and Spanish.

Other, more nefarious, signs also are evident. Spray-painted symbols mark the territories of the over forty gangs in the Greater Porter Crossing neighborhood. In the 1980s over 800 Lakeside youth were killed by gang violence. In 1991 more than 130 young men lost their lives—the highest count ever for gang violence in Lakeside.

Seventeen-year-old Tito is a member of the Zs, a Puerto Rican gang. On this morning, he and other gang members are gathered in front of a mom-and-pop grocery. It is an unusual sight for this hour since most members of the gang are still at home asleep after a late night of corner drug dealing. Tito, dressed in calf-length shorts and a hockey shirt, both with the same popular sports label, lounges against the graffiti-covered pay phone. His circular wire-framed sunglasses reflect the morning sun, and the three spikes of his carefully trimmed goatee identify his gang affiliation, making him instantly recognizable to both friends and enemies. The phone rings, and Tito begins to converse with a prospective customer.

A van pulls up, its side emblazoned "YMCA Gang Alternatives and Intervention" (GAIN). "Yo, Tito, what's up, man?" calls Cruz Sanchez. In his late thirties, Cruz is GAIN's director, and a former member of the Zs. Resting on the van window, his forearm reveals the word "mom" tattooed within the outlines of a cross. "Time to go to work," says Cruz. Tito cuts his phone caller short, "We're not conducting business. We gotta go to work." The boys climb in the van. Their drive to the Porter Crossing YMCA skirts Porter Park, which the locals call Death Wish Park. Cruz knows well which streets are safe. On the route he takes the walls and fences are marked with familiar and friendly signs—the Zs' gang symbol, interlocking horns, drawn turned up to signify positive greetings. Graffiti on the wall next to the railroad tracks create a veritable art gallery. The image of a large yellow tombstone dominates one underpass. A lance, the symbol for the gang's enemies, is turned toward the ground and covered with the letters R.I.P.—a chilling tribute to a dead rival. Part of the community work the gang members do at the YMCA includes painting over gang graffiti. Sometimes GAIN participants simply cover defaced surfaces with fresh paint. Other times they produce complex and colorful murals replacing the deadly communication by way of graffiti with art that is both more sophisticated and more benign.

Safety is of utmost concern to Tito and his friends and one of their main reasons for joining a gang. Tito says people always ask why adolescents join gangs, and his response is, "Why not be in a gang? If I'm not in a gang, I'm still gonna get whupped. [With a gang,] at least I got somebody to come to if I get whupped. They gonna watch my back." But Tito adds, "I respect these brothers 'cuz they respect me. But I don't trust no one except my family. Never trust no one, 'cuz they'll back stab you."

The need to be safe, to have some respect, to have a way to get some money is the reality Tito and many gang youth perceive when considering their futures. Cruz describes the economic dilemma this way: "If the kids are on the corner making $500 to $600 a day, you have to replace that with something and not with nothing. They're not going to just take ... McDonald's jobs when they can make $600 on the streets. But [a job] making $7.20 an hour is [seen as] respectable. It's steady money that makes the difference. And that's why I stress ... that to them every day.... You get a job, and I bet you won't be dependent too much on this corner. Because what it is, is they need money."

Tito explains that local gang members currently need money because the drug traffic has moved elsewhere, either as a result of a bad drug deal or a police crackdown. Limited by territorial gang boundaries, gang members are unable to follow the money. Even though one or two years ago some members were making up to $600 a day, that is not the current reality. In addition public perception that drug dealing is the job of choice in the inner city is wrong, says Tito: "[Nobody says] 'Hey man, you gotta deal these ten bags for me, 'cuz you with us.' It don't work that way. You deal if you want to. But everybody don't wanna deal drugs. Everybody wants to make money legally, just like everybody else does."

Tito finds that obstacles to legitimate jobs for Porter Crossing youth are real and profound: "There's jobs, but not for us. There's jobs for people that are doin' something—they got an education. Well, I got an education, but I don't got no high school education. They don't wanna give us jobs, ... or if they *do* give us a job, it be in a place where we can't go [or] it's too far to go.... Like I said, some of us are uneducated, some of us don't know how to catch the bus, some of us don't know how to get downtown."

Members of the Zs express a strong sense of alienation from official institutions other than the YMCA and the church, which they are most likely to go to for funerals. Schools, police, and the courts are all seen as threats. Schools are considered unsafe when rival gangs are fighting over the school as turf or when the building is already under the control of a rival gang. Moreover, teachers and schools generally are experienced as hostile, uncaring entities that label gang youth as "lessers" and treat them as if they were "invisible." What Tito recalls from his school days is that teachers "think 'cuz you're in a gang that you're just ... wasting your time [in school]. But ... you don't have to get up in the morning if you don't want to.... You get up in the morning, you get dressed, you take a bath, and you go there 'cuz you wanna go." Tito feels teachers are not even going to try to teach gang members. Yet he thinks that "all gangbangers need is somebody to talk to 'em. Sit 'em down and say, 'Hey man, this is the only way you gonna learn, man. If you go around like this, ain't nobody else gonna teach you.'" However, he says, "[Teachers] don't do things like that. They won't sit down. They won't come by me and say, 'You know, Tito, you should try to do this work 'cuz if you don't do it ...' They all let me sit there all day. [They] walk right past me."

Police are perceived as a rival gang. According to Tito, the police "think they're the toughest gang 'cuz they got a badge.... If we do somethin' to them, we're gonna face life in prison. If they do somethin' to us, they get around five years."

Tito and other Lakeside youth are frightened of the police for other reasons. Stories of police dropping gang members off in rival gang territories are legion. Latino youth like Tito and African American youth like Tyrone believe the police see them as "a game." And the resulting trouble, says Tito, is "not mostly our fault. It's the police too, 'cuz they provoke the shit. They'll try to bring somebody from the opposition over [here] and try to drop him off and hope that we can beat him up and then they could come get us and lock us up [for assault]."

The justice system sometimes offers opportunities for reform, but teenagers often see more risk than opportunity in such sentences. Tito was interested in a special school with a vocational training program to which a court remanded him after a drug possession charge, but when he found out that he had to cross several rival gang territories in order to attend, he decided not to go. He says, "I'm not gonna risk my life for nobody... for the government, for the judges, nobody. Because they ain't gonna go to my funeral."

For Tito and his friends, the GAIN program at the Porter Crossing YMCA (or Y) is the only positive opportunity that is within their neighborhood, and the only reason they have hope that their future may include something other than jail, a wasted life, or an early death. They greatly admire the GAIN program founder, Roberto Colon, for giving them this hope and support on their own terms. Tito explains, "There's a lot of people that just got out of the penitentiary, they can't get a job and the Y could get 'em a job.... It's a start.... If they don't take you, they'll tell you about some jobs that you'll go to. Train you for your future jobs. Like we're doin' now.... When we go to get a regular job we'll have more experience, and we'll say what we're gonna do. [We] learn how to respect people. We learn how to be responsible."

Finding a Different Road

Keisha, Rosa, Buddy, Tyrone, Teri, and Tito have found a different road from many of their inner-city peers. These teenage hopefuls have ducked the bullet. They have ducked the real bullet of daily gun battles and mayhem on their streets and in their homes. They either have ducked or are learning to duck the figurative bullet of becoming pregnant, catching a sexually transmitted disease, taking drugs, failing at school, and committing crimes. And they have done more than survive. These hopefuls are acquiring the skills and perspectives necessary for them to achieve a productive and responsible adulthood. When we last checked on the hopefuls, we found that their futures were still positive.

Keisha is making good grades in Big Valley High School and is full of plans for college and an athletic scholarship.

Rosa graduated from high school and is enrolled in a business program at the local community college. She works part-time to support herself and to help her mother with household expenses.

Buddy completed his first year at River City University on a football scholarship; his grades were not what he hoped they would be, but he is confident he can do better and intends to get help with his writing. He plans to spend his summers working with the Cooper House summer camp program and has decided to major in child development.

Tyrone has graduated from high school and been accepted into a selective program for pipe fitters.

Teri graduated with honors from her high school and will attend a prestigious university on a full academic scholarship. She plans to spend her summers tutoring in the BEST program and working with African American youth in Lakeside housing projects.

Tito is working with the Porter Crossing YMCA as a street worker and with the local major league baseball team as a groundskeeper. Although he dropped out of high school he is studying for his Graduate Equivalency Diploma (GED) and intends to pursue his dream of becoming another Roberto Colon.

Are the hopefuls special? Yes and no. As we mentioned earlier, they are not unusually gifted youth, and their lives have contained the same exposure to poverty, crime, violence, and lack of caring adults as the lives of other inner-city youth.

They are special in their expectation of a viable future, their belief that they can be and do something other than succumb to the desperate and dead-end prospects of their neighborhoods. The great majority of youth in the six programs we describe here are also hopeful and are realizing their hopes. All six youth believe in themselves. They feel they have found a road to healthy adulthood. They belie the frightening media portrayals, negative public expectations, and even their own fears about the destructive or empty futures ahead for inner-city youth.

The tragedy for our society is that all the hopefuls in all successful organizations are still a minority in U.S. inner cities. Yet what makes them hopeful is not beyond this nation's means. Moreover, it has nothing to do with sociology, demographics, or luck. What enabled the hopefuls to duck the bullet and choose a responsible and fulfilling future was their participation in an organization that provided the values, the support, the safety, and the competencies they needed before they could believe in their own futures. Teri, for example, contrasts her positive sense of her future with the view of Francis Homes teenagers who do not participate in a program like BEST when she says, "I think everyone is feeling a sense of *no* hope, desperation. 'Cuz it just doesn't seem to end . . . no matter what they do. It seems like it's always somethin' holdin' them down. I think [youth] just feel like givin' up."

We asked the hopefuls where they would be if not for the organization and activities that have engaged and sustained them:

Keisha: I have no idea.

Rosa: I'd be pregnant like most of my friends.

Buddy: I'd probably be selling drugs.

Tyrone: A drug user, a gang member, a convict or ex-con.

Teri: Nowhere.

Tito: Dead or in jail.

These adolescents and hundreds like them look to specific organizations as a source of support. But organizations that successfully transform inner-city teenagers' time from a liability that leads them into danger and despair into a resource that gives them a future are the exception. Too often, the programs and opportunities sanctioned and funded by government or charitable nonprofits are neither attractive nor opportune to these youth.

We saw that inner-city youth organizations that become places of hope rely on a special adult to lead them. In the next three chapters, we illustrate the roles these uncommon adults take in their uncommon organizations and describe both the diversity and the shared traits of these individuals. We look at them both through our eyes and the eyes of the hopefuls to whom these adults have made such a difference.

Chapter Three

The Wizards: Three Homegrown Community Leaders

The energy, passion, and mission of the program leader outshone the details of the program in each of the six inner-city youth organizations where we met hopeful youth. We call the leaders of these organizations "wizards" because they have succeeded where so many have not.[1] They have created environments in which youth from the tough streets of inner-city neighborhoods can imagine a positive future. Accomplishing what conventional wisdom has often held impossible, these wizards have fashioned organizations that capture urban adolescents' attention, time, and loyalty. They are successful with adolescents many in society dismiss as unreachable or irredeemable.

When Leaders Are Wizards

Effective leaders' wizardry is not magic, but it is almost as difficult to emulate because it is highly personal. As we will illustrate throughout this book, wizards' work does not lend itself to conventionally conceived "program replication," "dissemination" of activities, or "treatments." The genius of the six leaders lies less in *what* they do than in *how* they do it. That is why organizations and programs that look similar to those created by wizards may disappoint.

The characteristics, thoughts, and actions that make these leaders wizards are the subjects of Chapters Three, Four, and Five. We look at the missions and ideas that drive these leaders, the methods they have chosen to fulfill their missions, the paths that led them to work with inner-city youth, and what they have in common with each other. (The ways in which they staff and fund their operations are discussed in later chapters.) Although the details of the six leaders' lives and organizations differ, some major elements are exactly the same. All six have a love for and commitment to youth, a mission and a vision to serve others, and a passion for a particular set of activities. These then are the key elements. Love, commitment, a mission, a vision, and a passion are what create places of hope and draw youth to those places.

Some of the wizards described in this book run organizations with many programs, frequently for adults as well as children. Primarily we focus on a single program for each wizard, one that is especially illustrative of his or her goals and methods. The six wizards also have varied relationships to the communities in which they work. Three are insiders, steeped in local knowledge; the remaining three are outsiders, yet in their own ways just as successful. This chapter focuses on the insiders: Reggie Jones, Luanna Williams, and Roberto Colon. Familiar with families and neighborhoods, known to local youth and institutions, these three special leaders leverage their credibility by being "one of us" to the adolescents they serve. They are powerful role models, heroes and heroines who make hopeful futures seem possible.

Insiders' local knowledge may make it easier for them to plan activities youth will find interesting, attract youth to programs through the insiders' local stature, and appreciate the personal circumstances with which youth struggle. The ethnic and cultural backgrounds that they share with their adolescents allow special relationships to grow. Wired into local networks and institutions, insiders can continually monitor their adolescents' activities and concerns. Parents, community members, store owners, teachers, older youth—the myriad individuals youth interact with regularly—are critical eyes and ears for these leaders. "It's like he has a crystal ball," marveled Tyrone after some trouble at school triggered a query from Reggie Jones. "Somehow he finds out [and] he's on us all the time to make sure, to check out what he hears." Insiders have the resources to shape their neighborhood youth organizations in many subtle and complex ways. The special challenge to them

lies in spanning beyond the perimeters and the parochial institutions of their neighborhood and gaining access to the resources,
institutions, and opportunities of the mainstream community and
the establishment.

Reggie Jones, Luanna Williams, and Roberto Colon are all con-
summate insiders. Drawing from their personal commitments, first
and foremost to youth, and second to particular programs, each has
followed a different path to reach the common agenda—creating
a place of hope.

The Reggie Jones Gymnasts

Tyrone, a.k.a. Superman, squints in concentration, measuring the
distance to the trampolette placed in front of the gymnastic mats.
Nineteen of his red-and-white-clad teammates position themselves
in a tight row, forming a human bridge and a challenge to Tyrone's
strength and athletic skills. Nicknamed for another man of flight,
Tyrone is the finale for the afternoon's show. He takes a deep breath,
sprints down the gym floor, springs from the trampolette, and flies
over the backs of his teammates. He lands with arms raised, gold
chains glinting, and a smile that lights the room. The Gymnasts
line up for a final backflip and bow before the appreciative suburban crowd. Their leader, Reggie Jones, turns to face the audience
with his signature military salute that swings into a friendly high
five with the nearest youngster in the audience. Reggie—in his late
fifties, African American, and very athletic—carries a discipline in
his frame that sends dual messages of congenial warmth and firm
expectations—of himself and others.

"Let's move it out," he calls. Tyrone and the other boys immediately begin to fold mats and grab trampolettes, carrying them out
to be strapped atop the vans. While the boys pack, Reggie works
the crowd, passing out the Gymnasts' business cards, which bear a
list of corporate sponsors, including McDonald's and Coca-Cola,
and team action photos. Then the team heads to their fourth performance of the day, this time at a block party in an African American neighborhood.

With three thousand youngsters on his waiting list and a thirty-three-year history of success with the Gymnasts, Reggie Jones has a reputation as Lakeside's resident Pied Piper. Two youngsters on a street corner begin doing backflips and handsprings as soon as the boldly lettered team van comes into view. Inside the van, Reggie has taken on his habitual role of conscience to his young charges. He punctuates questions about the boys' school work or relationships with short sermons, favorite proverbs, and demands for the obligatory responses of "Yes sir, Mr. Jones." Reggie lives by his own set of mottoes and wants his Gymnasts to do so as well. Today he tells them, "A quitter never wins and a winner never quits, and if you want to be successful in life, you have to have a lot of intestinal fortitude and a lot of stick-to-it-iveness. Promptness and firmness and fairness, and a lot of those little things will carry you far in life. . . . Responsibility to duty."

At the block party Reggie delivers his standard introduction while the boys warm up: "These guys are not involved in anything negative," he tells the audience. "They get high on something other than drugs, and they are *not* members of gangs. The red we're wearing is Coca-Cola red and McDonald's red. Make no mistake about it. We're not hooked up with gangs." Reggie's energy and personality stand out around every aspect of the team. From his name on the uniforms (and the rarely needed prompt to a Gymnast to tuck in his shirt) to setting up the next routine, he seems to be everywhere, marshaling the Gymnasts with inexhaustible energy. Moving fast is essential if he is to handle the hundreds of performances the Gymnasts do each year in addition to his other responsibilities as an elected official and consultant to the school district.

After the show the Gymnasts are greeted by autograph seekers. Then the team heads back to Francis Homes. Like Tyrone, the rest of the Gymnasts usually feel comfortable navigating the divided gang territories of Francis Homes on their own, but after a late performance, Reggie drops them in front of the buildings in which they live. Few vehicles ever traverse the treacherous side streets of the projects late at night, but Reggie's highly visible van is known to the gangs and has safe passage. Before driving away, he sees that each performer gets safely inside.

After most performances Reggie stops by the community contact office that has been his workplace since he was elected to the county board of supervisors. The cramped space doubles as a team office and meeting place. At night he has time to check over pay schedules and performance requests left for him by Violet Vaughn, the secretary/office manager attached to his political position and unofficial mother to the team. Salaried staff for the Gymnasts include a bookkeeper, two drivers, and three assistant coaches. However, in energy and focus, the Gymnasts are still very much a one-man show.

The hall and reception area are as much museum and locker room as office. Old black-and-white photographs of Reggie playing ball on a minor league farm team and receiving a promotion in the Army offer a glimpse of the personal discipline and determination that also created the gymnastic team and its success. Another montage of visual milestones traces both Reggie's political career and the Gymnasts' athletic triumph. Interspersed among early black-and-white action shots of the Gymnasts and the more recent glossy promotional layouts, are pictures of Reggie with such dignitaries as Coretta Scott King and Andrew Young. On the shelves behind Violet's desk, various trophies and community service awards compete with each other for the limited space.

Around midnight, after posting the schedules and rosters for the next day's performances, Reggie heads for his security apartment on the other side of the tracks from Francis Homes. Some might ask why he doesn't live in Francis Homes itself when he is so involved with the residents but, as another highly effective youth leader in Francis Homes points out, to live in Francis Homes is to lose youth's respect. Any credible role model embodying an appealing future would live elsewhere. Tonight, like most others, Reggie will indulge in only three hours of sleep. That is the only way he can keep it all going—his job in the school district central office, his political duties, and his team. Divorced and living alone,

Reggie has made the Gymnasts his family and his total social life. The team is what drives him.

The Path to the Gymnasts

Known as a street fighter when he was growing up in the tenement neighborhood that Francis Homes replaced, Reggie Jones credits his high school coaches with being the adult male role models who helped him turn his life around. He attended college on a baseball scholarship, but his career in the minor leagues was cut short by military service. After fulfilling his military obligations he went back to school instead of baseball, earning a degree in education. Then he returned to his old neighborhood as a gym teacher at the local junior high school. With a college degree and reputation as a professional athlete he was something of a celebrity. However, Reggie Jones's "philosophy of life" is that "much of what I am today I owe to someone else." That philosophy made him decide it was "only fair" to give something back to the community.

In addition to his teaching, Reggie began working with youth in the evenings, through Lakeside's parks programs. As he witnessed the rising rates of school failure and gang participation among Francis Homes's male teenagers, it came to him that a gymnastics team would combine the discipline, mental and physical rigor, and novelty he thought necessary to attract these young men and turn them away from treacherous inner-city attractions. Since that time in 1959 the Reggie Jones Gymnasts have been a positive and attractive alternative to gangs for almost one thousand adolescents. Reggie and his group gave nearly seven hundred performances in 1992 alone, including a number of free performances for hospitals, churches, and children's groups. The team has approximately seventy-five members at any one time. Ranging in age from twelve to twenty-five, they are constantly engaged in practice and performance in addition to keeping their school grades up, their jobs going, and their lives "clean" and "free of anything negative." Van rides are just one of the regular opportunities Reggie takes to quiz each Gymnast on his school, work, family life, and plans for the future.

Reggie Jones's Mission and Methods

To Reggie Jones the elite performance team he has founded and sustained for so many years embodies the same elements that he firmly believes are central to his personal success—strong role-model relationships combined with athletics, clear rules, and quasi-military disciplined behavior. He also has a clearly defined mission that he expects these program elements to fulfill. It is "to enable youth to see a future, to make the Gymnasts a positive alternative to gangs, and to instill in youth the sense that there are rewards worth reaping from responsibility, energy, and determination." Reggie believes that his program achieves this mission by exposing the Gymnasts to people and cultures outside their neighborhood.

Reggie has made adherence to his strong set of rules and expected behaviors a prerequisite for team membership. The clear "Yes sir, Mr. Jones" that punctuates conversations between Reggie Jones and his Gymnasts is just one part of the discipline and respect for authority that characterize the team. Gymnasts may not drink or smoke. Swearing or "doing the dozens" (joking about someone else's mother) can draw a quick $10 fine. Reggie insists on certain norms of behavior for the Gymnasts at all times, from the ways they talk about their girlfriends to their care in disposing of trash to the ways they interact with audiences. He is the sole authority on sanctions. He tells the Gymnasts, "If you're ... in trouble with society then you're in trouble with me, and I think you'd rather be in trouble with the police than with me if I catch you doing something that is in violation of our rules and regulations." Reggie touts himself as an advocate of corporal punishment, but in practice he is able to make fines, probation, and the threat of dismissal from the team do the job of making most of the players "toe the line."

Reggie Jones stresses quality. He likens his requirements for team membership to the requirements for success in any job—

maintain quality, have good comportment at all times, and know well the full job of the working group. His markers of quality for the Gymnasts range from maintenance of uniforms to peak performance in even the simplest routines.

The discipline is accompanied by hard work. "Idle hands make for idle minds," Reggie pronounces. "And idle minds are the Devil's workshop." During the school year, the Gymnasts perform only on weekends to allow time for academics. During the summer, the schedule expands as Reggie meets not only the increased demand for appearances in this season of parades and block parties but also the increased need of the youth to be off the streets and out of the housing projects due to heightened gang activity. Summers in Lakeside are marked by gang retaliations for a winter's worth of offenses. Reggie aims to take his adolescents out of the neighborhood from dawn to dusk. He responds to the rhythms of gang life by making the Gymnasts' schedule an obstacle to the challenge, attraction, and danger of the gangs.

Another of Reggie Jones's responses to the gangs has been to structure the Gymnasts much like the gangs. The team offers the same benefits adolescents see in gangs, but it inverts the ways these benefits are applied, using them to support positive career and family-man behaviors and attitudes instead of violence and criminal activity. Both Gymnasts and gang members maintain a high-prestige profile through strong identity, marked clothing, assurances of safety, specific claims to fame, strict rules of belonging, and intense group loyalty.

In both groups, discipline is what literally keeps group members alive; either on the street or in performance each member knows every other member depends on him or her. Uniforms are the most visible marker of prestige. Gang members mark their affiliation by the colors they wear and by such signs as hats worn cocked to the left or to the right. The Gymnasts wear their own distinctive uniforms. Both groups relish the clear identities, but the Gymnasts' identity is very different in its results. Gymnasts' uniforms are tangible tickets to the outside world that Reggie thinks the youth will strive for once they have experienced it. To Reggie, the uniform is "a way in which the youth get a chance to communicate with others. [Because of] this uniform they wear, people start a conversation with them. If a Gymnast were walking along a downtown street and were to pass fifty people, I bet about thirty would stop and say something to him because he is a Reggie Jones Gymnast."

Safety is a major concern of all Francis Homes residents. For gang members, security comes from staying on their own turf under the gang's protection. Reggie fulfills his commitment to day-to-day safety for the Gymnasts through the reputation he carries in the neighborhood. He compares himself to Clint Eastwood, tough and unyielding, and attributes any troubles a Gymnast has with gang members to "newcomers" who do not know that "if you mess with a Gymnast, you mess with me." Team members also achieve a degree of safety because, as Tyrone has recognized, the gangs know the Gymnasts "are not a threat."

Reggie further ensures team members' safety by giving them a place to go to get away from the streets. He makes himself available on a twenty-four-hour basis for the team members as individuals, and he or a member of his support staff is in the office from 8:00 A.M. to 7:00 P.M. Gymnasts know they can stop by at any time to visit with Reggie, work out in the small weight room set up next to his office, or study or relax in another room.

Despite his emphasis on rules and discipline, Reggie does not neglect either fun or enrichment. "You're going to have to have something in your program that's going to be enjoyable as well as educational," he points out. "Something that's going to get [the youth] out of their immediate environment—cultural enrichment, recreational [activities]." Tyrone confirms Reggie's belief that performing and travel are the major immediate benefits when he says, "Being on the team lets us see the real world, not just the projects.... I love to travel. I love performing in front of a big crowd. I like hearing the cheers and knowing that those cheers are for me. It makes me feel special to know that I can display my talents and that people appreciate it."

When the team travels Reggie insists that all its members are to think of themselves as image-breakers and public relations ambassadors of Francis Homes in order to realize a further team mission—getting outsiders to recognize that these inner-city youth can thrive when given the right opportunities. Reggie encourages the team to respond positively when outsiders express curiosity and surprise at the behavior of "those kids from Francis Homes." "People are surprised at how well-mannered we are," Tyrone comments. "They don't expect that with us being from Francis.... We have to show them ... winning attitudes."

A Demonstration of Commitment

Team members often talk of Reggie as their father. Tyrone expresses the sentiments often repeated by his brother gymnasts when he says, "Reggie's the only father I've ever known. I'll never walk away from him because I know he'll never walk away from me." Reggie agrees: "I'm their father. If a mother's having trouble with one of them she'll call me. I'm the only father a lot of these young men will ever know and through my example and my commitment to them they will see the rewards that can come from hard work."

In his many roles as coach, manager, father-figure, and disciplinarian, Reggie is concerned with both the Gymnasts' present and future well-being. Acting as a one-man employment agency and scholarship scout he strives to ensure that all his youth have employment and educational opportunities that can lead to financially secure futures. His long experience in the city and wide knowledge of constituents in his voting district help him learn the job and scholarship possibilities. Gymnasts know that if they show their determination and willingness to practice and work hard, Reggie will follow through to help them find worthwhile employment or further education or training. He also helps those who take on family responsibilities to budget their earnings; he advises those in school to save their money for unexpected needs and future goals, such as licensing courses that will help them enter skilled trades. Many current and former Gymnasts now work as bus drivers, policemen, postal workers, mechanics, electricians, and security personnel.

Thus, like a loving parent, Reggie stretches his role well beyond the bounds of coach or teacher to encompass the whole individual. As a youth organization the gymnastics team is, as Reggie says, a "full-service organization."

Luanna Williams and the Arroyo Girl Scout Troop

"Where have y'all been keeping yourselves all morning?" Luanna Williams asks Keisha and the other girls who have just arrived at the city-sponsored Arroyo Community Center, a white-washed cinderblock structure that is the largest building in Arroyo and the last one before the railroad tracks marking the neighborhood's border. Luanna is a tall, large-boned, African American woman in her early thirties, the director of the community center, and the leader of Arroyo's one Girl Scout troop, Troop 10. In her blue jean skirt, pink teddy bear sweatshirt, and tennis shoes, Luanna looks ready to tackle another hectic day at the center. Although her words are slightly admonishing because she expects volunteers to have the same sense of obligation and responsibility as paid staffers, as usual she speaks with her musical, good-natured drawl.

Keisha and eight other Girl Scout aides herd the younger kids away from the air-conditioned front entry and the hallway that leads to the health clinic, housing office, and senior citizens' center and into the gymnasium at the other end of the building. A few teenage boys are already playing basketball, and by 8:00 A.M., the gym is filled with the chatter of over one hundred and fifty youngsters. The center is the only place Arroyo youth can find safe activities during the summer days. The basketball players help the Girl Scout aides get the children into several lines and then, as the Scouts move to the front of the lines to lead morning exercises, the boys take up positions lounging against the gym's back wall. Soon the gym is filled with sing-song chants and movement, routines the Girl Scout volunteers have learned in a series of training sessions that qualify them to be Scout program leaders and summer-camp aides.

After a few songs Luanna bustles into the gym, adding her strong, deep voice to the chorus and moving through the lines encouraging more energetic hand and body movements from the youngsters. "Wait a minute. Wait *one* minute," she calls above the din as she stops in front of one of the lounging adolescent boys. In an instant the gym is silent and all eyes are on Luanna and the sheepish young man. "Now, I *know* you know how this goes, Charlie, but seems you just might've forgotten. You wanna do us a solo?" The boy shuffles for a moment and then, with Luanna moving his arms, he joins in the fun and quickly hurries through a verse. "Everybody now," Luanna calls, and throughout the rest of the songs, every boy in the back row yells out the words in an attempt to sing louder than the rest.

After about half an hour, Keisha and her friends help the children split up into age groups. Depending on the day's schedule, the Scouts assigned to each group either stay with their groups in the gym or lead them to the day-care center, outdoor playground, or meeting room. They will stay with the youngsters throughout most of the day, helping Luanna, center staff, and visiting art teachers from Campfire with various activities. By the end of the day, Keisha is moving more slowly, tired out from her day's work, but the children hanging on her arm seem as energetic as ever. "Luanna, she's really all right," Keisha says. "But I don't know how she survives down here at the center. These kids are crazy. I couldn't do what she does." What Luanna has done for the past thirteen years, virtually alone, is to run her fifty-member Girl Scout troop (ranging in age from six to eighteen), be the full-time coordinator of the Arroyo Community Center, and hold down a part-time night job as an office cleaner. Recently she was also elected to the Girl Scout's city board as Vice President of Council Diversity.

The Path to the Arroyo Girl Scout Troop

Luanna Williams has been involved for most of her life in one way or another with the Girl Scouts, first as a member of her mother's troop and now as the leader of Troop 10. She models herself on her mother, and says, "I remind myself a lot of her because she was on the go all the time. She was always doing something, to the point where one time she was on four different PTAs [Parent-Teacher Associations] because that was during busing time, and there were four of us, and we were in four different schools." Luanna believes that "just watching" her mother and "wanting to make a difference" in Arroyo were part of what led her to the work she does now. Another factor was Girl Scouting itself: "I have to think in some ways they helped shape me. Therefore I just want to make sure that all girls have a chance to be involved."

Luanna strongly identifies with the struggle of women in contemporary society. Married to an alcoholic who works only occasionally, she strives to raise her son in the tradition of solid family values. Her primary wish for youth in general, and for girls in particular, is that they come to understand that they can be independent and self-reliant. She thinks that "girls these days need to know that they don't have to be followers all the time." To accomplish this, she says, "I try to let my girls know that sometimes, that if they don't step out, nothing's going to get done. I . . . push them into that."

Luanna Williams's Mission and Methods

Luanna Williams's mission is her commitment to youth and to Arroyo, the neighborhood in which she grew up. Her personal goal is to see that Arroyo youth have opportunities and exposure to more than the pressures and social ills endemic to low-income communities. To this end, despite her minimal budget and staff, she has successfully shifted the programming of the Arroyo Community Center to focus on youth. The center used to be "just a hangout," but over a five-year period, Luanna and her helpers have "turned it around. It's more oriented towards youth. . . . We've decided [that] it's the young people that we really need to reach."

Girl Scouting is a major part of that reorientation. Luanna sees Scouting as the particular strategy she can use to "push" her older girls. Scouting has "some important things to offer" even though the emphases of scouting have shifted from the cooking and sewing skills that were important in her day. The new programs are equally relevant, because "they give [the girls] a sense of their self-worth for one thing. To let 'em know that girls are important and that they're not there just to be there. That they are worthwhile human beings."

Scouting's message of self-worth differs sharply from the messages girls like Keisha hear on the street. When Keisha contrasts her feeling of being a woman when she is with the Girl Scouts to the way she is viewed on the streets, she says, "Outside it's like we're not females anymore. We're not ladies. We're totally different things.... We're, well, I'm not gonna say what they call us, but it's like, 'I got this girl.' But they don't call her that, and she's not really a girl anymore." Keisha thinks the Arroyo boys view the girls as trophies: "It's like they markin' down how many babies they got and each girl they got pregnant." Luanna creates a forum in which Arroyo girls can talk about their experiences growing up female in the inner city. She fosters a sense of self-worth in Keisha and her friends, in opposition to the largely negative images fostered by many boys and men.

The mere existence of Girl Scout Troop 10 is remarkable in a minority community that has rarely supported such traditional mainstream all-volunteer programs as Scouting, and the troop is also unusual in including a large group of older girls. In the past, girls like Keisha had come to the center sporadically to play basketball but never stayed for long. Girl Scouting and its image did not appeal to them, but slowly they developed an identification with Scouting. Luanna says, "It was real funny. A few years ago ... the girls didn't want anyone to know that they were a Girl Scout because it was a goody-two-shoes-type thing." If the Scouts had a Friday night party, "they didn't want anybody to know" they had sponsored it. Then, "like overnight, there was sisterhood.... I really think that it was the things that we were doing. They really started enjoying what they were doing."

The girls' identification with Scouting came not because the girls accepted the well-known mainstream images of "what Scouting can do for you" but rather because they enjoyed the consistent contact with Luanna Williams and the productive activities she and they shaped together. The first activities were dances and parties. Later the troop took on a wide array of more proactive community-oriented activities, at least in part, Keisha says, because the younger girls in the troop "need them." Scouts volunteer not only at the center but also at the local hospital and senior citizens' homes.

The large size and wide age range of Troop 10 is due to a lack of volunteer leaders, but Luanna has turned this apparent liability into an asset, encouraging the older girls to find responsibilities at the center and in the troop that set them apart. Thus at adolescence, when girls typically drop their Scouting activities, Luanna's girls are finding new opportunities in Scouting, and her troop is growing. Luanna points out that her Girl Scout helpers get discounts on field trips, and at the end of the summer she invites them to her house for "slumber parties and all that kind of stuff." She says, "They like those things. But I [also] think they just like being out [at my house]."

Luanna is committed to Girl Scout programs because she believes they "encourage girls to be independent [and] teach girls to be leaders, to become self-confident." For example, the camp aide and program aide training actually teaches "girls how to teach other kids, teach a song, . . . things like this that later on in life can spill over." Luanna nurtures this independence among her older girls by giving them responsibility not only for the younger girls, but also for planning their own activities. Luanna thinks she would get nowhere if she did not listen to what her Girl Scouts want and then respond to their interests. During weekly troop meetings, Luanna coaxes and pushes them to plan and think. While all her urging usually results in a busy schedule, occasionally they cannot come up with plans and she is content to let them adjourn. This flexible strategy has paid off. Although the troop has pitifully few resources, it is very active and, according to Keisha, "always interesting," because the youth are engaged in activities they care about. The older girls participate in activities ranging from baby-sitting to parties, from basketball to telethons, from community service projects to camp aide training and service.

Luanna wants her Scouts to focus primarily on activities that meet the Scouting objectives of service and contact with the broader community, and she thinks community service is a major reason for the continued success of the troop in attracting and keeping older girls. Learning the value of giving is particularly important for African American girls, she believes, "because they have so little opportunity to see themselves as capable of giving to others."

Other aspects of traditional Scouting, such as uniforms, prepared materials, and participation in camps and jamborees are less important to the girls' needs. Arroyo Girl Scouts do not work systematically toward earning badges. Such activities seem trivial to young women like Keisha who often have adult caretaking responsibilities and economic roles in their families. Girls of Troop 10 do not wear uniforms as they are too expensive. They rarely participate in camping or jamboree activities for the same reason.

Luanna has also adapted the Scout program to take advantage of her daily availability at the center. Typical Scout troops meet once a week, but many Arroyo Scouts are at the center every day. They come to do their homework, help younger kids, talk and relax, and work on annual and seasonal projects they plan during the weekly meetings. This strategy creates a sense of place and continuity. Luanna is always available to talk to the girls, and the Scouting program rests on the trust and give-and-take between Luanna and her Scouts.

There are rules, but Luanna couches them in a context of continual support. Her goal is to "be flexible" because that will keep youth in the program, where they have a better chance at a successful future. Only rarely is someone sent home. Luanna explains, "You work with some discipline within the program. . . . [If] you don't do what you're asked to do then you don't get to participate in field trips or you don't get the special treats or something like that." Luanna describes a lot of the discipline as "just conditioning. . . . When they know, 'Luanna's not gonna send me home. She's not gonna put me out. But I may not get to go on the field trip. I may have to stay here with [staff members] Miss Wilson or D'Andre while everyone else has fun,' then [you know that] the girls [are beginning] to feel a commitment to Scouting."

Luanna asserts that, in addition to enjoying the activities and responsibility and feeling needed, her girls stick with Scouting through their teens because she has kept pace with them. She thinks most troop leaders cannot keep up with the girls as they develop into young adults, and remarks that "if the girls stretch and the leaders can't stretch with them, they lose them." Luanna keeps her girls because she "plays a substitute mom. The troop becomes like a family with intense and intimate relationships. It's safe; it's supportive."

From that supportive base, Luanna actively seeks to open a door to the outside world for her Scouts. She talks of giving them an enlarged vision of possible futures and opportunities outside Arroyo, because, "right now in our community, they're getting trapped . . . in the drug trafficking and all that kind of stuff. . . . I think to break that cycle they have to get out and then come back into the community. . . . I would want them to experience everything they could possibly experience to show them that they don't have to stay in their community and shrivel up and die."

Troop 10 has many opportunities to move beyond the isolation and sheer lack of resources that, according to Luanna, characterize the Arroyo community. For example, the girls engage in the Girl Scouts' Wider Opportunities summer program for older adolescents. "Held throughout the country in different specialty areas," the program allows teenage girls to "experience something different, to experience what it is to be part of a larger organization . . . to give them a sense of, yes, we are part of a national organization chartered by the U.S. Congress." In this way, Keisha and her friends can feel a link to all girls, a symbolic breaking of their isolation.

Yet another benefit of an association with Scouting is that it gives Arroyo girls a mark of legitimacy they can use to their advantage. For example, the baby-sitting certificate they earn translates into work. Keisha believes that Big Valley's mainstream European American community looks at her differently when they know she's a Scout. "It's like being a Scout makes you okay—a positive thing," she explains.

A Demonstration of Commitment

Luanna faces many staffing and budget difficulties. However, she is determined to continue her Scouting work because the most important element of the Girl Scout program is that "the girl comes first.... *So* many times in our society, women get tossed aside or overlooked and treated unimportantly. Girl Scouting let's them know that it's really okay to be a woman in today's society. You can do just as good, you can go just as far as any man if you put your head to it."

Luanna is also committed to seeing her girls accepted within the larger Girl Scout circle. At present in her region, Scouting is predominantly a mainstream middle-class activity. Her faith that she can make—and has made—a difference in the lives of many girls through Scouting includes a belief that she can teach the Girl Scout organization to be more accessible and hospitable to African American adolescent girls from poor neighborhoods, if she just keeps at it. The national Girl Scout organization, Luanna stresses, "is committed to pluralism, diversity, and affirmative action. It takes a lot of work to live up to this on a day-to-day basis." Luanna Williams is a model to her own Scouts of that day-to-day hard work.

Scout leader, surrogate mother, big sister, and role model—Luanna is a part of her girls' lives in as many ways as possible, always giving them the same message—if you try you will succeed.

Roberto Colon and the Porter Crossing YMCA Gang Alternatives and Intervention Program

On a typically hot Lakeside August day, twelve Puerto Rican teenage boys from Porter Crossing are hard at work with rakes, shovels, and a wheelbarrow, cleaning up the debris in a large empty lot just a block away from their usual drug-dealing post. Bare backs, bent and glistening with sweat, provide visual testament to their affiliation. Above their left shoulder blades, tattoos in the shapes of horns (turned up) and lances (turned down) indicate that they are Zs and the killers of Gs, a major rival gang. T-shirts, deemed too hot for a temperature of one hundred-plus degrees, hang like kerchiefs from their back pockets. Emblazoned with the same symbol as the black-and-white van on the corner, the shirts boast of another affiliation—the Porter Crossing YMCA.

The boys have been at work since 9:00 A.M. Although the announcement of the day's job had been greeted with complaints of "I don't want to clean up no dirty lot" and "When are we going to paint again," the boys had set to work quickly when they reached the vacant lot located in the heart of their neighborhood. In these few blocks, the outer walls of stores, garages, and phone booths once sported gang graffiti, but now clear expanses of brick-red or cream-colored paint, also applied by these gang members, cover the spidery scrawls of intergang communication. This summer's efforts appear more successful than last summer's; it is already August and, although some walls need repainting, two-thirds of them are still clear.

The Zs are generally silent while they work. Goofing off is quickly squelched by Tito, one of the group's oldest members, with comments of "Don't you wanna get outta here? I wanna go to the beach, man." This diligence contrasts sharply with the joking camaraderie of the van rides, during which most of the teasing is directed toward Manny, their supervisor. Although twenty-seven-year-old Manny's job description includes caseworker and van driver, the Zs identify him most importantly as "an old man"—a term reserved for an older, respected member (or in this case, former member) of the gang.

Around noon, a middle-aged African American man approaches, wearing a baseball cap emblazoned "Security." A couple of the boys observe him warily until they see that he is carrying bottles of cola. He says, "I thought you might want something to drink. Sure appreciate what you're doing here." A few minutes later, a young Puerto Rican woman emerges from a dilapidated brownstone with a large pitcher of ice water and similar words of thanks. Tito relaxes and calls his thanks, adding, "We're just tryin' to do our part."

An hour and seven large garbage cans of debris later, the boys quickly load their equipment into the van and return to the Porter Crossing YMCA. Manny chooses a circuitous route even though it adds fifteen blocks to the drive. That morning Roberto Colon, YMCA regional director for five YMCAs in the Porter Crossing area, warned him that a rival gang member had been shot the night before. It is turning into a "hot" summer between the gangs, and the Zs agree that it is smarter to take the longer route than to cross three hostile blocks.

When they reach the Y the boys obey rules designed to keep gang members from contact with non–gangmembers. Careful not to talk to any of the younger patrons, they quickly file downstairs into the Gang Alternatives and Intervention Network (GAIN) office where windows separate them from the game room and children and youth who, to date, have avoided gang affiliation. A few of the Zs sprawl onto old sofas against the back wall. Tito sits down with Manny to go over job applications. Life-sized posters of local sports heroes hang next to a bulletin board covered with job postings ranging from receptionist to grounds maintenance at the local stadium. A flyer for the Safe Summer Street Understanding Dinner is a reminder that the Y is working to negotiate a peace between leaders of several local gang factions.

Planning for the future often seems futile amidst the climate of violence in Porter Crossing. "I'm not the kind of person that thinks ahead," Tito says. "I think day by day... 'cuz I don't know what's gonna happen tomorrow. I could get shot tomorrow." In spite of this view Tito is now one of the most regular workers in the GAIN summer jobs program and constantly reminds Manny that he wants a more permanent job. His connection with GAIN is beginning to offer him concrete hope for a better life.

It is GAIN founder Roberto Colon's dream for youth that is giving hope to Tito and others like him. "My mission is training youth for productive futures," says Roberto. "I want to give them opportunities, including opportunities to become the next generation of leaders in their community." Central to Roberto's success with GAIN is the fact that Tito and the other gang members in GAIN recognize Roberto not only as a "tie man" or "suit" and someone taken seriously by the outside world but also as "one of us."

The Path to GAIN

Now in his late thirties and the single parent of a teenage daughter, Roberto Colon grew up amidst Porter Crossing's Latino gangs. Unlike many of his peers, however, Roberto survived the streets and developed a career for himself in the Lakeside YMCA. He later acquired a master's degree in sociology from a local university, after years of part-time study. He attributes his success and survival to three factors—his family, a local YMCA, and a job.

Roberto's parents were Puerto Rican immigrants who created a strong family structure for their children. "They worked for us," Roberto says. Avoiding the gangs, he spent many after-school hours at his local YMCA, where he was introduced to basketball and swimming. While many of his close childhood friends remained heavily involved with gangs, Roberto got a job at the age of fifteen. Later, he found work at the local Y. Since then he has worked indefatigably to provide alternatives and hope for youth, many of whom, he knows, "already have a long history of probation." He wants to help youth who "live in a family that's totally destructive in that the [parents] are either alcoholics or drug addicts or even have been former gang members themselves." While he knows the worst about Porter Crossing, he also rages at the negative images of inner-city youth that blare daily from the media, and at the punitive regulatory policies that flow from policymakers' similarly negative conceptions.

While Roberto is concerned about prevention—keeping youth away from gangs, drugs, crime, and school failure—he has refused to give up on intervention strategies, even though they are difficult to fund. He believes that prevention and intervention strategies should go "hand in glove," that it is impossible to enact prevention programs without dealing with the "negative elements" in the community. Although "the model of prevention is great" in a "middle-class community or suburban community, . . . it just doesn't work in this community [without intervention]." Roberto also disagrees with those who claim that increased law enforcement is the only response for dealing with gang members. He asks, "Do we wipe out a whole generation of kids who need intervention in their lives?"

To start GAIN, one small program at one YMCA in an association with twenty-seven YMCAs, Roberto had to work hard to win over the larger Lakeside YMCA organization and the local board. His personal assurances that he knew the streets well, knew what to prepare for, and could guarantee that gang members would be kept separate from the other youth and children at the Y were essential to his victory. However, he feels that some YMCA officers are still struggling with the idea that youth can be helped after they have joined gangs. In addition, while Roberto was negotiating for approval from his own board of directors, he realized that he needed approval from the boards of directors of the streets, so he also met with juntas of three or four members at the top of each gang and convinced them of the value of GAIN.

Roberto Colon's Mission and Methods

Roberto Colon's general mission is defined by the lower-class Latino families and youth of Porter Crossing to whom he wants to provide access to better futures. Moreover, he is committed to a community-based approach to social service. "Location," he says, "determines the mission." As a YMCA regional director he is entitled to a downtown office, but he prefers to work out of the local Porter Crossing Y so he can stay close to the youth and the community.

There are so many programs at the Porter Crossing YMCA that the space given to the gang members in GAIN is not easy to find at first. The former bank building is filled with youngsters coming and going for swimming lessons, escorted by their big sisters, mothers, or grandparents. Youth come for tennis lessons, and adults come to work out in the weight room and attend aerobics classes. Youth groups from local schools and Scout troops attend special events here. Health and human development classes are held for teen mothers who learn everything from how to sterilize formula to ways to economize on buying equipment and clothing for their infants. There is also an employment training class offering job counseling and leadership skills to the Y's Youth Leadership Club. YMCA staff coordinate a Head Start program and work with a youth network to link area residents with more than thirty community organizations.

As in Francis Homes, a scant two miles away, gangs shape the social character of Porter Crossing. In response, one of Roberto Colon's immediate missions is to work with gang members to break the cycle of violence that continues to destroy both individual lives and the fabric of the Porter Crossing Latino community. For the community to develop, its youth must regain a sense of self-respect, but "how can we expect these kids to develop any self-esteem, any sense of pride . . . if their most basic element in their society, which is the family structure, is totally destroyed?" Roberto asks. "How can they function?" He declares, "There [is] nothing out there for these kids [and they] are killing each other. We've got to do something." GAIN is that something.

Roberto has designed GAIN with three components: outreach, case management, and summer jobs. All three are intended to draw gang members back into the system that they have rejected and that has rejected them. Roberto reaches out to gang members with a recreational hook—gym-and-swim nights for gang members. On these nights, the YMCA closes its doors at 9:00 P.M., according to its regular schedule, but reopens shortly thereafter for the gang members. The brief interval allows other Y patrons to leave without encountering the incoming gang members. On these nights, fifty to eighty gang members make full use of the swimming pool, weight room, and gym facilities until 11:00 P.M. To avoid possible "hits" by rival gangs, the schedule for these gym nights is kept secret. While members of the gang whose territory surrounds the Y usually arrive on foot, members of the Zs, whose territory lies several blocks to the west, are picked up by one of the Y's four vans.

Roberto's outreach strategy is to give gang members positive experiences in an institutional setting. GAIN staff use recreational activities to build relationships with gang members and talk to them about the jobs available through the Y's placement program. Once drawn in by the dual promise of safety and athletic activities, and given a chance to test the promise, gang members are encouraged to involve themselves in a complex of activities aimed at changing their relationship to each other and to the community and its members. Like Reggie Jones and Luanna Williams, Roberto Colon also starts by trying to fill up as much of the adolescents' free time as possible. As Manny puts it, "What we're doing is taking them off the corner. That will reduce the risk of them getting shot that night for three hours." For those in the jobs program, the risk is reduced by eight hours each day.

Roberto intends GAIN's case management program to place gang members either directly into jobs or into job-training programs that will lead to full-time employment. Thus GAIN offers safe, real work alternatives to gang participation. In the jobs program, gang members are referred to as clients. Each caseworker had between fifty and seventy clients on file before the end of GAIN's first year and worked on average with thirty clients each week. Caseworkers assist gang members with job applications, advise them on job or job-program placement, counsel them on school or GED opportunities, and follow up on the placement. The help needed can be considerable. Roberto reports that some gang members "can't even fill out résumés, even something as basic as that." Others may have skills but no access to the job market. One gang member had been trained to be a welder, "a pretty lucrative thing," while he was in prison, but he didn't find employment until Manny used his "connections" to get the welder "through that bureaucracy" of job applications and personnel offices to get him a job.

GAIN's final component, the summer jobs program, was developed primarily in response to the difficulty of securing long-term positions for interested clients. Roberto also knew that summer jobs were crucial because of the summertime rise in gang activity. The program in which Tito participated, for example, employed seventeen gang members to promote and carry out community cleanup that both benefited Porter Crossing and gave stop-gap jobs and training to the teenagers. Other goals of the cleanup included instilling the teenagers with greater pride and ownership in their community, and giving them chances to experience a better relationship with community members.

Unique in terms of gang work, Roberto's intervention program faces challenges not experienced in prevention programs. As GAIN director Cruz Sanchez puts it, "Intervention means you're goin' to come in contact with the elements. Prevention means they're goin' to stay inside and not get their hands dirty." Cruz feels that people who push prevention programs only "have no confidence" in inner-city youth who are gang members. "They don't think they are going to make it."

One of Roberto's challenges is to combat the strong gang identification. GAIN does this by offering gang members an alternative affiliation—the YMCA identity. It comes packaged in the form of T-shirts that proclaim the wearers are YMCA staff and that Tito and others wear while out on Y projects. In addition to giving the youth a new, more respectable symbol of identity, the shirts conceal their gang-related tattoos. "[Gang members] are so proud and they want to connect so bad with something that they are in control of or they are part of," Roberto explains. "[And] I've just seen so many kids with tattoos. . . . So I said, . . . 'you guys put on the shirts, the Y shirts.' . . . It's to cover up those tattoos, basically. And now they have hopefully some pride in [being part of the Y]." Being part of the Y is more than a surface affiliation. The YMCA identity comes with a clear set of expectations and a clear set of messages about preparing for a positive future and establishing a positive relationship with the community.

Another challenge Roberto and his staffers understand and must face is the perception and reality of "once a gang member, always a gang member." Rival gangs will either not know or not care that someone is no longer active in a gang. Part of GAIN's authenticity to youth like Tito is that the staff is conscious of gang members' special needs for safety. For example, when Manny is placing clients in a job or a training class, he says he would never send them to a particular site if he feels it's going to be a "danger to their life."

GAIN has yet another side, one without which it probably would not work. "We're getting [gang members] jobs and we're getting them into school", says Manny, "but we've got to give them something else too. Like something to have fun, where they can relax with each other and not be [on edge] all the time, watching their back all day." One of Roberto's ultimate goals is to develop opportunities for real dialogue among rival gangs so that they will no longer have to watch their backs. Thus in addition to providing recreation, jobs, and the Y identity, Roberto is working to help rival gang members communicate with each other face-to-face, rather than through the graffiti that so often lead to attacks and killings.

A Demonstration of Commitment

Roberto Colon's GAIN program has been successful largely because both program components and staff attitudes rest on local knowledge and the credibility Roberto's staff has as former gang members. The youth know that Roberto is a tireless networker and advocate for them and especially for Latino youth. He has served on as many as thirteen boards and committees at one time, both in his official capacity as a YMCA regional director and as a community leader.

Tito acknowledges the importance of Roberto's contribution when he says, "I think if there were more Robertos in the world, this world would be a better place. And that's a serious comment." What impresses Tito is that, "every time" he and Roberto talk, Roberto's "main objective [is] getting brothers into the right stage of life." Tito believes Roberto is especially trying to help "the ones that are on the corner," as Tito himself was. Tito's conclusion? "If we had a hundred more Robertos in the City of Lakeside, I think it'd be a happenin' place."

Roberto Colon's success also springs from his express commitment to being a local, reachable role model for youth, in the hope that they will become leaders as well. That commitment is paying off. On the street Roberto is known as "the Dream," something to admire and to be like. He says:

I can relate to them.... So when they say, "Everything is bad," I can come back and say, "No, it's positive.... I've gone through it too." These kids want to emulate me now.... They say, "Roberto came from this neighborhood, but look, he's wearing a tie. He's driving a nice car. He's got a telephone. What can I do?" And I say, "You can do it. But you gotta realize you gotta be willing to sacrifice; you gotta stay off that corner; you gotta pick up a book once in a while, make some sacrifices."

Being a role model is a responsibility that Roberto takes seriously. "It's amazing how the kids look up to me," he says. "So I'm always on the edge [in that respect]. The kids can't see me drinking a beer or cussing, because I feel like I'm a role model. If I do something to disprove that, then there goes their hope."

As a result, the adolescents in GAIN do have hope. They are learning to say, as Tito does, "We want respect as human beings, not gang members. . . . You gotta earn respect, and if we don't earn it, they ain't gonna give it to us. If you had a hundred jobs, almost all of 'em would be taken up by brothers from the 'hood. Nine outta ten of 'em would be linin' up." Manny goes on to describe how Roberto looks for those youth who are looking for a chance: "When Roberto finds one who says, 'Hey, help me, man. I need a job. I need to get back to school,' then we know [that person] will work, and I say, "Hey, oh boy, he's interested, man. Let's hook him up."

One final secret of Roberto's effectiveness lies in his tangible, everyday interaction with youth in the community. His commitment and his knowledge are such that he says, "I can take [commitment and interaction] *beyond* the job. I think that's the difference. That's what a role model is." Roberto acts as mentor, friend, job counselor, and role model for his GAIN youth. Because of its resident wizard, GAIN, like the Gymnasts guided by Reggie Jones and the Arroyo Girl Scouts led by Luanna Williams, is much more than a single youth program. It is in itself a full-service youth organization.

Chapter Four

More Wizards: Three Outsiders Who Have Earned Respect

Outsider youth leaders can be external to local settings in several ways. Besides being unfamiliar with local customs and history they also may differ from their youthful charges in ethnicity, personal background, and culture. Outsiders' mission to work with youth is often connected to their experience of a national organization such as the YMCA, Boy Scouts or Girl Scouts, Boys and Girls Clubs, or Girls, Inc.

Outsider youth leaders also bring to their chosen communities a range of skills and outside contacts that can widen adolescents' circle of experience. They face less of a challenge than insiders when they must draw power and opportunity from the larger community. However, outsiders face a greater challenge than insiders in establishing local trust and credibility and acquiring local knowledge. Yet they must gain this community support as it is the bedrock for places of hope. The often disillusioned youth and families of the inner city treat outsiders with suspicion, expect little, and trust slowly. Youth organization wizards are those outsiders who have succeeded in earning the trust of their newfound community and in demonstrating that they are *for* the community even if not initially *of* it.

The outsider wizards described in this chapter are Steve Patterson, John Peña, and Michael Carroll. They are outsiders to different degrees. Steve Patterson is a geographic outsider who nevertheless shares many values and circumstances with River City youth and their families; John Peña shares a Latino background with many of the youth who come to the Big Valley Boys

65

and Girls Clubs but is a stranger to the community's intricately choreographed society and politics; Michael Carroll is both an ethnic and a social outsider in the Francis Homes community where he works. Despite their potential handicaps, each of these men is succeeding in creating and sustaining hope among inner-city youth because each has recognized that his most critical test is winning youth's confidence.

Steve Patterson and Cooper House

It is 3:00 P.M. on a Tuesday, and Buddy lounges on a wooden bench in the Cooper House entrance hall. He starts front-desk duty at four o'clock, but right now he is reading *Sports Illustrated*. With a loud bang the great wooden entrance door falls shut and in rushes nine-year-old Ben, late as usual for his swim class. Buddy calls him over and, sending a meaningful glance toward the portrait above the marble fireplace of Mrs. Cooper, wife of the industrial philanthropist founder, pulls the cap off Ben's head. Ruffling Ben's hair, Buddy tells him, "Take your time Ben, and remember your hat." "Aw, man," Ben says. Then he changes tactics, leans against Buddy, smiles, and asks: "Will you play checkers with me after swimming?" "Sure," says Buddy, "you know where I'll be."

After Ben disappears into the locker room, Buddy heads over to Steve Patterson's office, where a group of Buddy's friends, including Marcus, are enjoying the air conditioning. Unbeknownst to the executive director, there is serious business going on in his office while he is in the gym teaching basketball. The older boys are practicing Mr. Patterson's problem-solving style. This activity started as a game a few weeks before, Buddy explains. "There was four or five of us. We walked into his office; we took turns pretendin' and sittin' in his chair, pretendin' we were him. We sat there for five hours! It felt like half an hour." The game turned into a secret plan to roast Mr. P., as they affectionately call Steve, at the upcoming benefit dinner. Now Buddy listens to four-teen-year-old Bill's attempt to capture Steve's style, but when Bill says, "Here's what you're gonna do," Buddy intervenes: "If you have a problem, he doesn't say, 'Well, here's what you're gonna do.' He brings up, 'Well, what do you think are the consequences of this?' And he lets you make your own decision. He leads you, but ... it's like the old saying goes—you can lead a horse to water, but you can't make him drink. [Mr. P. is] there to help you, but [he] gives you all the possible outcomes of any decision you can make and then you decide."

Today the role-playing is cut short when Steve appears at the door to say, "How about coming and helping in the gym? I want to give each of the kids some practice with jump shots. Do you gentlemen have some time?" All the youth except Buddy head upstairs with Steve, making bets on which juniors will be best at jump shots. After agreeing to meet his friends in the senior game room at six o'clock, Buddy takes over at the front desk. Hearing shrieks from the regular game room he gets up and pokes his head in the door to see six twelve-year-old girls lying across the pool table, laughing helplessly. Apparently, Heather has just sent her third ball into the far corner of the room. "Can you keep it down a bit?" Buddy asks, laughing too. He offers to give Heather a quick lesson, asking Mary to keep an eye on the desk.

By 5:00 P.M. Buddy is busy collecting permission slips from kids for a trip to the zoo, answering the phone with a polite "Cooper House. May I help you?" and describing the house to Joe, a newcomer who has just walked in. Joe has heard that Cooper House has a pool, and he wants to swim. Buddy smiles and tells Joe about Cooper House and its Boys and Girls Clubs affiliation. Joe cannot come only to swim; he has to become a member. Membership costs $3.50 a year for teens (and 30 cents a year for elementary school children), and members are required to attend two activities a week, one sports and one club activity. In addition, Buddy says, Joe can participate in photography and art classes, receive tutoring, receive instruction in the new computer lab, and use the newspaper and print shop. Buddy explains that Cooper House is "a very special place. You can't work with clay anywhere else. You can't take dance lessons for a cheap price. You can't take piano lessons for a cheap price. You can't do a lot of the things anywhere else." Joe wants to know if the rules are hard to follow, but Buddy assures him that "the kids don't mind the rules and stuff 'cuz they wanna be able to come [down the house]." He adds that he is sure Joe will fit in, and he asks Ben, who has now arrived, checkerboard in hand, to give Joe a tour. As the two youngsters disappear around the corner, Buddy hears Ben say, "The first thing you gotta learn is you always gotta take your hat off when you come in." During Joe's tour of "the house," he will see several game rooms, a swimming pool, a gymnasium, a kitchen, a disc jockey room, classrooms, and, in a rooftop addition accessible only through a third-story window, the new computer lab. A newcomer's tour is essential because there are no signs anywhere; they would go against the house's family atmosphere. "Are there signs for the bathroom at your house?" Steve Patterson asks. "We encourage them to understand that Cooper House is their house, and to treat it that way."

At six o'clock Buddy's relief arrives, and he and the other older boys gather in the senior game room, off limits to all under the age of fourteen. Time spent here is mostly unsupervised and unplanned. It is a privilege earned by attendance at required activities, and by fulfillment of work requirements if the senior is one of the many who have part-time jobs as receptionists, tutors, lifeguards, or supervisors for the younger members. At eight o'clock, the boys have their Senior Boys Club meeting to plan both social activities like dances and picnics, and service projects in the community. This evening they will have dinner together and present Steve with their plans for the Wacky Olympics. The idea behind the Wacky Olympics is to develop a set of games that everyone, even nonathletes, can take part in. The concept reflects Steve's guiding principle of providing everyone at Cooper House with experiences of success. In the same vein Steve thinks that "all facets of the program and of life should be recognized." For example, Cooper House holds an "awards banquet to celebrate everything." Prizes include a Gold Shield award that recognizes club members for anything the staff "see them doing that's positive." The object is "to catch them doing something right as often as possible." This award and the most outstanding member award are the organization's most coveted prizes. The shield, gold-painted plaster of paris mounted on black velvet, features the letters SCR, standing for service, character, and responsibility.

The Senior Boys Club members have embraced Steve's guiding principle, and to support it they have invented such Wacky Olympics games as straw throwing instead of javelin throwing and a portable miniature golf course in which ingenuity rather than athletic prowess will determine the winners. As Buddy explains, there's no "competition" at Cooper House. "You're all equal friend-wise, and you help each other out. At Cooper, everybody's one.... We just get along great, like immediate family."

The Path to Cooper House

Although most people would never guess it, Steve Patterson is, strictly speaking, an outsider to Cooper House, its neighborhood, and River City. But his cultural and moral background of strong family values focusing on hard work, discipline, and service to others parallels that of many of the club's traditional members and its founders.

Steve is a solid, athletic European American in his late thirties and a longtime youth worker. He grew up in rural Ohio in a strongly religious community, and his early development remains visible in his commitment to youth organizations. Married and with children of his own, he initially taught athletics and physical education in the public schools, much like Reggie Jones. When he left teaching it was to take a position in the YMCA, but the same strong religious convictions and focus on children and adolescents that led him to youth work eventually prompted him to leave the Y when he found the local branch focusing on income-producing activities rather than youth in order to stay in good stead with the national organization.

Unlike the Lakeside YMCA, which eventually acceded to Roberto Colon's desire to serve not only youth in general but also adolescent gang members, the River City YMCA structure within which Steve Patterson worked was moving away from accommodating the needs of youth, especially poor youth, and was instead designing programs to attract fitness-minded and dues-paying adults. In 1989 he almost accepted a high-paying job at a bank, but accepted the position of executive director at Cooper House instead.

What attracted him to Cooper House was a fit between his personal mission and that of the Boys and Girls Clubs organization, and the promise of enough resources to carry out that mission. For example, he has ten full-time staff members and seventy-two seasonal and part-time staff for a membership of around six hundred, swelling to four thousand in the summer. "The reason I wouldn't be in youth services anywhere else," he says, "is I could never be satisfied not doing my job again." He frames his job and his life's mission in terms of "focusing on youth" and creating environments to support their successful development. The original mission articulated for Cooper House by factory-owner Peter Cooper nearly one hundred years ago also focused on youth. Cooper wrote, "We want to make this a factory for character-building and good citizenship. It is our desire to surround the boys and girls of this neighborhood with such good influences that they will never want to depart from the right paths. Good citizenship is the purpose we shall keep in view. Character, which is the outgrowth of honor, will be the goal of our endeavors."

Steve Patterson's Mission and Methods

When Steve Patterson arrived at Cooper House, he initiated a five-year plan whose mission continues Peter Cooper's. The mission, Steve wrote, is "to provide a comprehensive youth service to the community through recreational programs which focus on building leadership and character development... to enable youth to achieve their highest potential." Buddy restates the mission from the adolescents' point of view when he says, "one of the things we do at the house is surround ourselves with positive influences; one of the ways to get out of a [bad] situation is to surround yourself with positive friends, positive influences."

Positive influences are at the very core of Cooper House's existence. The club exudes traditional values. The spirit of home and respect for elders and place pervade the whole of Cooper House's immense three-story brick building. Guides to character are literally part of the Cooper House walls. On the first-floor landing of the central stairway, a twenty-foot stained glass window enunciates the virtues of manhood: wisdom, courage, temperance, justice; womanhood's virtues encircle the companion window on the second-floor landing: piety, chastity, faith, and prudence. Cooper House has been home now to several generations of Housers, not a few of whom have married other Housers. Loyalty and a feeling of responsibility toward the house is strong. A current staff member and alumna remembers that thirty years ago, as today, "you never missed. Never, ever, never missed, unless you were deathly sick."

However, when Steve Patterson arrived the long-standing Cooper House traditions had begun to create problems. The house was finding it hard to remain in touch with changing urban youth and by the late 1980s few adolescent members remained. Youth saw the traditional programs as sissy and boring. Coming in from the outside, unencumbered by house tradition, Steve was able to view the organization with fresh eyes in his five-year plan and rethink procedures and programs, revitalizing the house and creating an environment that attracts and engages adolescents while it also retains some traditions that symbolize Cooper House for members, alumni, and the community. As a result, house membership is now about half adolescents, double the number when Steve Patterson arrived on the scene.

Susie Parnel, Steve's exuberant director of programs and a house alumna, says that the important difference between the house as it was in her day and as it is now is that Steve "has really brought the kids in in new ways." There are more coed activities, "'cuz that's what the kids want," and now, older members plan, run programs, and set and enforce the rules. Steve says his success in bringing adolescents back to Cooper House simply entails listening to them: "You gotta listen, because we'd rather have the kids down here hangin' out than on the streets hangin' out. So you do things that the kids *want* to do, and they're here.... We talk to them, particularly in club, about what their needs are. What's goin' on in school. Like we just suggested a program on AIDS, and they popped up [and said], 'We've had it up to here with AIDS; we don't wanna hear another word about it.' That's good input for us." Contrasting his approach to that of other youth organizations, Steve says that he fits programs to the youth rather than the other way around.

Particularly sensitive to adolescents' needs to express themselves and think for themselves, Steve points out that youth "don't want to be preached to. They don't want to be shown everything. They need to have input in the program so we started [saying], 'Okay, show us what you want. Help us to develop a program. Become a vital part in the creativity part of it.' And they've for the most part started doing that." Among the new programs Steve started after a series of talks with the club members were a car maintenance program that introduces youth to the complexities of car insurance and purchase as well as repair, a program for teenage girls that addresses issues of sexuality and futures for women, and a jobs referral course. In Steve's view, these programs have been successful because the youth did "real work" in launching them and carrying them out. "They made real calls to insurance agencies [to get] quotes and all the information—not mock calls or role plays."

One big hit with adolescents was an all-night dance, which Steve agreed to after the Senior Girls Club committee came up with rules, guidelines, and assurances to the conditions he set forth. Susie Parnel recalls that "the staff was hesitant at first. But Mr. P. told the staff [it would be all right] 'if you can get [the kids] to follow these rules,' [which were] no one is allowed outta the gym, they're not allowed to suck face whenever they're in the corner, [and similar rules]. I took it back to the girls and said, 'Okay, you can have it if we meet these requirements.' They did it and more. This year is our second year. One hundred and eighty people came—and not one problem."

Although he listens to youth in order to introduce a wide range of programs that meet their needs, Steve has not abandoned his programmatic goals of teaching responsibility and providing opportunities for growth. He believes club members have a responsibility to try things before they decide they do not like them, to at least test opportunities. Steve calls this his "take a bite" approach to programming, and it extends from trying basketball even though you are short to tasting all the food on your plate at camp.

Steve has worked hard to create jobs at the house that give youth opportunities to earn a small salary for working at a job with more responsibility than "flipping burgers." Older members have opportunities to develop leadership skills and earn modest salaries by working as junior counselors, both during the year and, in particular, at summer camp. Youth with interests in business are hired to work in Cooper House offices. More than simply offering kids money to stay around, the program for older youth is designed to mirror the real world. All youth must prepare résumés, write job applications, and undergo an interview by the staff to secure any house job. Youth are also encouraged to take responsibility outside the confines of the house, volunteering in hospitals, with the homeless, and at schools.

From his listening, Steve also learned that the adolescents needed a place of their own, because "if you ask them to participate in open forum on a constant basis, with kids seven, eight years old, it's not going to work. They need their own space. They need their own atmosphere. They need to be able to go into an area and talk about the things teenagers wanna talk about, address the issues that they need to address.... That opportunity wasn't available to them before ... and we needed to provide that." However, the senior game room was not simply given to them. Steve made the members' need into an opportunity by designing a way to give the youth more ownership in the house and real work experience as well as their own place, decorated in the red paint they wanted. In this way he blended his goals with theirs. He contracted a painting job to the youth, taking the money from the house repair budget. They had to go through the application procedure, plan the job, and present the plans for approval by the board of directors and the staff, and finally, paint the better part of the first two floors. The payoff, in addition to their salary, was the coveted red senior game room.

For many Cooper House members, youth who have been "told to" most of their lives, the decision-making and problem-solving support they receive is one of the club's most important benefits. Buddy says this is what Cooper House is all about: "It teaches you responsibility. It lets you be an individual and not a clump of people.... It lets you be your own person."

The importance to the house members of being responsible and being held responsible is yet another lesson Steve learned from listening to them. At one point he had decided to eliminate the obligatory attendance rules. Aiming to serve as many youth as possible, he thought looser rules about participation would serve to attract more youth. He quickly found that not only were the staff against the idea, but much to his surprise, so were the youth. They perceived that meeting the obligations of membership enhanced their sense of self-esteem and individuality and was also an important guarantee of group identity and cohesion. In Buddy's words, "Cooper House [is] not like a community-center-type thing. It's not come as you will and do what you want and then leave whenever you want. It's pretty structured.... It opens its doors to everybody, but it lays down certain rules. You have to come to gym-swim, and you have to come to club each week to be a member. You're allowed to miss. It's not like you miss one day you're out, but it teaches you responsibility and makes you an individual [because you have to account for yourself]."

A Demonstration of Commitment

Cooper Housers use family terms when they talk about their loyalty to the organization. Staff and youth have family-like roles and responsibilities, and Housers are full of "family" stories, tales about past members, leaders, and their own peers. "I think one of the fun things about Cooper House is there's ongoing jokes about each person," Buddy says. "Everybody has their little thing that everybody can laugh about, even themselves."

More important proof of Steve Patterson's success than the doubling of adolescent membership is found in the words of those adolescent members when they talk about the environment of personal contact that their Mr. P. has engendered. For example, Buddy tells a story about the hard time he was having when he was about fifteen. He remembers that "[Mr. P. talked to me for hours] and even called me at home to see how I was doin' and gave me his home phone number. Then he had to go out of town to a conference, and he called me to give me the number of his hotel. Just so I was never out of touch. I don't know nobody else that would do that for me." Another of the older club members agrees: "Mr. Patterson is always there. I really look up to him. I really respect him 'cuz if you're in trouble, if you need *anything*, ... if there's any possible way he can do it, he will do it for you."

Steve Patterson has created a home for youth in the Cooper House neighborhood, a home where participating teenagers typically spend around twenty-five hours a week. "Most times," says a friend of Buddy's, "you have so much to do down there, it's so fun, you don't want to leave." Steve sometimes defines Cooper House as "a getaway from school ... where everyone lays down all the hurdles that are in front of them, and they come on in. They're on neutral territory in our building. Our kids seem to say that teachers don't care, and they're looking for people who care about them. Like family."

Steve and his staff model in every way they can the importance of individual responsibility, of active problem solving and questioning, of care and respect for others. "Down here," says

Steve, "you're *never* told you can't do something. You're always told if you have the willingness to learn and the desire to learn, and if you go through these steps, you can do whatever you want to do. Even if you have one or two failures along the way, the outcome is better for them." Steve sees his overall role as that of the trusted adult who can listen and advise and that of the person who always has his focus on youth, both as director of Cooper House and advocate for youth in the broader River City community. Summing up that role he says, "You've got to always keep your eye on the ball. And that ball is youth. Anything you do that doesn't keep youth at the center is going to pull you off of what you should be doing."

John Peña and TeenTalk

The TeenTalk troupe is performing. A charged exchange between a senior and a pretty underclasswoman, played by dark-haired Rosa, quiets the teenage audience. The setting is a noisy party. The young woman has had a few drinks, and now the young man leads her toward his parents' bedroom. He starts to knead her shoulders.

> *He:* I'll take care of everything.
> *She:* I think I really need to go . . .
> *He:* No, everything's all right.

The young woman stands up and tries to pull away, but the young man grabs her hands behind her back. Saying, "Wait, wait. I've had enough," the young woman pulls away again, but the young man still has hold of one wrist. He whips her back toward him and forces her to the floor. He says, "You haven't had enough till you've had me." She screams. The two actors freeze.

With the rapt attention of their audience the TeenTalk players move wordlessly into position for the next skit. During the next half hour Rosa is, in turn, a pregnant mother, the bereaved friend of a drunk-driving victim, and the child of abusive parents.

When not portraying one of these characters she takes her turn as both backdrop and stagehand while other players act out scenes on issues from substance abuse to sexually transmitted diseases, including AIDS. Each scene ends at the midpoint of some action or decision, so that the audience is moved to question the characters' motivations and choices.

After the final scene, the eight players in this particular performance sit near the edge of the makeshift stage for a period of straight talk with their peer audience. The adolescents can ask questions of any character they have seen, and the appropriate actor will answer the question as that character. For another half hour the questions shoot out from the audience. The date rapist is asked, "Why did you do that? Just to get another notch on your belt? You must think you're pretty hot." (His toughest questioners are the young men in the audience.) His victim, Rosa, is asked, "What are you going to do now?" Rosa responds, "Well, I talked to a friend about it, and she gave me the number for the Big Valley Rape Crisis Line. They talked to me about my options. That I needed to get a test to see if I was pregnant, but that the most important thing was to find out whether or not I had contracted any sexually transmitted diseases. . . . I found it really hard to tell my parents."

During the van ride back to the Cougar Hollow Boys and Girls Club, most of the youth talk animatedly about their performance in a discussion led by Beth Walker, their soft-spoken yet effervescent and, the youth say, "slightly crazy" adult director. Rosa, commanding and emotionally raw onstage, sinks back into her usual watchful quiet. At sixteen she is one of the youngest members and the only Latina in the ethnically diverse TeenTalk troupe. She rarely fights for the floor in this talkative group. In fact, during her first few months in the troupe she spoke in front of everyone only once, during a summer training session on parental abuse and neglect. After learning factual information about statistics and help centers, the group also shared personal experiences that might provide fodder for later skit development. It was at this point that Rosa spoke, to say of her father, "He doesn't even know when my birthday is."

For the twenty members of the Big Valley Boys and Girls Clubs TeenTalk troupe, the group is an environment in which they can help each other deal with personal adolescent traumas and challenges, and a means to reach out to other youth throughout the Big Valley region, informing and helping them with similar problems and concerns. For Big Valley Boys and Girls Clubs executive director John Peña, TeenTalk is his favorite embodiment of the new direction he is giving to the Big Valley club affiliates, including the Cougar Hollow group to which Rosa belongs. Developing programs that combine both discipline and hard work with an emphasis on education, John is shifting the traditional Boys and Girls Clubs drop-in centers to places that offer youth more focused and demanding activities.

During off-hours, the boarded-up facades of the Cougar Hollow branch lend the old buildings an air of abandonment, but a brightly painted mural encircling the base of the firehouse suggests a myriad of activities. These activities spring to life during after-school hours and throughout the summer months when children and youth practically overrun the facility. Once inside the club's heavy steel doors, a visitor is caught up immediately in the bustle of many activities. The pungent smell of chlorine permeates the entry hall from the swimming pool, and the club also boasts art rooms, a gymnasium, a weight room, a closet for bicycles, study areas newly outfitted with computers and a modest reference library, the TeenTalk practice room, a game room, and a full-size boxing ring in the basement. Boys and girls come and go after school each day and all through the summer, taking part in scheduled events led by staff members in each of the club's special areas.

The Path to TeenTalk and Other New Programs

The genesis of TeenTalk reflects John Peña's own odyssey in adopting and adapting to his new community. Like Steve Patterson, John Peña has come to work in a multiethnic, low-income community that is not his own. A Latino in his late thirties, John was born and raised in the Southwest. With deeply held convictions about the importance of pressing for change from within (as opposed to agitating from without as many Latino activists urge), he followed a typical career path for a professional youth services provider. His first experience of prejudice ignited a lasting desire to be taken on his own terms. After his father was transferred to a predominately Anglo community John remembers "friends that I had just known for six months telling me [their parents said] that I couldn't hang out with them because I was a wetback Mexican.... I said to myself, 'I'm a law-abiding citizen.' I was not a troublemaker, hadn't stolen anything." Peña recalls confronting his friends' parents. "[I made] up my mind at that time that I was not going to let my ethnic background be a barrier for me... and that I was never going to use my background as an excuse for any failures or successes." He adds that "at fifteen, it was a big agenda."

He completed a degree in education, took a position in a parks and recreation department, and then served in two different cities as executive director of Boys Clubs. He constantly feels the conflict between his desire to be taken on his own terms as an individual and his ability to fill a role as a well-placed advocate for the Latino community. However, his personal mission to help youth rises above this conflict. He says, "Society doesn't pay enough attention to its youth. It doesn't support them enough. What happens with this generation of kids will determine the future of our society. There's nothing there for them. They're not stupid. They know no one cares."

John Peña's Mission and Methods

When John Peña and his family came to Big Valley in 1989, he was charged with revitalizing its Boys Clubs while simultaneously shifting them to Boys and Girls Clubs and making them particularly responsive to the needs of urban youth. (The national Boys Club organization became Boys and Girls Clubs in 1990.) The national club has seven affiliates in Big Valley, and John maintains his office at the largest affiliate, the 1500–member Cougar

Hollow club in downtown Big Valley. Another affiliate, the Parkside Boys Club, initially resisted a merger with the other local affiliates although John was eventually able to bring them together under one board. Under John's direction the clubs continue to provide a multitude of club-based activities including sports and games, but John has added structured educational centers and computer labs for his youth and such specialized activities as TeenTalk.

The fact that education altered John's life has had a great impact on how he translates his vision for youth into action. He says, "I want to see our [inner-city] kids come to the foreground, ... to let them know that if they work hard enough and try hard enough they can be successful, no matter what. But they have to be focused and have to stay on the track." For John the structured activities now offered by the club are tools to achieve his primary goal—breaking down the isolation that surrounds many Big Valley youth and exposing them to a range of opportunities. "The broad mission of our club," he says, "is to provide kids labeled at risk with activities and programs [and] to bring those programs into their neighborhoods. We want to give these kids something better than the street. They have enough to handle. They need somewhere to go."

In response to the insularity of Cougar Hollow and numerous other low-income neighborhoods in Big Valley, John has focused on club activities that will cross boundaries and break down barriers between members of different ethnic groups on the one hand and between the adults of the Cougar Hollow Boys and Girls Club and community youth on the other. Of all the innovations John has put in place in the Boys and Girls Clubs since he arrived, he is most proud of TeenTalk, a program that presses the heart of his personal mission into action.

TeenTalk grew out of discussions among members of a local youth services network, the Big Valley Youth Collaborative (BVYC). BVYC members believed that Big Valley would benefit from a peer-counseling drama troupe similar to ones developed in other big cities, often with Planned Parenthood taking the lead in their formation. However, BVYC members felt that Planned

Parenthood sponsorship would be too controversial for conservative Big Valley. If the troupe was to succeed in educating its primary audience of adolescents by dealing frankly with such volatile topics as sexually transmitted diseases and date rape, and if it was to cross barriers of class, race, and age, it had to be sponsored by an agency that would be welcome in many different institutions including churches, schools, and youth centers. John Peña not only guaranteed sponsorship by the well-established Boys and Girls Clubs but also expanded the program's scope to the point that similar groups from other cities now send enquiries about John's training materials and skit development process.

As a Boys and Girls Clubs program, TeenTalk gives adolescents opportunities to write, to perform, to communicate, and to become part of a tightly knit, supportive group. As an issues-oriented youth theater group, it has changed the atmosphere surrounding the arts in the local community. The traditional arts opportunities for youth were typically such established events as youth choruses and musicals and a celebrated piano competition that is hosted in Big Valley. In contrast, ethnically diverse TeenTalk represents the voice of all youth, with a strong emphasis on the experiences of nonmainstream youth. Finally, as a forum, TeenTalk takes youth issues directly to adults, to the Big Valley community, and of course, to youth themselves.

John Peña stresses that TeenTalk educates both participants and audiences. Because it is "a specific program with specific focus, the kids really learn about all the social issues that... kids are going through. Then they're in turn going back and educating other kids, because they can answer the questions. It's not just a performance without feedback and knowledge." In John's view, TeenTalk is effective "because it's kids on kids. It's different from adults or a lecturer talking to these kids, or talking *at* 'em instead of *to* 'em about what's right and what's wrong."

TeenTalk members, drawn from throughout Big Valley, take primary responsibility for the content of their program and management of the group. Each year, the twenty-member troupe under Beth's direction includes two junior directors, alumni from the previous year. The troupe members' year-long calendar of events begins in the summer and contains three general activities—learning about teenagers' issues, learning improvisational acting, and learning how to teach other youth.

To learn about the issues, the troupe completes fifty hours of training with professionals on such topics as AIDS, sexually transmitted diseases (STDs), teen pregnancy, alcoholism, depression, eating disorders, gangs, the occult, incest, drunk driving, date rape, abortion, and parental problems. They learn the facts about specific issues and where Big Valley teenagers can go for help. At the end of the summer each TeenTalk member must pass a competency exam that covers such details as precise medical terms and symptoms for STDs, adolescent suicide statistics, the major indicators of alcoholism, the legal ramifications of drunk driving, and the medical, mental, and legal services available to Big Valley youth. The survey of required information is so detailed that many adult youth workers would have difficulty in satisfactorily completing the posttraining exam. John Peña himself ruefully admits he could not answer "the detailed questions they get about things such as the complete symptoms and treatments for AIDS, or the annual date rape figures for Big Valley."

The process of becoming a team member develops the adolescents' ability to be open and truthful as well as creative. They develop a common knowledge and vocabulary that enables them to discuss teen dilemmas more directly and probingly. Moreover, they are challenged to step beyond their own understanding and opinions to encompass all the potential views of an issue. As they develop skits through an intensive process of group work, they are helped to come to an understanding, and the subsequent portrayal, of the concerns of a typical teenager in a particular situation. The performers develop a sense of unity as they work through the details of plot and character together. They must reach agreement as a team because members interchange roles and must be able to play any role they fall into. "We're not portraying anything," Beth says, "We're dealing with reality.... [There is] no type casting [based on ethnicity or social class when it comes to teen issues]."

Through the skits and the realities they describe, the TeenTalk performers can successfully broach issues that are especially sensitive or touchy for teens and the general community. The troupe does not try to directly instruct its audiences about racism, for example; instead it acts out experiences of interracial relationships. The stage characters illustrate the issues in the hope that volatile concerns and social realities can be communicated across the boundaries of parental assumptions. Rosa explains:

Even when the group performs for only adult audiences, parents, business people, it's just as moving because they see kids being kids. I think they see some of their kids.... And it's done in such a way they say, 'Gosh, I should have known that.' I think it opens adults' eyes, too, 'cuz you know how adults are. They don't think . . . that kids are out there doing stuff that they're doing. Then they find out that they are, and they're like, "My kid?" And their eyes get all wide.... It's like they started to think, "Well, maybe my kid is . . . doing that stuff"—which is what we're there for. Yeah, your kid is doing it.

Writing the skits is extremely intimate work, forcing the youth to draw upon personal experiences. Almost half of them come from divorced homes, a number come from abusive homes such as Rosa's, and all have had to deal personally with incidents that range from pressures to have sex or use drugs or alcohol to the need to be supportive of a best friend who is a teen mother. The respect the troupe develops for one another over the summer training translates into respect from the audience during the performance cycle. The long hours of training, writing, and rehearsing result in a remarkably effective teen-on-teen education tool.

The group functions with a minimum of rules, but one rule is inviolate because it affects group cohesion: all members must attend all rehearsals and performances. Lateness or absence must be excused in advance, and missed training sessions made up through viewing videotapes of the session. Members who miss more than two sessions without first calling Beth are "put before the jury," and their peers decide if they can continue with the group. One tacit rule is equally important— be supportive of others at all times. Adherence to another simple though essential rule establishes the group's general ethos. That rule is, listen. Listening is important not only because it encourages community but also because it maintains order among the diverse and gregarious group. Beth gently establishes this rule during the early weeks of training, softly harnessing the energetic talk by informing people that "we're not getting out of here till y'all start listening to each other." Negative talk, even in jest, is not allowed. Following performances, troupe members applaud each other and discussions of the performance are punctuated by positive remarks and by protective words of encouragement if the audience has been particularly harsh on an actor. This often occurs to the young man playing the date rapist when audiences have difficulty distinguishing the actor from the character.

The troupe's supportive intimacy also allows behavior that is unacceptable in other settings, such as a boy's crying. Among the troupe, such behavior is not only accepted, but welcomed as an expression of the sincerity that is allowed. The members' acceptance of each other is further encouraged by the fact that TeenTalk has no stars. Roles are constantly rotated to maintain an environment of equality and to prevent the development of cliques or status distinctions.

Finally, the same group cohesion and mutual understanding that allow the TeenTalk troupe to present real, often personal and raw, issues also "provide an atmosphere for [TeenTalk] kids to sit down and talk about issues that hit them all and close to home," John says. "They are forced to work together and come up with alternatives to their problems—not solutions, alternatives. This program is as good for the kids performing as it is for their audiences."

TeenTalk embodies all the goals John has for his overall agenda of educating youth and preparing them for their place as future citizens in society through helping them confront the issues of survival and ethics that they must navigate successfully in adolescence. TeenTalk also demonstrates that part of the success of this broad objective will depend on program developers' recognizing that the most effective channel for communicating with youth is other youth. John says that he has "never come across a program that crosses the barriers and gets teens talking as well as TeenTalk." He points out that, from the adolescents' point of view, "it's not a bunch of adults [or] me talking to them, or talking at them, [saying,] 'Hey, I'm smarter than you are because ... I'm a graduate.' ... And by the time [the adults] get to the real meat and potatoes, they've lost the kids. TeenTalk gets right into the ... social issues or personal issues that some of these kids are going through."

A Demonstration of Commitment

John Peña is straightforward about the nature of his commitment: "These kids need someone they can count on, someone who loves them." John plays that role for the adolescents in the Big Valley Boys and Girls Clubs. Moreover, John says, "I enjoy what I'm doing. I believe that kids can be successful given the right direction, given the right support system. Kids are gonna make mistakes. I think that it's my responsibility to change the attitude of the community about [their] feelings [that these kids are no good].... And I'm doing it."

Michael Carroll and Building Educational Strategies for Teens

"But I'm not really into relaxing this morning," sixteen-year-old Teri protests, as she and other junior staffers settle down on gym floor mats at Building Educational Strategies for Teens (BEST). It is 7:30 A.M., and the tall thin woman at the front of the mats invites the thirty or so young men and women to "lie down, breathe deep, and relax; enjoy the quiet; it's the last you'll get today." The teenagers laugh knowingly. Once their twenty minutes here are over, they head out into BEST's halls to corral their classes of six- to ten-year-olds for the day's activities. Teri stretches to her full five feet six inches on the mat and closes her eyes. She is worried that the energies of two especially active six-year-olds in her group will outstrip her class plans, but she knows she can cover this worry in the afternoon debriefing session when junior staffers talk about their teaching problems with curriculum director Renee Jordan.

As a BEST junior staff person Teri tutors small groups of the more than two hundred students who crowd BEST's colorful rooms each afternoon. Although she came to BEST's summer day-camp program when she was in grade school, Teri had had little other contact with the organization until she returned as a paid tutor for fifteen hours each week during the school year. Now Teri spends her after-school time at BEST even on her nonworking days. While it was the tutoring job that drew her to BEST as a teenager, it is the spirit and community of the organization and the "other mother" figures such as Renee, who also grew up in Francis Homes and is a product of BEST, that engender Teri's loyalty.

When Teri began work, BEST was in an old two-story church building right across from two of Francis Homes's most notorious buildings. Stray bullets from rival gangs' cross fire made the projects' playgrounds and open spaces unsafe for youngsters so they came to BEST partly because it provided safe territory within its brick walls. By the end of Teri's first year as a junior staffer these youngsters had become too numerous for the church building, and BEST moved its youth center several blocks north of the projects to the old education building of another vacant church. The original building now houses primarily adult education programs.

Everyday life at BEST in many ways resembles the typical family as many Americans imagine it. Youngsters come in after school, get themselves a snack (from the machines in the entry hall), do their homework at tables with their "brothers and sisters," take breaks to play games or work on special projects, and occasionally settle down with staff or other members for serious talk about long-range plans for a Saturday visit to a museum, the zoo, a big game or even for college or travel. While focused as an educational program, BEST provides both personal and academic resources as well as broadening experiences for the children and youth who come to the after-school activities and to summer day camp.

The purpose of all programs at BEST is education and self-development. BEST's cultural base is personal initiative coupled with service to others. The educational focus contrasts with the other programs we describe, yet BEST is not a narrow, curriculum-driven endeavor. The building that houses BEST, its staff, and its youth has become a refuge and a warm, welcoming family place for the young people of Francis Homes. BEST has evolved into a program that embraces and recognizes the whole child, not just the student. Youth are drawn into BEST through their desires for personal development, an educated future, safety, and a place to "be at home." Studying goes hand in hand with a safe place to help others, express oneself through drama, join in recreation, and just relax.

Teri and others at BEST agree with director Michael Carroll's view that safety, security, and a chance to "do something" matter, but they also credit the team of adults who make up the BEST "family." Teri remembers hearing Edgar, a young member of BEST with the nickname of Tiger, tell the following story on himself and his affection for BEST. Nearing the building on foot he heard a shot, jumped behind the hedges marking the north end of BEST's grounds, and threw himself flat on the ground, his heart pounding. Then he heard the laughter of several men standing around an old car parked across the street as they discussed its backfire. Sheepishly he crept out from behind the hedge and made a run for BEST's only entrance, double doors covered with double-run steel webbing. Once he was inside, Teri, on duty at the receptionist desk, simply called out, "You okay, Tiger?" And Harriet Caldwell, the grandmother who for more years than she would ever tell had been the combined greeter, social chair, and household manager for BEST, gave him a quick pat and said, "I wish Randy would get that ol' car out there fixed; every time he and his buddies get out there and make it sound off like that, I think my heart's gonna stop." Later, Edgar was able to laugh about the experience, remarking that no one had spoken about the fear all of them feel when shots ring out in the neighborhood or commented on his sprint behind the hedges.

The Path to BEST

Michael Carroll, the wizard who imagined and built BEST, is a European American who looks more like an assistant professor in a college history department than a youth director in a major African American inner-city community. Carroll has remained committed to BEST and its youth through more than a decade. Living nearby with his wife and two teenage children, he bikes to work each day, usually arriving early enough to open the building. Once he narrowly missed being hit by a stray bullet from a local gang battle, but he continues to downplay his own safety and to put that of the youth first. Giving youth a sense of security goes at the top of Michael Carroll's list of ingredients for program success in the violent context of Francis Homes. He describes BEST as "kind of a sanctuary for the kids." There is "chaos" outside, but when they come through BEST's heavy steel door they can hope to find calm and security.

Lacking a shared neighborhood heritage, ethnic identity, and class background, Michael Carroll was a thorough outsider when he first came to the Francis Homes neighborhood in 1977. While Reggie Jones, Luanna Williams, and Roberto Colon built upon their inherent understanding of their local communities and Steve Patterson and John Peña grew up knowing class or ethnic challenges similar to those of their chosen communities, Michael needed to be educated about the youth and culture of Francis Homes. What he did bring with him was a tough, practical, and firm belief in human potential, along with a sense that people's fundamental needs cross cultural, ethnic, class, and racial barriers.

Michael was raised in Oshkosh, Wisconsin, in a family he describes as a "Leave It to Beaver" household. He holds a master's degree in religious education from an evangelical college. Not an obvious candidate for developing a grass-roots organization in Francis Homes's tough and suspicious community, he was tapped for the job by the European American congregation of the nearby Grove Street Church. The church was looking for someone to create a bridge between its congregation and the African American youth of Francis Homes and to expand its small fifteen-year-old youth tutoring program. Michael was eager to take on the challenge. After a rough stint of teaching in the inner-city schools of St. Louis, he had acquired a seasoned understanding of the bureaucratic vagaries that burn out so many students and teachers, but he had also developed an appreciation for education's potential impact on the lives of urban youth. He saw education as the most reliable ticket out of the despair of the inner-city housing projects.

Over the following fourteen years, Michael Carroll developed the church's fledgling tutoring program into Building Educational Strategies for Teens. Today, BEST is an agency with over three hundred and fifty active students, two hundred of whom, like Teri, are in some form of college scholarship program. From one intern, a budget of $25,000, and a church-basement site, the program has expanded to include twenty-four full-time staff, fifty teenage staff, and over two hundred and fifty regularly participating volunteers; two Francis Homes community building sites; and an operating budget of well over $1,000,000. Michael's long-term commitment to BEST and the Francis Homes community enabled such success.

Michael Carroll's Mission and Methods

Michael Carroll's mission involves touching and nurturing the potential of inner-city youth, enabling them not only to imagine but also to grasp a positive future. He achieves his mission through expanding educational opportunities for Francis Homes youth and enhancing educational development in the community. "Why do tutoring?" he asks. "It's not to just help kids do better in school. [Tutoring is about] revitalizing communities through what you're building with these kids."

One strong component of BEST's character and effectiveness is Michael's comprehensive approach to programming. Each program has specific parameters. For example, three of BEST's five scholarship classes consist of students who are all at the same grade level and who have been promised a college scholarship if they maintain certain standards at school and at BEST. The students and their BEST leader stay together until the students graduate from high school. Other scholarship programs are designed to include students from multiple grades. Students from all programs meet after school, often on Saturdays, and throughout the summer in study, work, and performance programs that require specific academic, social, and cultural development. However, great flexibility is allowed in the ways students reach the general developmental guidelines. As a result, the five scholarship programs bear little resemblance to each other. During the summer months some meet on a daily basis with a full schedule of student activities. For example, one group meets for tutoring each morning, followed by afternoons filled with tennis lessons, visits to ethnic communities, art classes, and student production of a sex-education video. Another group meets twice each week to watch and discuss films such as *Cry Freedom* and *School Daze* relating to the African American experience. Still another group of mostly older scholarship recipients simply checked in with their supervisor weekly while maintaining full-time jobs at BEST and throughout Lakeside's midtown area. Teri feels youth like to come to BEST not just because of the educational opportunities but "basically because they make the program so that it's fun.... If they're doing math ..., they play math bingo or something like that. And I think that's fun for the kids because they don't feel that they're back in school again." Educational activities are also developed to be relevant to the lives of BEST youth. In an annual literary magazine produced by the youth, they use poetry and short story to express the frustrations, insights, fears, and joys that come with life "in the 'hood."

BEST's high levels of participation and the waiting list for admission are remarkable given an educational focus that many might consider too dry. Teri believes that young people "wouldn't be in the program if they didn't have something special going for them, [if they didn't] have motivation. You have to come every day. And parents, as hard as they try, they can't make their kids come every day; you have to be willing to do it. And the kids in the scholarship program, they have a lot of requirements that they have to meet.... So they have to be motivated." Edgar is an example of the personal motivation that inner-city youth can have. When he first applied for the scholarship program, he could not be taken because his mom never seemed able to make the required parental visit to BEST. He persisted in calling Jennifer Adams, the director of the scholarship program he wanted to join, and after numerous phone calls to plead to be included, Jennifer did some checking. She learned Edgar's mother had few sober days. Indeed most of the time, Edgar was parent to her and his younger siblings. Realizing that Edgar's mother would never get to BEST, Jennifer accepted Edgar without that required visit.

A second component in BEST's success is staff development. BEST has grown to the extent that it can provide many youth with their first paying jobs. The school-year junior staff of forty expands to over one hundred youth during the summer. Numerous community adults have also come to work at BEST, and programs have expanded to include adult continuing education, job training, and GED preparation. BEST works to make effective use of volunteers and youth staff and maintains a high ratio of staff to program participants.

BEST's third component of success is the extent to which Michael Carroll and his staff allow older youth to be a vital part of both daily and long-term decision making. BEST's strong familial and community environment and commitment to youth encourage youth and their families to reciprocate with a commitment of similar duration and energy to BEST. Michael has designed BEST's programs to enlist and sustain the involvement of young people and their families from the youngsters' early grade school experiences through their part-time jobs, college graduation, and career placement. BEST does not think of "serving" youth but of making youth active agents in the enrichment of their own lives. Through BEST, youth also contribute to the development of their own community through a broad range of projects from long-term cross-age tutoring to recording of community oral histories.

As part of their holistic approach to the life of the community, building upon and moving beyond basic educational needs, Michael Carroll and his staff recognize the varying degrees to which their youth can rely upon individual family resources. Renee Jordan, the young curriculum director who grew up in Francis Homes, says, "[Parents] see us as a place that can help them or can help them find the appropriate assistance.... Some of our kids would still be doing fine [without us] because they do have a strong family unit and their moms, grandmas, or just whoever, would make sure that they're being developed. [However] some of our kids might not realize the options at an early age if we were not here."

Moreover, in contrast to programs based on minority talent searches that cream the most likely to succeed from the local community and take them to an outside centralized location, BEST retains the highest achievers within the community while allowing for self-selection and self-direction among all BEST's youth. Renee says:

We're not just concerned about the kids who just do well in school, who get the A's and the B's. We have kids here that don't do well in school.... We'll give a scholarship to a kid who someone else might not give a scholarship.... If a person has demonstrated that they want to go to school and they can articulate why they want to go, and they have the desire, BEST has been there to give them money. And I like the fact that we're not just working with the bright kids, because . . . the average person would look and say, "Oh, there aren't a whole lot of bright kids [in this neighborhood]," but we look at our average kids and say, "Yeah, they're bright and they have the potential." So we provide avenues and actions to see to it that they have money to go to school.

A Demonstration of Commitment

BEST has had great success in bringing adolescents from Francis Homes safely through their school years and enabling them to reach for and grasp high school diplomas, college acceptance letters, scholarship offers, and places in competitive training programs. But none of this could have been accomplished had Michael Carroll failed to establish and sustain trust among Francis Homes's embittered and embattled African American residents, made cynical by repeated negative experiences with "do gooders" from outside their neighborhood and culture. Winning acceptance and trust from this community was Michael's first objective. From his perspective, issues of ethnicity and social class mattered less to the distrustful residents of Francis Homes than did commitments made and kept, respect given, and honor established. Therefore he established trust and a place in the community through building BEST slowly, to ensure consistency and program quality. He fulfilled promises and provided programs that were "as ongoing as possible, so people can know what to expect." He made his programs "responsive to community needs." Michael says, "There is so much b.s. that [is promised about] Francis Homes; you can't promise what you can't deliver. What was important for me was to build a program as credible as possible for me, for the kids in the community, the funding community, the potential volunteer community, and the church. It's no problem to go slow and let it build slowly. The bottom line is that the program should sell itself."

Michael relies on the individual talents of his staff members to develop and sustain a wide range of activities as BEST's success and Lakeside's demand for his expertise in shaping the city's youth policies increasingly remove him from BEST's daily operations. As advocate and visionary for BEST, he must operate in two worlds, the local sphere of Francis Homes and the wider resources of Lakeside, acquiring outside support that respects local needs. Nonetheless, the environment, the sense of place, and the hope that surround BEST continue to fulfill his initial mission, engaging the youth and adults of Francis Homes as vital resources that contribute to the BEST family, the community, and the broader society.

Chapter Five

What Matters Most? Common Traits of Wizards and Their Organizations

The six successful youth organizations we studied are diverse in their particular purposes, organization, leadership, and location. The personal attributes of the six wizards who guide these organizations are dissimilar on almost all dimensions: socioeconomic status, education, previous career, family status, special training and skills. None of these factors stands out as necessary to successful leadership. We found that insiders and outsiders can be equally effective; ethnicity and gender do not determine the ability of an adult to work with urban youth.[1]

However, there are important similarities among the six wizards and among the organizations they have built to attract and embrace young hopefuls. Again, they are not the traits sometimes thought to matter most, but they are the only ones we consistently found in the organizations that youth themselves said were successful in changing their lives and futures. We identify the similarities among the wizards first and then among their organizations and programs, concluding with brief portraits of the sheer range of activities that each organization has come to encompass in order to meet as many of inner-city adolescents' needs as possible.

The Six Wizards

Reggie Jones, Luanna Williams, Roberto Colon, Steve Patterson, John Peña, and Michael Carroll share five broad characteristics. They see genuine potential in their youth. They focus on youth, putting youth at the center of programs. They have a belief in their own abilities to make a difference. They feel they are giving back something they owe to a community or society. And in everything to do with their organizations, they are unyieldingly authentic.

Seeing Potential, Not Pathology

Successful leaders of inner-city youth organizations have a passionate commitment to young people, particularly to underserved and disadvantaged youth. This trait is so strong as to constitute the most elemental aspect of youth organization leadership. Wizards have no hesitation in viewing inner-city youth as valuable assets to society. "The youngsters who live in the housing projects are some of the most talented and nicest kids you'll find anywhere," says Reggie Jones. "But they're right on the cutting edge—they could go either way. That's why I'm here, to show them the positive [way]." Steve Patterson echoes Reggie's image of youth engaged in a critical balancing act. His young Cooper Housers are "walking the fence and could fall on either side.... We want to be such a good influence that they will never want to stray from good paths."

When wizards frame their personal and organizational missions they consider inner-city youth as resources and youth organizations as opportunities to develop those resources. They see potential, not pathology; therefore they design settings to guide youth through the mingled violence and indifference of the inner-city environment and to engage them in the types of learning and experiences that will transform these adolescent boys' and girls' sense of their own abilities and expectations so that they can duck the bullet.

The six leaders described here do not see the youth of U.S. inner cities as people to be fixed, remediated, or otherwise controlled but as young people of promise, largely ignored, wrongly perceived, and badly served by society at large. John Peña speaks for all six wizards when he phrases his personal mission as providing "leadership for youth at risk." For John, seeing potential instead of pathology is a question of personal philosophy. He says, "I just love it when somebody tells me, 'You can't change those kids. Those kids are no good.' They're never *our* kids, it's *those* kids. And my philosophy is that they're *our* kids. They're *my* kids, and they're *our* kids, as a community."

This deeply felt, unforced focus on the positive lies at the heart of the six leaders' conception of youth and strategies for connecting with them. Roberto Colon declares:

What I'm tryin' to do is get people to understand that there's a way to work with that [inner-city youth] population, that law enforcement and drug marches and protests are not the only way to deal with it. [When I hear] all the community uproar about gangs [and the] community fighting back against gangs, I say to myself, "Those are the kids of those people that live in that neighborhood, so who are they uproaring against, their own kids? Where do these gangs come from? Do they come from underneath the sewers at night, and they don't belong to anybody or belong to anything? They belong to the community." I hear the media talking about "the communities are angry and they're fighting back!" This is not a war. These are their own kids!

Successful leaders locate "the problem" of inner-city youth and the dysfunctional behaviors and attitudes associated with them primarily in the larger society and the general failure of social institutions to understand, support, or care for these teenagers. "Kids can be saved with a loving agenda," says John Peña. "Fear of failure drives people back to their own environment. It takes a lot of one-on-one reinforcement to get a kid to set goals, think about the future."

Loving agendas and positive missions with productive and healthy purposes set successful youth leaders apart from those who aim to "control" the "youth problem" and its impact on society. Remedial programs and substance abuse or other prevention efforts that take an epidemiological view, labeling youth as delinquent or categorizing them according to various pathologies or "conduct disorders,"[2] are rooted in negative conceptions of inner-city youth. Our wizards avoid negative labels, especially those that mark

youngsters as deficient or deviant and concentrate instead on raising expectations and providing settings where youth can gain the
attitudes, confidence, and measure of expertise necessary to remove
themselves from the inner city's despair. The general public may
regard inner-city youth who break society's rules or fall short of
mainstream expectations as outsiders, but wizards insist these youth
can never be outsiders. Our six wizards accept inner-city youth as
"our kids" and strive to respond to the desolation and chaos of
these adolescents' everyday world by replacing punishment and
rejection with acceptance and feasible notions of a better life.

That youth will not elect to participate in a program or organization that demeans them or labels them as somehow unacceptable or unworthy seems self-evident.[3] The leaders featured in
this book succeed in attracting in youth in large numbers while
others with apparently similar missions do not. We visited YMCAs
empty of youth, talked with coaches discouraged by poor turnout,
and sympathized with Scout leaders who said it was "impossible"
to attract teenage girls, especially Latinas and African Americans.
We observed tutoring programs where tutors outnumbered the
tutees, and youth clubs with disappointing membership figures for
teenagers. For inner-city adolescents, creating an environment of
success, of affirmative self-identity is absolutely essential to their
continued participation. In this environment youth seek opportunities to learn, to stretch, to take concrete steps toward becoming responsible adults.

Focusing on Youth

The successful leaders' commitment to youth also means that they
focus on youth before organization, program, or activity. They see
youth organization technology and the models that policymakers
focus on and try to replicate only as vehicles for turning commitment into a practical reality. Wizards' personal agendas contrast
with those of well-intended leaders whose primary passion is their
program or institution—the baseball coach whose love of the
game sometimes overshadows concerns for the kids, or the Scout-
master whose devotion to the Scouting movement sometimes

eclipses his view of the needs of the inner-city Scout, especially African American or Latino Scouts.

This question of primary motivation is complex and our intention is not to disparage other talented leaders. It also is not to say that youth are indifferent to content. As Michael Carroll maintains, quality and relevance in youth programs are of first-order importance, and youth of the inner city are perhaps the most stringent judges of that quality and relevance. Nonetheless, the practices of most successful leaders make the question of primary motivation a critical one. We found that the wizards put youth's interests first with a clearness and consistency that distinguished wizards from their dedicated colleagues with a different focus. For example, we spent considerable time in an organization we will call Harmony House, an academic center similar to BEST in terms of official mission but less successful in drawing youth into a sustained relationship. In their practice, the very talented leader and key members of his staff focus more on designing the best possible tutoring program for youth than they do on the variegated and changing realities of the inner-city youth with whom they work. To a person, Harmony House staff have devoted their lives to working with young people; yet their intellectual and earnest purpose results in a program that is focused first on providing the academic assistance youth require, rather than on their immediate nonprogram needs and concerns, which sometimes go unnoticed.

Such differences in focus matter less in neighborhoods and families where youth can find sources of caring and support other than their youth organization. But focus matters enormously in the barren, harsh neighborhoods of the inner city, where youth test leaders' commitment and caring at every turn and where what is normal is often unpredictable and brutal. For inner-city youth, a leader's being always available and responsive to daily realities supersedes the content of any program. Indeed, this responsiveness is the only way leaders can signal the sincerity of their commitment to individual youth.

Wizards themselves are aware of their special focus and criticize many in the youth program and policy sector for failing to "keep their eye on the ball," for affording higher priority to a particular program concept or policy rather than to youth. The wizards know that, more often than not, adolescents do not share adults' assessments of what is "good for them." Steve Patterson, for example, believes that focus is perhaps the biggest problem for youth organizations because "too many people try to develop a program that fits the kids into the program, instead of looking at the kids and developing the program for the kids."

As our later discussion of organizational similarities will show, the organizational result of keeping the focus on youth is the "full-service organization" identified by Reggie Jones. To a person, the wizards we met refused to define their responsibilities and roles in the narrow terms of a job description. In addition to carrying out their basic responsibilities, all six also serve as youth employment counselors, school advisors, bankers, baby-sitters, advocates in the world of purported helping institutions, and more. Wizards never forget that meeting adolescents' basic survival concerns is integral to those adolescents' ability to acquire competencies, belonging, and hope.

A *Sense of Efficacy*

Wizards' commitment to and focus on inner-city youth is reinforced by a strong sense of personal efficacy. While countless other youth workers or policymakers stress that "it is too late for teens," that "you have to get to them when they are young," these successful leaders have a firm conviction that they can and do make a difference in the lives of teenage youth from even the bleakest urban settings. John Peña's declaration that it is his "responsibility to change the attitude of the community about [inner-city youth]" and that he is, in fact, meeting that responsibility could have been made by any one of the leaders introduced here.

Because the six leaders also believe that they make a difference through their example as well as their work, they all agree that youth leadership is a total commitment, on the job and off. Roberto Colon, the wizard who works so effectively with gang members in Porter Crossing, shows how acutely he feels this responsibility when he says:

[If] these kids... find someone they can relate to, a role model, and there's options for them, [they] have at least a 90 percent chance of coming out of [the gangs]. That's how strongly I feel about it. I can't prove it to you. But just in talking to these guys ... [When I started GAIN] my boss asked me, ... "Are you sure you wanna do this, Roberto? You're opening up a can of worms." I said, "George, I can't go home every day, passin' these guys up, lookin' at them, seein' them hang out, knowin' that the Y is here and we're not even attempting to do something here."

Giving Back

Part of wizards' consuming commitment to youth results from their wanting to give back what others gave them as they grew up. They want to pass opportunities along. Reggie Jones is repaying "what I owe for what I am today." Luanna Williams wants her Girl Scouts "to have the same chance to be involved" that she had growing up with Scouting.

The six leaders also hope their adolescents, in turn, will develop a commitment to give opportunities and brighter futures back to others. Reggie Jones describes that hope this way: "My personal mission is to try to help as many young people as I possibly can to come through this world and benefit from this program and go out and be productive citizens. I don't want them to be on public aid. I want them to be gainfully employed. I want them to be educated. I want them, once their feet are firmly planted on this Earth, to do what I have done, and that is to give back to their community."

The salience to the wizards of giving back explains why these talented, energetic individuals choose to work in a field of notoriously low pay, little or no recognition, and limited upward mobility. All of them see their work as a mission and vocation, not simply a job or even a career in the traditional sense (a theme that harkens back to days of Jane Addams and community service work before the days of professionalism). They are not seeking to move up and out of the positions that bring them into regular contact with youth. They share the feelings Luanna Williams had when her supervisor asked where else in the city she might want to work, as a promotion, and she said, "Nowhere, because every other job in the city is administrative or it's out of touch. That's not what I want to do.... There needs to be more people working *in* neighborhoods like Arroyo."

Wizards define their vocations in substantive rather than hierarchical terms. Steve Patterson, for example, says:

It's just extremely difficult to describe our profession. I tend to just say that we're in [the] people business. I know that's really broad, but our jobs are really broad. We have to do counseling; we have to do program creativity. My particular job is more administrative than it is anything else. In fact if you'd asked the board of directors what my job is they would say, "He's the administrator; he's the business person for our operation," and I am. But I have a firm belief that if you let your executive director, your CEO, whatever you wanna call him, lose touch with the floor program, then you also lose touch with your management. You've got to keep a hand in there so you feel what your staff is going through, what the kids are experiencing, what's working, what's not working. You have to keep some sense of touch.

While the majority of our leaders are similarly engaged in administrative duties, they all are set apart from leaders in similar organizations—especially building-based programs such as the YMCA or Boys and Girls Clubs—by their resolve to stay in contact with the day-to-day doings of youth and staff. It is clear that wizards intuitively distinguish between managing the organization and leading it and are dedicated to doing both.

Authenticity

Each wizard manifests a different personality and programmatic interests, with the result that each successful organization has some characteristic that is a special draw for youth. Wizards create programs for musicians, thespians, scholars, athletes, artists, and young people who simply want a supportive group to call their own. The moral here appears to be that one-size-fits-all programming misses adolescents' need to do their own thing, to feel they are pursuing interests and goals they themselves have selected. Wizards too need to do their own thing, and so they mesh their personal talents with their work. Michael Carroll, for example, does not try to be a father to Francis Homes youth in the way that Reggie Jones does. Michael feels he could not be fully successful in this role. Instead he gives Francis Homes youth his strengths as enabler, encourager, and organizer of others' skills and energies. Youth demand such truth to self from their leaders.

The wizards we came to know also demonstrated the authenticity of their commitment through becoming part of their inner-city communities' fabric and soul. They serve in many ways—through many memberships on organization boards and policy commissions and through many hours of advocacy work on youth's behalf. The six leaders' common motivation of giving back and sense of vocation also underlie the authenticity they show to youth. Through their daily enactment of commitment and respect, these wizards leave little doubt of their genuine caring for inner-city youth and of their high assessment of these adolescents' potential. The wizards' authenticity is what bonds sometimes ordinary features into an extraordinary organization that, as Luanna Williams puts it, "smells good" to cynical, suspicious inner-city teenagers. "You can't be phony," she says. "These kids can see through you if you are really not genuine and really don't care about them. They can completely see through it."

The Six Wizards' Programs

The places of hope created by the youth leaders we feature here have little in common in terms of program focus or physical environment. Luanna Williams's Girl Scout Troop functions in the context of the multiage, multipurpose Arroyo Community Center. When not on the road, Reggie Jones's Gymnasts must make Reggie's county supervisor's office their hangout. Cooper Housers are the most privileged hopefuls in terms of place, personnel, and program opportunities. We found no model of "treatment" or facility for policymakers to disseminate. Nevertheless, from youth's perspective, the six substantively different organizations have striking commonalities. They offer safety. Their direction is taken from needs youth themselves express. They are generous in the number and types of opportunities they offer. They provide real responsibility and real work. They encourage self-discipline through their clear and consistent rules and attitudes. And they are future focused, encouraging youth to develop "real life" as well as educational skills. All these qualities add up to positive self-identity, tangible successes, respect, responsibility, and autonomy for participating youth.

Safety

Safety is one of the first organizational qualities identified by both youth and adults associated with effective youth organizations. In gang- and crime-ridden inner-city neighborhoods, leaders must provide safe passage and protection. Adolescents' development and growth can take place only when personal safety is assured. The effective youth organization finds many ways to protect its members from alienation and potential abuse at home, from the dangers of pregnancy, drugs, alcohol, and violence on the streets, and from the isolation and deadening sense of personal insignificance that youth construct from their inner-city experiences.

Thus "keepin' 'em off the streets" means more than physical safety from gangbangers or street violence, although that is vital. It also means protection from the psychic harm dealt daily to many youth by the police, the school, and the family. BEST's Michael Carroll describes how "it sometimes takes us two hours in the afternoon after school to undo the damage done to these kids. All they hear all day is how bad they are. We can't even begin [our work] until we can make them feel okay, [feel] good about themselves." The leaders of successful youth organizations explicitly take their adolescents' broad view of what safe passage means in the inner city. The result, seeing young people of promise duck the bullet one by one, is enough to sustain many wizards through the tough challenges they face as directors of organizations that more often than not operate on shoestring budgets, far from the public eye and public praise.

Listening to Youth

"Keeping your eye on the ball" and your focus on youth, as Steve Patterson admonishes, does not simply entail acknowledging youth's interests and needs but also listening to youth and allowing them to take part in decision making. The young people of the inner city, most of whom are burdened at an early age with responsibilities for self, family, and support, reject settings where they are "told to," ordered around, or excluded from any say in how the organization works. Of course even the most insightful of wizards cannot always anticipate or understand youth's needs or concerns. One of the few criticisms of Reggie Jones leveled by his Gymnasts, for example, was his failure to understand that the Gymnasts' shorts were simply too short compared to the current baggy, mid-thigh fashion. While the Gymnasts pleaded their case as a matter of comfort, what they really wanted was to be with it. However, for the most part, the six wizards do pick up on what their youth are saying.

Steve Patterson attributes listening to his youth as an important reason why he was able to revive Cooper House as a magnet for community teenagers. Luanna Williams says flatly that she would have no older girls in her Scout troop if she did not respond to their interests and needs. "Who's it for, anyway?" she demands. She confirms Steve's view, saying, "A big factor in success is just listening to the kids. What *they* want. One of the things that I'll do at a Girl Scout meeting is say, 'Okay, y'all, tell me what you want to do. 'Cuz if you don't want to do anything there's no reason for us to keep coming.'"

Wizards believe that the genuine and active contribution of youngsters in building the organization also teaches them responsibility and affords them a sense of ownership. A strength of TeenTalk lies in the teenagers' role in setting the troupe's rules and adjudicating infractions. Much of the educational payoff at Cooper House derives from the lessons youth learn as they man the front desk, staff field trips, plan for events, negotiate with Steve for special privileges, and develop activities and curricula for club activities.

Successful leaders attend to the special needs of older youth, recognizing their status as elders in the organization and their need for a place of their own where they can "get away from the little kids," hang out with their friends, listen to music, and talk about matters of interest to them. The "older guys" at the Cougar Hollow Boys and Girls Club, for example, are excused from carrying their membership cards at all times, a strict rule for younger members. Older youth, experienced in the organization's activities, are given special coaching responsibilities and opportunities for leadership at Cooper House and the Arroyo Community Center. Programs with no space of their own, such as the Reggie Jones Gymnasts, cannot give older youth a special physical place, but they too can acknowledge and reward seniority with special assignments. Senior Gymnasts, for example, have responsibilities for scheduling, transport, and managing the group. This recognition of their different needs and skills as young adults is part of what attracts older youth to the wizards' programs. These adolescents feel they are being treated with respect and as individuals.

Listening to youth, allowing them to have a major say in the organization's character and relationships, is the keystone in building youth's trust. Wizards understand the difficulties their inner-city youth have in trusting unknown adults or other adolescents.[4] Wizards know that the topics of so-called normal discourse—family, school performance, personal relationships, free-time activities—can be threatening and painful subjects for inner-city youth. Successful leaders relate to youth not simply as Gymnasts or Girl Scouts or representative adolescents but as whole people whose lives and circumstances are unpredictable, demanding, and largely missing the multiple supports and resources available to middle-class youth. When youth are allowed to take the lead in building trust and to establish ground rules for disclosure and intimacy, they are more likely to feel accepted for who they are. As John Peña points out, "Trust is impossible in a situation where someone is trying to change you, to dictate to you. You've gotta meet the kid where he or she is, and go with that."

Offering Opportunities

When youth talk about what makes an effective youth organization and why they belong, they also point to "opportunity." But wizards have learned that opportunity from the perspective of a marginalized inner-city youth has particular dimensions. Therefore successful leaders build these dimensions into their programs. Youth told us that the programs they go to and the responsibilities they are given there mean more than just "fun" and offer more than safety. These places and responsibilities are chances to learn concrete, relevant skills as diverse as word processing, pitching, editing, or mainstream social behavior; they are chances to glimpse alternatives to the hopelessness found on inner-city streets. The six leaders attend to many skills and habits mainstream youth learn early—learning to dress, saying please and thank you, using alarm clocks, being a host or hostess, reading a bus schedule, using the right tableware in a dinner setting.

Another critical opportunity inner-city youth want is the chance to break out of the boundaries imposed by their isolation, to imagine and experience new things previously unimagined or unimaginable—"all the things you could be doin' besides standin' on a street corner, all of the things you could be besides a loser or in jail." Travel outside their immediate neighborhoods enhances their worldview. Wizards know what most outsiders to inner-city life do not: many youth like Tito or Tyrone who grow up in neighborhoods where the most important maps are drawn by gang boundaries have never ventured more than a few blocks from their home, have never been downtown, have never ridden a city bus. Reggie Jones remarks that, on one level, his gymnastics team is "really just a juvenile prevention program. It's designed to provide the seventy-five kids on the team with some cultural enrichment, to take them out of their immediate neighborhood—living in hotels, traveling to various cities, performing before various organizations [and] before large [audiences]." As Reggie points out, giving back requires first getting out. Luanna Williams also says, "Right now in our community, [youth are] trapped in the drug trafficking and all kinds of stuff. I think to break that cycle they have to get out and then come back into the community."

John Peña told us that, for his adolescents, "going across town is like going to New York City . . . just getting them out of their neighborhoods. One kid, when we took a trip to the other side of Big Valley to meet with some folks, wanted to know if we were still in the state!" For youth lucky enough to travel farther than across town, the impact can be mind-changing. Roberto Colon recalls Tito's reaction when the Porter Crossing YMCA sent him to a youth conference at a Wisconsin lake: "He came back and he said, 'Roberto, the world is incredible! There's so much out there!' He says, 'All I know is the four blocks that make up my 'hood!' He says, 'I don't believe it man.' He says, 'There's so much out there. Yeah!'"

Real Responsibilities, Real Work

The opportunities and activities that attract young people embody real responsibilities and real work. They are concrete, result in learning of value to the broader society, and have clear significance to the local community. They match the deadlines, rhythms, and demands of real work, requiring youth to be disciplined, committed, reliable, and serious about an endeavor. They demand long hours of dedicated work more than they promise good times, and they have a visible payoff that is of value to the youth and honored by society. When the wizards give real responsibilities and real work to inner-city youth, they also give them the opportunity for achievement and accomplishment and the structured learning environment that mainstream youth usually find in school, family, or community.

All the wizards' programs also have a built-in rhythm of peaks and denouements that result in concrete short- and long-term successes for the youth who participate. This is as true for Luanna Williams's Girl Scouts when they plan and put on their yearly Valentine Day dinner as it is for the TeenTalk actors and the Gymnasts whose performances are more clearly marked and more regular. The youngsters in BEST work according to the academic calendar, participating in reviews and celebrations at community events along their way to the culminating achievement of graduation. Cooper House offers youngsters concrete rewards through job success, award banquets, signs of status within the organization, and athletic challenges for those who participate in league contests. All these activities aim at culminations, singly or in series, where youth can see the results of their labor and often display those results to people outside the organization.

Clear Rules and Discipline

Inner-city youth want the security and predictability that accompany clear rules and consistent discipline. Contrary to many adults' expectations, inner-city youth are especially uncomfortable in anything-goes environments. They also flee settings where they see rules as rigid or unfair or where discipline seems erratic or harsh. Youth are comfortable in the wizards' organizations because wizards' rules and expectations depend on voluntary compliance rather than constant monitoring and sanctions for their overall effectiveness. All the successful programs we saw operate on the basis of a few rules that are based in the cultural authority of the group. Wizards recognize that people become environments for each other.[5] Thus youth are integral parts of successful organizations' culture, part of decision making, part of their own discipline.

Focus on the Future

All the wizards' programs work to encourage the value of education. Even though Michael Carroll is the only leader whose program places a primary stress on school-based learning, all the programs support educational activities in some way—through encouragement and rules about school achievement (Reggie Jones), access to peer tutoring (Luanna Williams and Steve Patterson), resources set aside to augment and reinforce progress in school (John Peña), or active recruitment for and provision of GED classes (Roberto Colon). However, the wizards' organizations do not treat education as a virtue in and of itself but as a means to achieving a positive future. The goal of all of the organizations, perhaps most poignantly described in Reggie Jones's terms, is that inner-city youth need tools for their own future, not just skills, but the pride and discipline to work hard to achieve goals. Thus the young men in the Reggie Jones Gymnasts are doing more than "ducking the bullet." They are doing well in school (a requirement of membership), graduating, and becoming productive members of society at an age when most of their peers are involved in crime, housed in jail, or dead. As Tyrone put it, "Mostly everybody that I grew up with is in a gang or selling drugs or something.... I just chose a different road." Reggie Jones showed Tyrone that road, and helped him navigate it.

Chapter Six

Making Vision a Reality: The People Who Make It Work

Wizards imagine positive places for youth where young people always have something to do and someone to do it with. To create the full-service organizations inner-city adolescents require, wizards rely on professional and junior staff who can translate mission into practice, creating and sustaining places of hope consistently day after day, supporting organizational norms and values, constructing environments where youth feel cared for, included, and valued. Wizards' youth organizations feel like families and induce hope in all their members because the staff members reflect the wizards' abilities, attitudes, and actions in addition to individual staffers' own exceptional abilities. In wizards' organizations the staff are true wizards' assistants, an essential part of the magic. In this chapter we discuss the role of staff in the successful inner-city youth organizations we studied. Chapter Seven describes how our wizards find and retain helpers who share the wizards' commitment and focus, and Chapter Eight discusses the essential role of volunteers.

Good staff not only have values that are congruent with the organizational ethos established by the leader, they must share the leaders' commitment to young people. As we have illustrated, the kinds of transformative outcomes hopefuls describe can be accomplished only within the security and shelter of a cohesive group. Staff must be as integral to the group as the leader and the youth, contributing of themselves in order to belong. Effective staff bring organizational plans to life, give the mission and the programs human faces and concrete meaning, day to day and minute to minute. Staff make the daily decisions that keep youth at the center of activity, driving programs rather than being driven by them.

The nature and mix of staff in each of the six organizations we studied depended on many factors—the nature of the programs, available funding, policy guidelines, and local availability of personnel. Simple numbers of staff also varied widely.

The Reggie Jones Gymnasts function with the small salaried, part-time staff of a bookkeeper, two drivers, and three assistant coaches. As mentioned before, Reggie's secretary and manager of his county supervisor's office, Violet Vaughn, gives the group administrative assistance and her personal attention too. Over the years she has mothered and enabled hundreds of boys as they collected in Reggie's office to dress for a performance or just to hang. Luanna Williams has no paid staff to support her Girl Scout Troop, but weaves the activities of Troop 10 in with Arroyo Community Center programs so that her Girl Scout activities are supported by the limited center staff while the older Scouts support center activities by volunteering as junior staff members.

Roberto Colon's GAIN program, located within the organizational embrace of the Porter Crossing YMCA, changes staffing patterns with the seasons. During the school year one full-time and two part-time street crisis workers, or caseworkers, are on hand for local gang members. During the summer, as the street action heats up and healthy outlets for youth are few, staff is increased by six additional street workers. Cooper House has a complex staffing pattern that blends adults and adolescent club members in full-time, part-time, and seasonal roles. Leading a staff of ten full-timers and twenty-five part-timers, plus about forty-seven individuals working in such seasonal activities as ball teams or summer camping, Steve Patterson enjoys an unusual breadth and depth of human resources for Cooper House's year-round membership of 620 and summer membership of 4,000.

John Peña in Big Valley has many fewer resources with which to staff his Boys and Girls Clubs. John runs the 1,550-member

Cougar Hollow Boys and Girls Club with eight full-time staff, one of whom works full time with TeenTalk. His staff for all the Big Valley Boys and Girls Clubs is approximately thirty-five. Michael Carroll has overseen the growth of BEST from the first years when he was the only full-time staff, assisted by a single summer intern, to the present complement of twenty-five full-time academic and support staff members.

Junior staff play an important and considered role in each of these effective youth organizations. These adolescent members are actively incorporated into organizational leadership, program development, and program delivery, although specific responsibilities vary. Steve Patterson employs approximately forty senior Cooper Housers not only to assist his professional staff but also to forge additional organizational connections with seniors. For Steve, youth staff positions are yet one more opportunity to furnish Cooper House members with the experiences and responsibilities necessary to support a productive adulthood. At BEST and the Reggie Jones Gymnasts, youth who grow up in the program are thought of as invaluable repositories of the organizations' ethos and skills, and for this reason, they are systematically integrated into the paid staff. At the Porter Crossing YMCA's GAIN program, local and current knowledge of gangland realities is so crucial that it has become the number one criterion for selecting staff.

Organizations' different staffing patterns create different staff problems and possibilities. John Peña and Steve Patterson, for example, strive to accomplish the same goals with vastly different resources. In each of the six organizations, however, the leader uses the talents of all staff to build a cohesive core from which the organization's programs and identity can develop. What was most striking in the very different environments where we met hopefuls and wizards was the common, if tacit, conception of the role of staff and the expertise needed to be an effective wizard's assistant. These roles and expertise relate to the tasks of creating a family-like setting, adapting environments to each youth personally, modeling behavior and outcomes, and teaching and monitoring organizational discipline.

Creating Familial Settings and Contexts for Hope

Because successful youth programs function like families, drawing youth into activities that enable them to move beyond the dead-end or deadly futures of their previous experience, staff must function as family members: caring adults; helpful older brothers or sisters; concerned aunts, uncles, or grandparents. Wizards' assistants carry out wizards' missions and vision by finding ways for inner-city youth to experience being valued as young adults but also sheltered as children. Inner-city youth who have responsibilities beyond their years for themselves, siblings, relatives, or even for their parents, need a protective haven that nurtures *them* and allows them to explore childhood imaginings and play.

Wizards' assistants may be professional staff responsible for providing the program or support staff responsible for running the office and cleaning and maintaining the facilities. Whatever their tasks their shared role is to perpetuate and reinforce group values and assure youth of a positive place in the organizational family. A nasty response from a receptionist to a young person's greeting or request for assistance can be as destructive to that youth's self-esteem as an athletic coach's impersonality. In this respect all staff are equal. Consistency and stability matter significantly in constructing a familial environment. For many inner-city youth, relationships with youth organization staff may provide the only human constancy in their lives. Rafael, Rosa's boyfriend, singles out Rick, a Cougar Hollow game room staffer, as one of the more important adult figures in his life. Rick has been Rafael's personal and reliable friend for years, and Rafael talks about him with a happy familiarity: "He's the one really that taught me how to shoot pool. Me and him have good games together. He's good. But he can't beat me no more! I can take him!"

It was Rafael's high regard for Rick and the value of that relationship that helped attract Rosa to the club and TeenTalk and away from her abusive family. In TeenTalk Rosa finds the personal attention and caring she misses in her home. From TeenTalk director Beth Walker's point of view, the family-like ties she works to develop among TeenTalk members not only benefit those members but are also essential to the high-quality performances that help teen and adult audiences talk about difficult issues. In addition, because the members of the troupe have shared many intimate details of their lives, they behave like a family, tending their norms and values and meting out their own discipline. Beth finds herself caught up in the lives of her TeenTalk youth, developing a special protectiveness for individuals like Rosa who face daily challenges and dangers from a crisis-filled environment. However, Beth also recognizes that many of her youth are already living adult lives, and she makes a conscious effort to treat them as young adults. Successful staff, like the wizards they assist, try to understand and respond to young people in their own terms and contexts, providing care and loving support. For such staff members, the first program objectives are their charges' growth and well-being.

The Cooper House hopefuls chorus the importance of the consistent and caring attitudes of everyone "down the house." To them, house staff appear as "safe" or "second" parents because "you can talk with them about things, tell them stuff, you'd never tell your parents." Cooper House staff themselves describe their roles in explicitly parental terms. When asked what her role encompassed, program director Susie Parnel says, "Everything! I am an educator, their friend, their adviser, their confidante. I mean anything! I take so many different roles for them. [For example, if] they're having problems, I tell them they can just come into my office. We'll shut the doors, they can say anything they want, and it'll go no further, never come out of my mouth again. That's all kids need, lots of times—someone to listen."

For Buddy the friendships and support he has found in house staff over the years bring him back every summer even though he has more lucrative alternatives available. He says, "All the people down there are just . . . like a grandmother. They're always there listening, and they always tell you 'if you ever have a problem, you ever need something, just come and let me know and we'll work something out.'" Buddy stresses that this sense of caring permeates the organization: "Cooper House in general, the secretaries, the program directors, just all the staff, the custodian, they're always there. . . . Everybody's there for you."

For Teri in Lakeside, BEST is truly a family affair because of her mother's and sisters' involvement. But the organization itself also exudes a "family feeling" and that is what Teri likes "most." At BEST, she says, it seems like "everybody just talkin' all the time, walkin' around, talkin' to everybody." Across town, in Porter Crossing, Roberto Colon sees the personal connections and caring attitudes of the GAIN staff as an essential asset. Roberto, Cruz, Manny, and a third staff member, Carlos, believe that even the hardest core gang members can be reached once they establish strong relationships with GAIN staff. Roberto describes one young man to whom the staff "gave a thumbs down" at first, thinking "he ain't gonna make it." The staff thought "he didn't want to survive. Didn't care about nothing." But the young man did make it through the program to a job, and Roberto attributes the youth's turnaround to the sense of belonging and family GAIN gave him. "Manny, Carlos, and Cruz became his family. . . . Manny became his big brother—to the point where when he told him, 'I'm gonna kick your butt if you don't do this,' [the young man did it]."

An effective family not only nurtures and protects its members but also prepares them to succeed outside the family. Susie Parnel tells of her staff role in the triumph of a young woman who gave a speech at the Cooper House awards banquet: "Everyone at the banquet was in tears because they were so proud of her, and she was too. It was *her* speech. She just didn't have the skills to put it down on paper. And so I helped her do that. They were her words, her thoughts, but we put them in an organized manner. . . . She was a star."

Steve Patterson sums up staffers' family role when he says, "We want to let kids be kids again, but still prepare them for their future."

Creating Personalized Environments

"Everybody knows me there." "There is always someone to listen." "I really feel accepted." A sense that they are recognized and accepted as individuals is the first reason youth mention for valuing their membership in one of the six organizations we studied, and it is staff who provide that one-on-one contact for these inner-city youth who so often find few steady or loving relationships at home or recognition in school. The warm and personal environment created by staff in places of hope distinguishes these settings from the herd programming of many youth organizations and the sense of anonymity youth experience there.

But providing a personal and caring environment for youth is a challenge for all the wizards. Even Steve Patterson who has thirty-five full- and part-time staff for six hundred and twenty year-round members could make use of more staff. Compared to these numbers, John Peña's eight full-time staff for fifteen hundred Cougar Hollow members seems paltry, especially as he has been moving the character of the city's Boys and Girls Clubs in the direction of Cooper House's more contact-intensive program. Altering the traditional Boys Club drop-in, gym-and-swim environment to a new family-like, personalized setting in which gym-and-swim is just one part of a program that stresses social, academic, and other aspects of youth development requires ever greater numbers of qualified staff.

Gym-and-swim programs are easier to manage and staff than programs that attempt to give youth all the kinds of opportunities middle-class families give their members. A drop-in club typically requires only one or two staff members for each recreational room within the facility. Since each recreational center—swimming pool, basketball court, TV room, game room, or boxing ring—can engage a large number of youth at one time with little direct staff involvement, a small staff can sustain programs that attract a high level of active membership.

But wizards' mission is to develop youth and give them hope, not just games and sports alone. Leaders like John Peña, Steve Patterson, and Roberto Colon believe that they are providing not only family opportunities where traditional families are not functioning but also educational opportunities that, increasingly, inner-city schools do not provide. As a result, they are adding computer labs, libraries, study centers, and training opportunities to their traditional community youth organizations. However, an education-oriented focus requires staff to provide more individualized and small-group attention to young people.

John Peña's primary concerns are whether or not some of the old program staff will be able to adapt to his new focus and whether enough additional staff can be funded to develop and sustain that focus. John sees installing the new program as an uphill battle. While he credits his success so far to the commitment and talent among many existing staff, he could "use another one hundred and fifty or so staff persons for the Big Valley clubs." With present staffing levels that stretch his staff to the limit running old recreational activities alongside new activities that require individual attention to youth, "it's really tough."

Role Models

Effective staff open their lives to the youth with whom they work. For inner-city adolescents, staff's other lives become tangible examples of "makin' it," of moving off the streets, of effective problem-solving, and of handling the disappointments and challenges that enter lives in any setting. Successful leaders' staff model roles that are accessible to youth. Staffers are not idealized sports heros and movie stars but individuals who live and work in the adolescents' neighborhoods, have faults as well as strengths, and show themselves to youth as survivors and optimists. They are pragmatic about how to survive the streets. Common background and perspective matter. Roberto Colon's strong belief that gang members who have a role model "have at least a 90 percent chance" of getting out of gang life is echoed by Manny, who says, "[Staff's] bein' from the neighborhood" matters because youth then see it is possible to move out of the grip of gangs and the drug business. "They saw us hanging out, dealing drugs and whatever, and they see us change. That's opening their eyes that there's something else out there for them."

Must staff role models come from youth's ethnic group to be successful in planting hope and fostering confidence about the future? Leaders, staff, and youth are of two minds about this important question, although their thoughts are not necessarily contradictory. They seem to say that a common ethnicity can be very important but that, at the same time, encouragement of militant ethnicity is to be avoided.

Thus most adults stress the importance of racial or ethnic identity as a component of a youth's self-esteem. They feel that, ideally, ethnic identity and awareness would be positive characteristics that youth could attribute to themselves. However, these adults also feel that youth may face a substantial hurdle in finding their ethnicity's positive values because, in their circumscribed inner-city neighborhoods, there often is little value or pride ascribed to being African American or Latino. In Porter Crossing, says Roberto Colon, "you don't see anything around you that supports any pride in who you are. [You just see negatives.] The local gang leader's Puerto Rican, the local drug dealer's Puerto Rican, all the guys hangin' out are Puerto Rican."

Inner-city youth of ethnic minorities see few representatives of their ethnic groups in professional jobs, aside from careers that are "outta this world" and out of almost everyone's reach, like professional sports or entertainment. Instead these adolescents see the adults around them in dead-end or menial jobs or, more typically, in no jobs at all. Many of these youth have no working adult living in their household. They also feel that the job market is racist and that they are its victims. "Its gotten to the point," says Reggie Jones, "that young black men don't expect anything of themselves or of their peers." Self-hatred permeates places like Francis Homes and the talk of its youth. In this environment, with its shortage of positive same-ethnicity role models, many youth organization leaders express that their first choice in staff would be someone of the same ethnic group or from the same neighborhood.

However, while youth workers and wizards believe ethnic awareness and pride can impart to inner-city youth a critical sense of richness, personal history, and identity that these youth are currently missing, no one we talked to supports the militant position that John Peña calls "ethnic chauvinism." The wizards and staff also agree that ethnic commonality is less important than caring for youth and understanding the conditions in which they live. Pointing to the lack of Latino role models available when he was growing up, John Peña states, "All the role models I had were non-Hispanic. And I never looked at them as being white, black, brown. They were just people that you could talk to and trust, that would give you feedback, that would give you discipline when you needed it. I think we're trying to get too culturally sensitive. A role model is a role model. . . . We need more role models of *all* races. A kid's gonna like somebody that pays attention."

Reggie Jones agrees with John Peña that ethnicity should be played down as an explanation or focus of life: "One thing I try to teach my young people is that you don't have to spend one second of your time [stressing] different ethnic backgrounds. The bottom line is that I teach my young people citizenship, brotherhood, fairness, and sportsmanship. When they go out they look at people how I look at people, and that is that color is nothing."

In fact some successful leaders of programs serving youth of diverse ethnic backgrounds worry that emphasis on ethnic identities will undermine group cohesiveness and the kinds of attitudes they intend to inculcate in their members. Staff are charged to create an inclusive and accepting environment for all of the youth who participate. For example, at the Cougar Hollow Boys and Girls Club, youth from different ethnic groups are at worst in conflict and at best indifferent to other ethnicities in the increasingly integrated yet polarized neighborhood outside the club. John Peña describes the situation as each group wanting the club for itself and his job as "trying to get [the groups] to see that [the club is] everybody's." He feels that the club has "potential because it has different races. . . . Kids are learning that they're not special because of their color and that someone else [is not] less because of their color." The ethnic makeup of the Cougar Hollow club changes substantially over the course of a year. It is pretty evenly balanced between European Americans, African Americans, and Latinos during the school year, but the summer membership brings new youth so that the club may be predominantly Latino one summer and predominantly African American the next. Despite this constant change, staff members' attitudes and behaviors must reflect John Peña's vision of the club as a wellspring of ethnic harmony in the face of Big Valley's racial tensions.

Although the staff for all the Big Valley Boys and Girls Clubs is "white-heavy" (three African Americans, four Hispanics, and thirty European Americans), John believes that their positive behaviors and attitudes can be models not only for youth but for the broader community. In response to the community's ethnic tensions, club staff assiduously avoid any words or actions that could provoke slights or disputes based on ethnicity, and they downplay ethnic differences, to an extent that bothers some members of the Latino and African American communities. John Peña explains, "We make a conscious effort not to make race an issue for being successful or for failure. We want each member to be proud of his or her heritage, but not to use it as a reason or cop out in any situation. El Cinco de Mayo and Martin Luther King holidays are viewed as days to educate all our members regardless of their ethnic heritage."

Nevertheless, while the wizards and wizards' assistants we met agree about the need to downplay ethnicity as something that sets youth apart from one another, they also believe that ethnicity can play an important function. In a place where "hope isn't a word you hear too much," youth need more evidence that others like them have climbed out of the despair of inner-city neighborhoods. Roberto Colon thinks that staff like Cruz, Manny, and Carlos are able to bring youth such as Tito out of gangs and into the embrace of the YMCA in large part because they share the youth's Puerto Rican background and that "makes it easier for a kid who's constantly being harassed [and] depressed to say, 'that person's just like me. He made it, why can't I?' These kids have pretty much given up on themselves and when they see Latino people like Cruz, me, and my staff here, then hope becomes real. It's tangible all of a sudden."

In general the six wizards and their assistants say that the more staff-youth connections spring from real life the better. Cruz can relate on many levels to Porter Crossing's Puerto Rican gang members who have dealt drugs, been to jail, dropped out of school, or fathered a child because he has experienced each of these himself. Certainly ethnicity and geography matter. But while Cruz may be most effective in his neighborhood, he also would be an asset to youth in the Arroyo Community Center, the Gymnasts, BEST, Cougar Hollow, and even Cooper House. His caring, his "no bullshit" approach to youth, his own persistence and success would make him an effective role model for youth in any context.

Teaching and Monitoring Rules of the Game

Group solidarity arises from members' consistent and reliable adherence to the group's rules and norms. While overall adherence to rules is voluntary in effective youth organizations, successful staff know they must monitor members' everyday behavior in ways that show youth that the group is a safe and stable place to be. Monitoring requires staff to achieve a delicate balance between their roles as family members and friends on the one hand and as accountable adults on the other. Youth want to be treated as "young adults, not children," as Rosa puts it, but they also want confidence that someone is in charge. John Peña repeatedly asserts the need for caring adult figures in the lives of youth, but he also emphasizes that "staff can't be big kids to little kids... because these kids need discipline. It's important to have staff who can be in charge as well as be a friend."

The success with which staff can monitor and enforce group understandings and rules depends on the extent to which youth see expectations and rules as fair and reasonable. Youth, even those who like attending organizations run by wizards, do not deny that sometimes they misbehave, but they also resent rigid "command-and-control" attitudes or harsh enforcement. Rafael, who has gotten into his share of trouble at the Cougar Hollow Club, feels staff there have treated him fairly: "They're nice to people even when we do bad things. They'll stay calm. They won't be mad about it. They try to look at it from your point of view, not from what *they* think is wrong or right." Other hopefuls also return again and again to the importance of calm, positive staff reactions to youth's varied behavior. Buddy approves of Paul Zwicki, the Cooper House basketball coach and camp director who only "screams" at the youngsters "when he yells 'GO! GO! GO!' [or] somethin' like that!"

While recognizing youth's perspective is an essential part of being fair in any setting, in inner-city organizations being fair demands special sensitivity. The youth who misses a scheduled activity may have had to care for a sick sibling while a parent went to work. A youth "going off" may have been awake all night because of gunshots outside his window. Wizards and their assistants know that "you just gotta be aware of their stressful life, all they have to endure." Luanna Williams applies her primary directive of being "flexible" when she develops programs and trains staff: "I tell staff that unless a child is just totally out of control, you don't send 'em home.... I may make 'em carry out garbage or do something else. But my thing is to keep 'em in the program because my biggest thing is, we don't know what it's like at home. And they have no place else to go."

Effective staff also see rule enforcement as an important opportunity for teaching youth broader lessons as well, and allocate time and energy to that task. "We're very disciplined here," says Cooper House's Susie Parnel. "We don't take much from any of the kids. They've signed up to be here; they don't have to be here. If you don't want to follow the rules, don't be a member of the house. Don't come." But Susie's strict tone masks the care and concern with which we saw her and other staff monitor and enforce house rules and work to make sure youth understand the reasons for them. Susie herself gave this example:

What I do first is give them a verbal warning, explain why they shouldn't be doing this type of thing. Then I let them tell me why because if they don't understand, I haven't accomplished anything. Then after that, if they do it again, there is some kind of punishment. [When a girl was] throwing cans out in the ballfield, I've gone around with [her] and we've picked up all of the cans and all of the *other* garbage. She won't litter again because she thought it was *disgusting* to pick up somebody else's garbage. And I said, "How do you think our custodian feels when he has to pick up your garbage?"

Being able to make decisions on the spot, adapt rules to a youth's particular situation, or ignore rules altogether is a critical staff attribute and one that poses a difficult challenge. Rigid enforcement of rules corrupts the personalized, youth-focused environment. Loose monitoring and enforcement threatens the solidarity of the group and cohesiveness of the organization. Shared understandings embodied in rules for behavior are a kind of organizational glue. To be effective, staff and leaders must constantly assess the appropriate responses to youth's inappropriate behavior. For example, Cooper Housers on the traveling basketball team learned an important lesson about commitment and obligation when Moochy, a team star, had an opportunity to go to a U2 concert that conflicted with the team's required practice time. Moochy asked Paul if he could miss practice to go to the concert, and Moochy recalls that Paul "said I knew the rules, that if he let me go, everyone could do the same, but that it was my decision." Moochy went to the concert, but when the first game came, he found himself "sittin' on the bench." He says, "I turned to Mr. Patterson and said 'Are you guys mad at me or what?' Mr. Patterson just said, 'U2. Arghhh.' I learned that a team rule had to be enforced and it was a commitment thing. I knew I let the team down." Discipline is important, but going strictly by the book proves as counterproductive in youth groups as it does in schools or other people-focused institutions. The astuteness with which staff manage these contraries day in and day out matters fundamentally to the stability and long-term health of youth organizations.

The Job of Wizard's Assistant

Effective staff are confronted by demands to be role models, family members, and mediating agents between youth's everyday experience and the broader environment. They negotiate, guide, and push. As youth make their transitions from the inner city they know to places in the outside world, youth organization staff must sustain these adolescents' new skills and roles and furnish bridges across boundaries of experience. If they do not assist at these borders, youth will not know how to respond to the organization's images of a life different from their inner-city routine. Staff sustain youth and their places of hope by tending internal boundaries as well. Conventional wisdom says youth are prone to avoid demands and discipline, but the organizations that draw the hopefuls are tough, rule-governed, "no bullshit" environments. From youth's perspective, they also are fair, engaging, respectful, and fun.

Staff work at all the boundaries to undergird youth's sense of safety within the walls, real or invisible, of the organization. That safety may be physical. GAIN staff have smoke-colored windows in their vans and take circuitous routes in respect to gang boundaries. In many other ways, safety for inner-city youth is psychological, allowing youth to let their guard down and speak in their own voices without fear of ridicule or betrayal.

Successful leaders' staff do not deliver programs impersonally. They love their jobs. "I thank my lucky stars everyday for this being my first job—this is a wonderful experience for me" is an expression of the kind of enthusiasm that pervades all the places where hopefuls gather. Such narrow job descriptions as baseball coach, camp director, club room supervisor, or office manager do not begin to capture what staffers actually do. They teach, listen, counsel, run interference, tutor, chauffeur, and baby-sit, in addition to their formal responsibilities. They are sister, brother, aunt, uncle, mother, father, and older and wiser friend. It is their willingness and ability to play these diverse roles for youth that makes them wizards' assistants and enables them to create havens for the hopefuls. The activity that first draws youth to an organization produces, retains, and sustains hopeful youth only when its staff give those youth caring, nurturing, and direction.

Chapter Seven

Building the Program's Family: The Challenge of Finding and Keeping Staff

Wanted: A caring adult to work long, unpredictable hours in a youth program. Must be available evenings and weekends. Job may involve risk to person or property; requires skill in all areas of human communication. Pay is low, opportunities for job advancement limited.

Such an advertisement would prompt few inquiries. But the qualifications it lists are closer to those needed to be a successful wizard's assistant than are the formal task-specific job descriptions compiled by many youth organizations.

All the wizards we met concur that finding and keeping staff is one of the two greatest problems they face in carrying out and sustaining their mission. (We take up the second problem, finding and securing resources and support, in Chapters Nine and Ten.) The quality of the program is directly correlated with the quality of the staff, say all six successful leaders. Therefore when finding and retaining staff is a problem, that problem threatens the fundamental character of the environments that nurture and engage the hopefuls.

Wizards' Requirements for Staff

The successful leaders of inner-city youth organizations want stability in their staffers and experience in working with youth who are out of the nation's mainstream. Many of them also want individuals with extensive local knowledge. But the prime requirement is that staff share the wizards' commitment.

Commitment

The six wizards agree that the staff qualifications most important to them are commitment to poor youth, knowledge of inner-city teenagers' backgrounds and circumstances, willingness to love these young people unconditionally, and passion for the particular enterprise within which youth are served. We found ex-athletes running sports programs, ex–Girl Scouts promoting Scouting, and alumni of Boys Clubs or YMCAs committed to providing youth with the opportunities these staffers believe enhanced their own lives. Cooper House alumni are particularly loyal. Most of the current staff grew up "goin' down the house," and working there fulfills a long-held dream. Susie told us, "My grandmother was a member here. My father was a member here. My mother was a member. All of my aunts and uncles were members. And so was I. And my staff—we all came here together. The three of us would always say, 'Yeah, we're gonna take over so and so's job whenever we get older.' One of the things that I can't believe [is] that I'm actually *here*!" Paul Zwicki says he is there because it is his turn: "God works in mysterious ways; I ended up at Cooper. They say life is a circle.... The reason I'm here is that I had excellent people workin' with me [when I was a member].... So you talk about passin' the torch. I guess my time is now."

For the leaders described here, commitment is as important as technical qualifications, if not more so. John Peña looks for qualifications—"Can that person completely perform the job?"—and then for "personal characteristics":

I want someone who is approachable, a good listener, patient. It's really important to get someone who has had experience working with kids who haven't had a lot of adult supervision. [Applicants] can be the best [people] in the world, but if they don't understand where that kid's coming from and what he's up against, they won't have the patience to listen a little longer or try a little harder. It takes a little extra to work with these kids cause they'll push you, they will. And the kids have enough to take care of out of the club, they don't need to put up with [impatience] in the club.

Since Boys and Girls Clubs professional staff must meet a college degree requirement, the majority of John's staff come from communities other than the lower-income neighborhoods where most Big Valley Boys and Girls Clubs are located. According to John, being an outsider can be a problem, and many prospects fresh out of college do not have the sense of reality or commitment needed to work with his kids. He finds that "a lot of them . . . want to move into a management position right away and not learn from the system." He looks for graduates who have "a background in the type of environments that they're gonna be working in, so they understand what it is, as opposed to coming in with their own philosophy and never having been in those communities. Sometimes they come in, and they want to change the world without understanding that world in itself." John also looks for individuals who can make "the commitment to the kids" and do "whatever it takes to get the job done, which is not always a forty-hour-a-week job."

The individuals who staff effective inner-city youth organizations willingly work long hours, and like the Wizards, describe fuzzy boundaries between their personal and professional lives. Susie Parnel laughs when she says, "I can't even count the hours! I work forty hours a week here, not including camp weekends, not including evening stuff, not including the time the kids come up to my house to hang out, . . . not including the time you lie in bed thinking about . . . What did this person say to me tonight? What kind of program am I gonna run next week? I've gotta do this, I've gotta do that. . . . And, I do *try* to go out, to have a social life. I have a boyfriend who's very understanding—he even chaperoned! The kids love him."

Commitment of staff in the hopefuls' organizations distinguishes these settings from others youth have come to know. Paul stresses the importance of working with youth over time in order to appreciate and celebrate growth and accomplishment. He points to a youngster who is "one of the most improved guys on the house team this year, but if he were goin' from coach to coach, or director to director each year, like at school, none of that hard work, none of his accomplishment would be appreciated. You gotta stick with [the organization] 'cuz it all goes with dealin' with a person, relatin' to a person better."

Experience with Nonmainstream Youth

John Peña stresses that he specifically asks prospective staff about their experience working with African American or Latino youth. If they are inexperienced, he "puts them into a probationary process and takes them through [to] see if they work," and he reveals that "a lot of times we have to go through the process three or four times before I find the right one."

Stability

The six wizards look for staffers' stability, their commitment to the community and the particular youth organization. To prove to youth that they care and are committed, staff must be predictably available. Words are cheap in the inner city, and commitment must be shown in action, not simply spoken. While it is difficult to find staff willing to stay twenty-five years like Rafael's pool-room friend Rick, the wizards all say they carefully consider each applicant's pledge of stability. With staff like club director Doug Wilder and TeenTalk's Beth Walker, John Peña is beginning to secure the stability he so strongly desires for his youth. After four years of seeking out the "right" kind of staff, he is able to say:

I've picked my staff so that I have people who are willing to take the time to get know the kids individually. They realize [the kids'] weaknesses and strengths. We don't have a high turnover rate in staff [and that was one of the problems with the club when I came]. Now, the people are here day after day and the kids know it. The kids have people going in and out nightly [at home], but not here. Here is their stability. And the kids get attached to the staff. You can ask the kids and they'll tell you, "It's one place I can go and always feel good about myself." They trust people here.

Local Knowledge

Another critical qualification for effective staff is knowledge of what youth go through in the networks and neighborhoods in which they live. Some of the six wizards rank local knowledge and preexisting ties to the community at the top of needed staff expertise. Luanna Williams underscores the importance of local experience as she describes what qualities her replacement at the Arroyo Community Center would have to have. That person would be "somebody that had some strong ties in Arroyo or that lived in Arroyo." Without that connection, the person wouldn't have the necessary amount of "concern or the caring." The person would also be "willing to stay—not somebody that would come in here and get tired and would be ready to leave, but somebody who would have the dedication to [Arroyo to] come in here and stay, regardless of the pay or the hours."

Roberto Colon knew from the inception of his gang intervention program at the YMCA that only complete "insiders" would be able to carry out GAIN's mission. Searching for a director for GAIN, Roberto did not look first for someone with YMCA experience or for a professional with a degree in social work. Instead he turned to Cruz Sanchez, whom he had known during his own youthful days in Porter Crossing's streets as a force to be reckoned with among gang members. Later Roberto had occasionally rescued Cruz from police roundups. While acting as cochair for the Lakeside Intervention Network (LIN), an unfortunately brief citywide initiative for gang intervention, Roberto became reacquainted with Cruz, who at thirty-six, three years Roberto's junior, was a street worker for LIN. Witnessing Cruz's work firsthand, Roberto came to respect Cruz's dedication and effectiveness and his knowledge of the streets of Porter Crossing. Roberto hired Cruz as GAIN's director, or as he puts it:

I hired someone who has a Ph.D. in the streets. [Cruz] had been working the streets for the last ten years. He knows the whole structure. He knows how the gangs are structured and run out of prison.... I found a guy that got out of [gang life] but understands it and can relate to it.... He's not a threat to them. He's not out there to bust their drug operation; he's not out there to bust the leadership; he's not giving any information to the police. He's out there to say, "Look, the Y has a program. Here's some viable choices for you. We can help some of you guys if you want to get the help."

In order to maintain the YMCA's neutrality and lay a foundation for negotiating peace in the neighborhood, Roberto and Cruz decided that the intervention work initially needed to target at least two of the numerous rival gangs in the neighborhood. The next step was to acquire gang contacts. As Roberto describes it, Cruz "went right to the two gangs, and he looked and he found Manny, [then] a twenty-five-year-old, and he found Carlos, a twenty-six-year-old, who still live in the neighborhood [and] who had been what we call ... one of the main heads, and they command respect. And now they come in, they got a van, they got insurance, they got jobs, they got school opportunities, they got training opportunities, these guys got some weapons now. They got something to [make deals] with. They are not a threat to the gang."

Manny became Roberto and Cruz's crucial link to the nearby, though by Cruz's gang standards foreign, territory of the neighborhood the gangs call Dark Crystal. Like Cruz, Manny lacks the traditional credentials for a career in the YMCA's professional culture. He did not complete high school, but as Roberto stresses, he has other essential qualifications: "He has the respect of the guys in this neighborhood. He could go over there and bring one hundred of 'em over here if I wanted 'im to.... He knows who the main head guy over there to talk to is." Manny's credibility on the streets is essential to GAIN. He carries a beeper for easy and familiar access, and he lives on the same streets as gang members he recruits for the Y. "Savin' the brothers" requires being able to get near them, but gang members are extremely suspicious of all outsiders. Staffing GAIN with former gang members has forged vital bonds of trust. Manny says, "If somebody else came up to [gang members] out of the blue and [said], 'Hey, we got a program goin' on over here,' they're gonna look at you crazy. . . . They're gonna think you're a cop. But I come to them, they know me and I know them, they're gonna have confidence in me. They're gonna trust me."

Tito, the young gang leader who participated in the graffiti cleanup program for two consecutive summers, explains his relationship with Cruz as one not only of trust but also of respect. That relationship is the reason he comes to the YMCA. Tito believes a Ph.D. in streets is an irreducible requirement for a program like GAIN: "If we got four guys from the university in here, and we trained them, we tell them, 'Okay, go out there now,' [the gangs will] eat them alive. Why? Because [the gangs] don't see that craziness in their eyes—that they were a part of this."

Few of the African American youth in BEST have had the GAIN participants' sustained and deep involvement in gangs. Therefore BEST director Michael Carroll stresses a different kind of local knowledge to make BEST successful. He expects staffers to have cultural sensitivity and personal knowledge about youth and their problems, such as conditions in a youngster's household or difficulties at school. He relies on senior program staff to "confront the issues which are bound to come up for kids who come to BEST."

The makeup of the staff and their attitudes also reflect BEST's long-term community affiliation. Two-thirds of the full-time staff are African American. BEST currently employs six parents of BEST participants as secretaries, van drivers, or classroom aides. Harriet Caldwell, the forceful, funny grandmother-figure, knows youngsters' parents well enough to chide them with both humor and persistence if they fail to support their children in every aspect of the program. It took untold telephone calls and admonitions of "C'mon, girl. Get your fanny in here," but Harriet managed almost perfect attendance from mothers at a parents' meeting. Finally, BEST links itself to the community by developing more community leaders, both through the adult education program and the policy of employing local adolescents to assist with the younger children.

Hiring Qualities That Can't Be Taught

Overall, wizards are looking to hire qualities that they know are essential and that they believe cannot be taught. Cruz, the director of Roberto Colon's GAIN program, points out that for his two-man staff, Carlos and Manny, training was what they already knew—the streets.

We just don't have a thirty-day seminar on how to became a youth worker. I just got in the van, took them out there. And our main objective is to come home in one piece. You've got to be on your toes, always. A shooting can come at any point in time on the corner.... It could be a retaliation shooting ... or a bad drug deal took place minutes before we got there and here comes the guy all crazy and stuff shooting the whole place up, and we're right there. So we need to read situations in the streets so we can identify whether or not we should even be there on that given day at that given moment.

Courage is another attribute training cannot instill. Roberto praises highly the dedication of his staff in the face of "the risks that they take out in the streets every day." The GAIN staff's former gang affiliations, necessities for making contacts with prospective clients, are never forgotten by former rivals. According to Manny, even though the staff's new YMCA connection gives them added respect in their old neighborhoods because "they're helping out the brothers," that connection is little protection against the long memories of old rivals. What a former gang member such as Cruz is now doesn't matter. "It's what he did ... back then. It's like it's not what you be, it's where you live that makes all the difference," explains Carlos. "And people grow up in certain areas and ... the rivals always look at you in that perspective.... Cruz will always be an enemy to them. Just like me."

Although the other wizards' staff requirements are less acute and dramatic than are those Roberto Colon faces, these wizards also distinguish between what a staff member can learn on the job and must bring to the job. For example, Luanna Williams told us that "the part that can be taught is how to be flexible, how to juggle schedules, how to deal with disciplining kids, and stuff like that. The part that nobody can teach is how to be genuine, because that has to come from inside. And one thing I've learned is that kids can smell it. That I don't think you can teach. That has be a part of you." Even though the organization he leads and the setting in which he works differ in significant ways from Luanna's, Steve Patterson echoes her thoughts:

My program director [Susie Parnel] ... did not have the major that I was looking for, but she had every quality that I would want in a staff person. She's enthusiastic; she's very caring [and] sympathetic; she loves kids; she loves people. She has a good set of what I would classify as values. I think she's a very honest person, a very sincere person. And those things you can't teach. You can take the most well-trained person in the world educationally, and you can't teach those things. Those things people either have or they don't. Being around a person like Susie makes *you* enthusiastic. I can teach someone how to run a program, I can teach someone to develop organizational skills or anything like that—those things are very teachable. The human qualities aren't teachable.

John Peña and his senior staff give new staff the flexibility to develop specific activities relating to their own interests, on the belief that a staffer will do best what he or she loves to do and that youth will respond to that genuine enthusiasm. From athletics to arts and from computers to tutoring programs, Cougar Hollow staff are free, as are Cooper House and BEST staff, to tailor activities to mesh with their own talents and their up-close assessment of what the youngsters need most at any given time. Staff see this flexibility as a key appeal of their jobs. Susie Parnel at Cooper House is enthusiastic about the "room to innovate.... Mr. Patterson is fan*tas*tic because if I have a program, and if I can run it successfully, or even *try* it so that it's organized, then I have the okay to do that.... That's really important to me, to have his trust to develop my own stuff." Steve Patterson considers "growing up good staff" as part of his broad mission and as a policy that results in an important contribution not only to Cooper House in the short term but also to youth organizations generally in the longer run: "Susie and Paul, they've been such good employees that if they left right now, I'd still be ahead of the game. It's okay to lose good people, because [the field] gains."

Raising Up Staff

All of the wizards stress the significance of hiring their own youth as junior staff and teaching them skills and attitudes that can help them succeed in the job market. But beyond training youth for future employment or community responsibilities, wizards see themselves "raising up leaders" for youth work, making an investment that will benefit the next generation of the community's children.

Cooper House has a policy of hiring its own teens for work both at the front desk and in the locker room in order to give them opportunities to earn money and to operate in a business setting. Even though the year-long positions are few, several adolescents told us these jobs are important education in learning about being on time, representing the organization to the public, fulfilling obligations, and being responsible. The academic-year routine of required and voluntary athletics and Boys and Girls Club activities is broken by summer camps, one for boys and another for girls, held at a nearby rural (and very rustic) campsite that has been part of Cooper House for decades. The Cooper House summer camp relies heavily on the house's teenagers and recent graduates to serve as counselors or counselors in training (CITs). As trainees, the teenagers once again receive financial incentives (a $10 deduction on the camp fee per session), but the rewards of privileges seem more highly prized. CITs relish their own camp "lodge," later curfew (meaning they have free time after the younger campers are asleep), and occasional sanctioned raids on the camp kitchen. In the Cooper House tradition, with these privileges come such added responsibilities as seeing to the development, safety, and entertainment of young Cooper Housers. Counselor-in-training Moochy sees CITs as "second in command. We're in charge of whatever the counselors don't do, to remind 'em if they forget. We're like their little brother, . . . and if the kids need to talk to someone and they don't feel like talking to a counselor or a staffer, they can talk to a CIT. [If the counselor is not there,] you have to be the head guy, so you pay attention to what your counselor does so when he leaves you know what to do."

The young counselors learn primarily through observing. "You just pick things up here and there," Buddy says. "Paul and Steve, they're there for you all the time." Buddy affirms that role modeling, an ethos of relationships, and leadership permeate the Cooper House environment. He sees that Paul and Steve model roles for him and that he has to do the same: "You have to play that role for those kids because you want them to say, "I can go to Buddy for any problem I have. I can go to see Buddy about how to do this and what I should do about this." And you're just there for them. The whole counselor deal is not 'Do this. Do that.' It's 'What can I do for you?' . . . That's what teaches you, people you're around. Paul wouldn't have hired us if he didn't feel that we was people that put our time into the kids."

Discontent can arise even in wizards' organizations when youth staff are not allowed to assume meaningful organizational responsibilities. Senior members of the Reggie Jones Gymnasts chafe at Reggie's apparent reluctance to trust them by sharing operating and management responsibilities. Tyrone says, "We could do it, but [Mr. Jones] just won't let us. We could take a lot off his shoulders if he would let us. It sorta makes us feel bad." The frustration Tyrone expresses is ironic given Reggie Jones's increasing weariness with the team's grueling schedule and unremitting demands, and his oft-repeated requests to find an understudy to take over so he can cut back substantially, if not retire, in the near future when he reaches sixty. Reggie has made token attempts to share responsibilities with the older Gymnasts, but delegated responsibility must be genuine. To be designated "coach" without access to the locker room or equipment can be frustrating. To be asked to take charge of a performance and have Mr. Jones "stop by to see how things are going" can be demoralizing. Youth want significant and genuine responsibilities ("to be treated like he has confidence in us"), and they sense that duties assigned without confidence are little better than no significant responsibilities.

Staff Compensation

Low pay and long hours make it difficult even for successful leaders to attract staff to their youth organizations and difficult to keep good staff on board once there. Cruz and Manny earn about $11,000 a year for the dangerous occupation of GAIN street worker. Beth Walker, who supplies the spirit, love, and wisdom to TeenTalk and holds a master's degree, earns barely $30,000 a year. Renee Jordan, the "locally grown" educator at BEST who also holds a master's degree, earns about the same. Wizards' gifted assistants work at their jobs for reasons other than money or career mobility. Cooper House's exuberant, talented Susie Parnel wonders, not entirely tongue-in-cheek, if perhaps the low pay serves a positive purpose: "Money's not *that* important ... because you're making an impact on the kids. You know, they're going to *be* our future. And maybe without realizing it, society is making the wages [of those] that work with kids ... low for a purpose, because if teachers were makin' hundreds of thousands of dollars, everybody would wanna become a teacher, ... and it would take away from [the dedication and caring], and it would become a business."

Staffers draw much of their reward from the successes of their charges. Trite but true, "making a difference" motivates staff just as it does their leaders, inspiring "parental pride" toward all their youth's accomplishments. Susie describes this reward when she says, "Whenever I have the privilege of naming all of our twenty-five outstanding females at Cooper House, I tell all of the parents that I feel exactly like them. I am so *proud* of these kids because I have seen them work *so* hard all year long that I'm just as proud as their parents."

Manny and Cruz understand that their streets are a realm of life and death and conduct their work with an almost missionary zeal, tempered by stark realism; they cannot accomplish all that they would like. Cruz says bluntly:

What we work here for is lives. To try to alter minds, not to go out there and shoot. We can't stop them from dealing drugs. That's the financial situation that I found myself in and they find [themselves] in. We're working here to reduce the gang violence in our community. . . . Not stop it, because we can't do that, but reduce the gang violence in our community that our own kids are going to someday face. . . . Whether it's by one murder a year or whether it's by a hundred murders a year, so that our kids might have a better chance. That's the bottom line right there.

Manny believes that the combination of jobs and schools can help young men accomplish the difficult trick of getting out of the gangs without having to be "violated" out, the usually brutal exit ritual.

I hope they just see another way of life, because it's like a hundred chances of them getting caught up [in trouble]. . . . Working legally, what's the most that could happen to you? Probably get a ticket for driving your car too fast or being late for work. That's about it. There's no risk in working, unlike dealing drugs. We may not be able to save a lot of brothers out there, but the brothers I do save, I go home feeling good [about]. Because it's not the money I make, it's the impact I make that makes the difference in my life. And I go home feeling good.

Staff whose youth work is a way out of the violence of the streets and gangbanging also find other rewards in their positions. For them the wizard's habitat serves as sanctuary and supportive family just as it does for youth. Both Manny and Carlos have been kept from jail by Roberto Colon's intercessions. For example, as a former gang member, Manny had a reputation with the police and a prison record. After he was accused of selling drugs to an undercover officer on a day when he was working at the YMCA and could not have made the alleged sale, Roberto arranged for the YMCA president to write a letter in Manny's behalf. Because Manny also had the backing of the community, Roberto was able to orchestrate an outpouring of support for him when he went before the judge. On the strength of this show of others' confidence in him, Manny was released. "He owes the Y," says Roberto. "He owes the people."

But staff members' strong ties and commitments to the youth, the organization, the leader, and their own personal mission often prove insufficient to retain gifted staff when circumstances in their lives require them to "earn some real money." Jennifer Adams, a brilliant teacher and extraordinarily able mentor to the youth involved with BEST, will soon complete her final year with the program. Now in her late twenties, she had made a "personal commitment" to "get one class through—six years, from seventh grade to senior year." But Jennifer and her husband, with plans to start a family, can no longer make do financially. Jennifer says, "It's time for me to get on with other parts of my life."

Paul Zwicki, whom Buddy calls "best friend," agonizes over whether or not he can afford to stay in his job:

I am really happy here and love working with the youth. [But] one of my big concerns now is I have a family on the way. And as everyone knows, it's financially difficult in this profession. If I could support my family, I could see myself ... working with young people for a very long time.... Soon after I took the job with Cooper House, the Washington Redskins called and offered a job working in their scouting department. And I turned that down to stay with Cooper House so I think that says something about what the house means. But it's a problem.

Like senior staff, junior staff prize the intrinsic rewards of work, opportunities to model themselves on people they admire, responsible roles in the organization family, and the long-term benefits of their current work. These youth are respected as vital human resources in the life of the organization and the community. They are encouraged by adult staff to be actively engaged in shaping their present lives as well as creating their own futures. Perhaps the most vivid example of the benefits junior staff receive is the familial loyalty they feel, a strong connection that they believe will be lifelong. Teri says, "Being at BEST [I] realize if some-one hadn't helped [me], then I wouldn't be able to come where I'm at. I have to help someone else. It's a responsibility. BEST sort of ties you up. . . . Once you're there you're always a part of BEST, no matter what."

Chapter Eight

Volunteers:
A Mixed Blessing

Creating places of hope for inner-city youth, a demanding, highly labor-intensive enterprise, requires many hands, hearts, resources, and talents—many more than budgets afford. To bridge the gap between resources and needs successful leaders look to volunteers from the neighborhood and the broader community to offer time, love, personal resources, and talent in order to benefit the hopefuls. Volunteers can help staff transform organizations into families and broaden the experiences and resources available to youth. Sometimes they make possible events that are beyond the reach even of wizards and their talented assistants. Volunteers can also be powerful ambassadors for youth. In short, effective volunteers are human resources, economic assets, and political capital for the wizards and their organizations.

Volunteers are vital but they are not without cost. They require training, supervision, perks, and other organizational resources if they are to be effective and committed over the long term. Further, although the kindness of strangers and the succor of friends usually are well-intended, volunteers may fail to live up to expectations and their failures can disappoint youth and diminish organizational effectiveness. Recruiting, managing, and rewarding volunteers are the critical pieces of wizardry discussed in this chapter.

Volunteered Assets

Volunteers benefit youth organizations in many essential ways. They contribute person power to field trips, sports teams, and fund-raising events. They provide shoulders for comfort, ears to listen, and arms to hug. They bring specific expertise often impossible to have on staff and unaffordable from consultants.

TeenTalk's effectiveness as a teaching agent depends on the generosity of experts who volunteer to instruct the performers on the array of topics they dramatize, from incest to AIDS. Youth in the organizations run by John Peña, Roberto Colon, Michael Carroll, and Steve Patterson are taken across town to visit lawyers, architects, accountants, and other professionals who have volunteered to spend an afternoon talking with youth about what they do and how they prepared themselves to do it. The generosity of these individuals opens futures previously unimaginable to inner-city youth, and "the suits," as the youth call them, learn something about these youth. John Peña stresses both the reciprocity and opportunity in these field trips when he says, "The contacts [the kids] make are important in terms of broadening their horizons, and they work both ways. Get a kid involved in a conversation with a lawyer, for example, and the kid learns about a career and the lawyer learns that [inner-city kids] are not 'bad kids.'" Many of these professionals make further contributions, mentoring youth, assisting them in school, and helping them have experiences relevant to their newly imagined futures. Youth leaders rate the payoffs from such encounters highly: they get youth out of their neighborhoods, introduce them to "downtown types," offer them opportunities to experience and act in the mainstream world of corporations, professional offices, and civic agencies, and give them confidence that they can construct a better future for themselves. But youth in these organizations point out that it is also important for the "suits" to come to the neighborhoods as well. "They got to do more than just drop off a T-shirt. They need to spend time *here*."

Wizards use volunteers with special talents to attract cynics to the organization, youth who think "that's for kids" or "wusses," or that "nothin' fun happens" there. The volunteered talents of a popular African American rapper enticed a number of African American youth to the Cougar Hollow Club, for example. A local baseball hero draws crowds to Cooper House. "To get kids to come and to stay, you make it fun. We need help from the community [and people like the rap artist] to accomplish that," says John Peña.

Volunteers permit ambitious programs that cannot be carried out without many extra hands. The all-night dance that was such a hit with Cooper House teenagers depended on almost twenty mothers and fathers who agreed to chaperon the event, "no way we woulda been able to have that dance without them," says Steve Patterson. When John Peña's youth wanted to experience a formal dinner, a small platoon of Big Valley parents and community members came out to cook, serve, and oversee a candlelight sit-down dinner for forty Boys and Girls Club youth in the midst of "one of the highest drug, shootin' areas in Big Valley. A housing project where only four males live permanently." The event succeeded beyond even John's expectations as a positive experience for the embattled community and as an opportunity for youth "to learn some social skills, learn how to treat a lady. They had to get dressed up. And they held the chair out for the girl to sit down and I mean, it was *unbelievable!*" John says the adolescents still talk enthusiastically about the evening and have requested another such event, a hopeful counterpoint to "the sounds of guns goin' off " they heard as they left the dinner.

BEST's rich academic program depends on the talents and generosity of many individuals in the broader Lakeside community. Michael Carroll is forthrightly opportunistic in using whatever resources he can attract to develop curricula and experiences for BEST. Within the stable atmosphere provided by the permanent staff, BEST's students encounter a wide range of experiences, from art lessons by professional artists to tennis instruction by tennis club members. A group of young professionals from the African American professional community give BEST's high school members insight into the business world during bimonthly meetings, and serve as additional role models. Through long-standing relationships with several area colleges, BEST has channeled the idealism and vitality of college students into the core tutoring programs, making one-on-one tutoring available for each BEST student several times a week. Michael Carroll and his staff succeed in attracting talented individuals to BEST, encouraging program flexibility and affording their youth the services of artists, technicians, athletes, and professors. The large number of volunteers means each student gets more personal attention and establishes an atmosphere in which the pursuit of higher education is a norm. The personalized environments valued by youth are reinforced and sustained by volunteers in many of the successful youth organizations we found. Volunteers join the family-like environment, and says Buddy at Cooper House, are like "experienced friends."

Recruiting Volunteers

Recruiting volunteers is an ongoing, time-consuming, and often frustrating job for effective youth organization leaders and their staff. BEST and Cooper House are remarkably successful in drawing volunteers, owing both to the talents of their leaders and to the particular characteristics of their organizations.

Michael Carroll has been able to tap into established university and church networks in the Lakeside area by exploiting BEST's twin identities as an educational program and a Christian service organization. He attributes his success to "always seeing [a contact] as a resource," and he tells others, "Search out how [each contact] can be useful to you.... Every phone call is a potential resource. Maybe not what you thought, but if you have a shopping list of real needs you can usually come up with something conducive." Michael encourages church members to see BEST as an opportunity to help with a mission and fulfill their commitment as Christians, and college students to see BEST as a chance to gain experience or academic credit in multicultural education. Michael's constant pursuit of academic expertise has reached beyond college students to their professors, who have donated program design consultation and staff development assistance to BEST. Through Michael's imaginative handling of contacts and harnessing of volunteer energies, talents, and assets to BEST's structure and focus, BEST has been able to engage numerous volunteers from the broader community at a time when many youth agencies lament the lack of volunteers.

Cooper House benefits from a large group of alumni who are loyal to the organization and eager to contribute so that their sons and daughters can profit from the same experience they did. "Volunteers," says Susie Parnel, are "really the main reason we exist." The alumni group is stable largely because the immediate community is stable, and several generations of Cooper Housers have lived in the same neighborhoods, often in the same houses. This constituency has supported and maintained the house's original mission statements and provided many volunteers. Although such intergenerational relationships are now becoming less characteristic, and the neighborhood is noticeably changed in some ways, Steve Patterson says that the "economic value [of alumni volunteers] is immense; they are an unbelievable resource for us. Everyday, almost, somebody drops by and says, 'I'm back! I wanna volunteer!'" Without the hundreds of young adults, parents, and other community members who give thousands of hours a year to the house, Steve's highly personal, comprehensive, and responsive programming "just couldn't happen." Moreover, Cooper House volunteers stick with the organization. In 1991, for example, two men and one woman were honored for thirty consecutive years of volunteer service.

Roberto Colon's YMCA gets some assistance from young adult alumni, as do the other wizards' organizations. Because they have given youth shelter and hope and served as families, these organizations often find that young alumni with time on their hands turn up to hang out, to be part of the organization again. The same program features that attracted them as youth pull them back as young adults. They hope to be included once again and offer to help out in exchange. "Hanging around the Y is like a comfort zone for them," says Roberto. "They're around people they know. They're off the streets. They're accepted."

Summertime brings out the most volunteers in Arroyo, as in other communities, and youth are Luanna Williams's biggest volunteer resources. She says, "The major thing is teenagers want to belong. They want to have a sense of responsibility. They want to feel like they're doing something. And I think that's what's always done it for them. They get to come down [here]. They get to actually help out in their own community. It's sort of a prestigious thing because they're labeled as a volunteer at the center. And they are told at the beginning that they will be treated just as our paid staff." Each summer the center draws on the energies of twenty-five youth volunteers. To the amazement of their parents, these young people display a responsibility that could be markers of a paid position. "The kids are really serious about getting to their jobs on time," Luanna says, and parents have remarked, "I can't believe this. It's like they're punching a clock." Luanna gives her young volunteers training before day camp begins and makes the volunteer experience as much like a paying job as possible. Volunteers sign in and sign out, and if they are going to be late or absent, they call in to their supervisor. One parent called and asked, "What are you teaching these kids? My girl wants me to write a note saying she's sick 'cuz she missed a day."

Young alumni just show up. Finding and engaging older adult volunteers is an extraordinarily difficult challenge for the wizards who lack the adult alumni resource of Cooper House or the strong support networks of BEST. Luanna Williams struggles mightily with the task and succeeds primarily because of her deep neighborhood roots, her directness about needs, and her forceful, positive representation of the Arroyo Community Center and the Girl Scouts. She says, "I just try pulling in the people that I know. My biggest problem is that we have the role models in the community, but they don't want to get their hands dirty. They don't want to take the time to talk to these guys or take these girls out camping. The ones that I have I just work to death."

Luanna also capitalizes on the presence of senior citizen services at the community center to add human resources to her youth programs and to strike a "balance between the old and the young." She asks senior citizens who come to the center to "volunteer to help the kids learn ceramics or quilting," and she says, "Whatever we need them to do, they're willing to help out with the kids." She also has gotten tough with the parents of her young people. She says she expects parents to sign up to chaperon at least one field trip during the summer, and "in the past, we've said, 'Okay, parent, you need to sign up,' and they never showed up. So this year we said, 'If you miss your assigned time your child stays home with you.' So far we've done real good."

Luanna also exploits every contact with men in the community in order to corral them into the center. Carl, a thirty-three-year-old postman who grew up at the center, began dropping by to play basketball when he returned to town and was soon drawn into Luanna's sphere of volunteers, taking on several of the boys teams. Other young men were similarly pulled in when they came in to play basketball, and some of her girls' fathers decided to coach because she would "talk up on 'em," haranguing them about their duty to help out.

By using every conceivable ploy Luanna has secured a small cadre of committed, reliable volunteers from the tight-knit Arroyo community. Luanna's difficulty gathering volunteers highlights a perception we heard from several youth organization leaders—that securing African American volunteers seems particularly difficult. Youth leaders in both Big Valley and Lakeside note the differences they see between Latino and African American neighborhoods in terms of voluntarism. In the Latino communities, parents and adults can always be found to cook a breakfast for a field trip, put on a dinner, chaperon a dance, or tend a child-care program. As one Latina activist told us, "We take care of each other. Community *is* family for Hispanics. Whether it is an enchilada dinner, Neighborhood Watch, or helpin' out at school, we'll be there—even though, [if you're a single parent,] after a ten-hour day, you just want to come home, kick off your shoes, eat, and go to bed. But we support our kids and community."

African American community leaders tell a different tale and express their frustration with getting adults to give time to youth organizations. An African American social studies teacher in Lakeside, the volunteer coach of a winning Francis Homes basketball team, was saddened and infuriated that "not *one* parent, not even one, came out for the awards banquet" honoring the team. Reggie Jones worries about the next generation of African American youth as well as the resources available to this generation: "Volunteering is a modeled thing; you just don't have it in the black community." John Peña, commenting on differences between Big Valley communities, echoes Reggie's words: "In the black community kids just don't see a whole lot of parent volunteers. There are no role models for volunteering in the black community. I worry about the next generation; they're teaching their kids the wrong lessons." In River City an African American civic leader concurs on the lack of African American volunteers: "African Americans who have made it move out to the suburbs. A major problem is to get these commuters to go back to the old neighborhood . . . and spend some time with the organizations and the youth there."

Localized struggles with attracting and retaining volunteers go largely unnoticed at the wider community level. In each of the three urban areas we studied, civic leaders praise the city's philanthropic spirit, and rightfully so. (Indeed, the presence of this spirit was an important reason why we selected these cities for our research.) But the majority of volunteers in all three cities are typically middle- and upper-class European Americans. While they have great spirit, energy, and talent to offer, they seldom move out of the circle of United Way agencies and the familiar national organizations to involve themselves in inner-city grass-roots groups. Parents who live in the suburbs or wealthier parts of the cities understandably volunteer their time and resources to the organizations that benefit their own children—their neighborhood YMCAs, Scout troops, and athletic teams. So even though some communities enjoy a high level of voluntarism on the whole, these human resources are distributed unevenly and rarely show up in inner-city communities to coach ball teams, lead Scout troops, drive for field trips, or bake or sell cookies to raise money. These outside volunteers are least likely to show up when the inner-city youth organization is homegrown and unfamiliar to mainstream adults.

In inner-city neighborhoods where adults feel shut out of the mainstream and lack confidence, the training and experience that they get when they volunteer can be a powerful enabling strategy, making them not only more reliable volunteers but also community leaders. But the extent to which volunteers and volunteering represent a resource for local residents depends to a significant extent on whether leaders successfully resolve what effective leaders call the Lady Bountiful problem, the dependency and alienation that often result when people from outside the neighborhood come in to "do" for the locals. When nonprofit organizations compete for funding there is a great temptation to use outside expertise in order to produce visible, short-term results. But unless managed carefully, this particular kindness of strangers can inhibit the development of neighborhood volunteers.

The key to alleviating the Lady Bountiful dilemma is, as a Lakeside Girl Scout official put it, to "move from a model of Mrs. Wilson is here to lead the program in the church with the help of the ladies, to Mrs. Smith is here to help the ladies of the church lead the program." The latter strategy uses volunteer positions to develop local leadership and empower adults in the neighborhood, while also minimizing future dependency on the Mrs. Smiths and Wilsons of the world. BEST, for example, has enabled many adults in the Francis Homes community to complete their GEDs, or even go on to college, as Teri's mother did. BEST provided the initial impetus through volunteer opportunities and later through financial and other supports. Local volunteers who have provided assistance in the classroom, supported social activities, and organized fund-raising affairs have subsequently assumed leadership roles in the Francis Homes community, buoyed by their experiences at BEST. Adults trained by BEST also have moved confidently into positions outside Francis Homes. When Lakeside's school district was restructured to decentralize authority and invest decision-making power in local advisory councils, BEST's corps of committed parents and staff were already trained in educational issues and ready to serve. BEST representatives on eight neighborhood school councils have forged vital links for the expansion of BEST programs into local schools and allowed BEST volunteers to influence schools beyond the immediate neighborhood of Francis Homes.

Another challenge and opportunity for wizards is to recruit volunteers from outside the neighborhood who can provide entrée and access to the larger community and leverage additional economic, social, and political resources for the organization. When kind strangers can be transformed into friends they become advocates of the organization's mission and organizational ambassadors to the community. They cease to be "checkbook philanthropists," keeping their distance and insulating themselves from the problems of their beneficiaries, and become partners, concretely involved with the organizations they support.[1] Effective leaders understand the educational function these volunteers perform by advocating inner-city youth organizations in their corporations, professional groups, social clubs, boards, and other networks as the most important, long-run contribution of strangers turned friends. Once enlightened and informed, these volunteers reduce the isolation of inner-city youth organizations and correct their own peers' misperceptions about inner-city youth. The resulting political capital often means more to the organizations than do dollars or other material forms of support.

Managing the Gift Relationship

The nature and terms of a gift establish a relationship between benefactor and beneficiary, and this relationship, in turn, influences significantly the perceived value of the gift to both. When wizards manage volunteers they are managing a gift relationship.[2] Therefore the main questions they consider are, Who gives and why? and, What are the terms of the relationship? Even though volunteers frequently talk about what they do and why they do it in moral terms, pure altruism seldom motivates volunteers. They come to a youth organization for a purpose, and usually for more than one.[3]

Like wizards themselves, many volunteers come to a youth organization wanting to pay back gifts they were given at some point in their lives. Cooper Housers, the Arroyo youth, Cougar Hollow members, students at BEST all benefit from the commitment of adults seeking to repay. Carl, the postman who volunteers at Arroyo Community Center, sees his "main reason" as "being involved with the kids. Giving back.... Too many black men have been doin' too much negative. . . . I'm doin' it because of what they're not doin' [and because] of what some people did for me."

Others volunteer in youth organizations out of a more generalized sense of duty—to a religious mission, to ideals of public service, to norms of mutual support within a community—or out of a sense of noblesse oblige. Volunteers who belong to such charitable organizations as Rotary Clubs, Junior Leagues, or Kiwanis Clubs work with youth organizations in conjunction with the mission of their own voluntary organizations, a mission generally rooted in promoting social change and giving charity to the less advantaged. Still others volunteer out of "enlightened self-interest." They mean to enhance their résumés or community status, or garner social approval, credits, or contacts needed for other purposes. And some adults volunteer simply because it is fun, a chance to engage in sports, theater, the arts, or some other activity they enjoy. They meet two objectives at once, doing good and having fun.

Different expectations, assumptions, and levels of commitment accompany these diverse reasons. Effective leaders understand these differences and try to provide the right motivation and rewards to encourage various volunteers to continue giving of their time, talent, and love. Some, of course, find their own motivation. Carl, the postman, takes his reward [as do the wizards and their staff] in the successes of the youth: "Some of the boys getting scholarships. That's the thing I'm most proud of myself. All these little fellows that I know, that I've been watching grow up over the last years, some are going to college next year, or on to somethin' positive. If I had any kind of hand in that, I'm glad."

However, extrinsic rewards count too. Wizards make rewards for volunteers a part of the organization's rhythms. Youth and volunteers are honored together at Cooper House's annual celebratory banquet. The occasion links volunteers to past and future accomplishments of the house and reinforces volunteers' desire to contribute to youth. Another favorite perk that Steve Patterson uses to make volunteers feel special is to designate the Tuesday and Thursday gym nights "only for volunteers. A thank you. They really like it." And of course Luanna Williams also rewards her Girl Scout aides with special privileges.

The leaders we talked to also confront the fact that not all volunteer contributions are positive. Sometimes, especially when volunteers are unfamiliar with the youth and the organization or neighborhood, the gift relationship can be a damaging one. Luanna Williams realized that well-meaning donations of used Girl Scout uniforms to African American Scouts in Big Valley, for example, would be received as a patronizing affront. "You just don't toss second-hand stuff at black girls," scolds Luanna. "Used uniforms from white folks are an insult."

In the same vein, do-gooders who come to an inner-city youth organization intending to "fix" or change the youth who gather there send all too familiar negative messages to youth about their worth. For example, volunteers may focus on getting inner-city youth to college—a noble end, but perhaps an undesirable objective from the perspective of some youth or realistically beyond the reach of others. Unwittingly, these volunteers give youth the message that not going to college means failure. Caught in their own value systems, volunteers sometimes fail to understand and support feasible and honorable futures based on accomplishments other than academic achievement as conventionally conceived.

Volunteers who consciously or unconsciously belittle youth's families, personal circumstances, and cultural backgrounds demean the very youth they intend to benefit.[4] For example, Michael Carroll knows that BEST profits greatly from the vigor, idealism, and commitment of his small army of volunteers, but he and senior staffer Renee Jordan also know that volunteers from outside the Francis Homes neighborhood can bring with them destructive attitudes or naive beliefs about African American youth, compounded by stereotypical views of life in the housing projects. Senior and junior staff make a concerted effort to educate volunteers about the youth, the community, and the ethos of BEST. Outside volunteers are schooled in community sensitivity and the importance of consistency. College students receive a two-hour training session in the fall and sign a contract committing themselves to meet weekly with one BEST student for at least one year. They continue to be monitored closely by permanent staff throughout this time. With this careful preparation many of the relationships developed between tutor and student expand beyond the classroom, in the form of day trips around the city and overnight trips to nearby colleges (upon approval by BEST staff), and often extend through and beyond the tutor's college years. Michael says that training outsiders to be sensitive to community youth is "tough." He believes "there's a real sensitivity about this whole thing by a good majority of the staff, but you do get into these problems of bringing on people who are pretty naive and seem to want to learn, but you're really not quite sure how open they really are, and they've been brought up in certain ways." As a junior staffer, Teri's experience of helping to train volunteers has led her to similar, less diplomatically phrased, conclusions:

A lot of times, especially if people come from Christian colleges, they come right down and mention the faith: "We're gonna save them from themselves. So they won't go to hell," and such. And we have to tell 'em it's really a turn-off to do that to people. I told 'em that they should act like *they're* learning something as much as the kids, instead of trying to save them. And I don't think they're familiar at all with inner-city life and that culture.... And they probably just come in 'cuz they had to take a class or something.... A couple of years ago, kids from a Southern state came to volunteer. And I don't know whether it was ignorance or [what, but] they were making wisecracks about black people. To the black kids! Like expecting them to laugh with them. And they were just really ignorant.

Even Steve Patterson, rich in alumni volunteers, has to manage the downside of their enthusiasm and commitment to the organization. This downside is an emphasis on "the way it used to be." By and large his volunteer pool is committed to the mission and the program of Cooper House as they themselves experienced it. Yet changes in the status of Cooper House youth over the past twenty years have been dramatic. For example, almost 70 percent of today's Cooper Housers come from single-parent or blended-family homes. A majority of these homes are stressed by layoffs at River City's mills and factories. African Americans have joined Cooper House's previously all European American membership roster. Alumni resistance to new faces and a changed agenda was evident when Steve failed to find any volunteer help for Cooper House to participate in a youth conference with a focus on racism. Some alumni have also expressed concern about house discussions on date rape, AIDS, and teen pregnancy.

In addition to monitoring volunteers' attitudes, leaders also watch their behavior. Failure to follow through on commitments is a typical problem that volunteers visit upon youth organizations, and the penalties of adult insincerity or thoughtlessness fall particularly heavily in the inner city where disappointment is already a daily occurrence and trust a scarce commodity. Our six leaders are especially protective of their youth and work to ensure that volunteers do not renege on commitments, but disillusionment still occurs and always stings. John Peña cites baseball teams and other activities that fell apart because adult volunteers failed to show up or bowed out in midseason. Luanna Williams speaks forcefully about adults who agreed to work with a Scout troop but then decided "they didn't have the time." Such disappointments still happen on occasion, even though she carefully screens her volunteers because "these girls just don't deserve that. They don't deserve another disappointment, and it's just one more disappointment when troops don't last." Although inner-city youth organizations cannot exist without the kindness of strangers and the succor of friends, these gifts of time, energy, and presence have a cost. Leaders strive to give volunteers sufficient satisfaction, status, skill development, and perks to attract them and then sustain their interest, while at the same time minimizing the costs of insensitivity to youth and the inner-city culture, unreliability, broken promises, and potential pernicious dependencies.

Leaders stress volunteers' essential contributions and can tote up all the hours, in-kind contributions, economic assets, and political capital that volunteers contribute. But the nonquantifiable aspects of the gift relationship are perhaps the most powerful and the most problematic. No gift of volunteered time can be completely impersonal or detached. Ideally the gift relationship between volunteers and a youth organization is one of reciprocity and equality, rather than a unilateral transaction. Both volunteers and the members of the organization are assumed to have something to give, something of worth to share. Obviously the first challenge to leaders is to successfully invite the gift of time, energy, and affiliation. Then they must work to create environments in which volunteers can both give and receive resources, especially the scarcest resource of all, love. Because of the importance of fostering integration of inner-city youth and the broader community, the particular talent of the six wizards lies in using the gift relationship to redraw the implicit social contract between volunteer givers and youthful receivers, to make friends of strangers, transform outsiders into insiders, and dissolve the barriers between "them" and "us," between inner-city youth and the institutions of the larger community.

Chapter Nine

Finding Resources: The Struggle to Fund Neighborhood Programs

Attracting and keeping talented staff and volunteers is only one of the two greatest problems in achieving their vision that our six wizards identified. The second, and often more difficult, obstacle to sustaining places for the hopefuls is finding sufficient resources. Organizations for inner-city youth lead uncertain existences. They must compete for support with other youth programs, with social initiatives for other parts of the community (particularly senior citizens), and with public policies that draw dollars away from social services and into such public services as transportation, facility maintenance, fire, and police. Youth organizations also compete with other institutions and causes for scarce volunteers, media attention, gifts of building space and equipment, and all the other direct and indirect economic, political, and social resources that enable nonprofit organizations to exist.

In all the cities we visited, youth and especially adolescent inner-city youth, simply were not a high priority, and few public dollars or other resources were allocated for them. Public policies reflect public preferences. In U.S. urban areas, adults with children in schools make up less than 20 percent of the population, and children have no vote. So it is not entirely surprising that support for youth trails behind support for pothole repair, services for seniors, and beefed-up police protection. "Sure, we care about our kids; they are a priority," said a Big Valley community leader, "but the fact is there are never any dollars left by the time we get to them on the list."

Private resources for inner-city youth are constrained in somewhat different ways. Philanthropic organizations, social agencies such as the United Way, and corporate sponsors define funding priorities, eligibility guidelines, and opportunities according to their own perspectives on problems and promising solutions. Such perspectives are mainly shaped by a community's political economy, available resources, and social history. Too often potential funders for inner-city youth organizations have no direct knowledge of the youth or contexts they hope to affect. Policymakers, professionals, and others who develop social policies and programs are outsiders to the youth, foreign to their culture and value system and uninformed about what they require to survive, let alone flourish, in the inner city. As a friend of Buddy's who has taken an active role in planting pocket gardens and creating playgrounds complains, "There's a lot of things goin' on around here that you gotta see. When you don't have nobody [come] down here, like political people, to realize what we need down here, [it's frustrating]. And it's not the fact that we're not tryin' hard enough. It's that they're not givin' us the opportunity to do it. . . . They just won't let us or help us."

Difficulty in lining up financial support for inner-city youth organizations is universal, but the wizards' battles are local, even when programs have a national base of support such as the YMCA, the Girl Scouts of America, or the Boys and Girls Clubs. Therefore, just as successful leaders' organizational success derives from crafting programs that fit specific youth's needs and interests, success in obtaining organizational support depends on these leaders' skill in maneuvering through community resources outside the organization. Each community poses somewhat different problems and presents somewhat different opportunities. In this chapter we discuss how John Peña, Luanna Williams, and Steve Patterson cope with fundraising in Big Valley and River City. In Chapter Ten, we look at the methods Roberto Colon, Reggie Jones, and Michael Carroll employ to keep their programs alive in Lakeside. While one leader heads an organization that is relatively rich, the other leaders show that it is not necessary to be financially well-endowed to run a place of hope for inner-city youth. We also show just how fragile the success is of even highly successful organizations, given the scarcity of resources to be had.

Reconciling Them and Us in Big Valley

Luanna Williams and John Peña work in the same city, but their search for resources focuses on two different aspects of the local political economy. John Peña works with traditional private sources of funding, while Luanna must concentrate on public funding since the Arroyo Community Center belongs to the city.

John Peña and the Big Valley Establishment

When John Peña first arrived in Big Valley in 1988 it was obvious that he had come to a city proud of its reputation as "a United Way kind of town" that was "taking care" of its own. The old firehouse and church facilities of the Cougar Hollow Boys and Girls Club, the downtown flagship club where John has his office, had been donated by men who had also started two of the most prominent downtown foundations and who were namesakes of the oil barons and cattle ranchers who helped to build Big Valley. Street signs above the red-brick roads downtown often carried an additional placard boldly lettered "United Way." Seemingly every other bus carried a colorful reminder on its side to "Give—The United Way." And as John quickly discovered, practically all community resources for nonprofit noncity agencies were funneled either through the United Way or through a small cadre of foundations that work in close conjunction with the United Way in determining funding priorities. During John's first year in Big Valley over 90 percent of his operating budget was covered through United Way contributions.

Named to the executive directorship of one of Big Valley's oldest and largest youth institutions, with a mandate to "rebuild" the Big Valley Boys Clubs, John was faced with the challenges we mentioned earlier of merging with the Parkside Boys Club and orchestrating the transition to the Boys and Girls Clubs. He was also to initiate a capital campaign to refurbish and expand cramped, worn facilities and to redesign programs. However, perhaps his greatest challenge has been to make the clubs' needs known to a funding community that has been historically conservative in its view of services to at-risk youth and nonmainstream populations, seeing youth as numbers to be served rather than resources to be tapped.

Traditionally populations out of the mainstream have had little voice in Big Valley's social services agenda. Although the Big Valley ideal of "taking care of our own" expanded during the 1950s and 1960s to "taking care of our minorities," services to the nonmainstream population were designed in keeping with the definitions and diagnoses of the establishment elite, who perpetuated a them/us distinction between European American civic leaders and poor, nonmainstream families, often thought of, says John, as "those who received the Christmas hams." Nonmainstream representation is rare in positions of power and influence throughout the Big Valley agency and funding community, and grass-roots organizations that could serve as advocacy and power bases for nonmainstream populations are also noticeably absent. While the centralization of resources for community services has built a strong funding base for traditional agencies, including the Boys and Girls Clubs, this centralization has allowed little room for grass-roots organizations to develop.

The lack of nonmainstream representation also hit close to home for John Peña in his own boards of directors. While overseeing a merger between the downtown and Parkside clubs, John found he had to merge two distinct director styles. The Parkside board, he recalls, was of "the working type. The board member has the time to spend at the clubs, but doesn't have the ability to go out and get a lot of resources for us in the community." The downtown board consisted more of "movers and shakers," board members with access to serious resources. By 1992, the merged boards had evolved primarily into a board of movers and shakers, able to attract funds but not highly representative of Boys and Girls Clubs youth. While seven of the forty board members were women, at a time when the board was reevaluating the organization's direction in regard to girls, only one African American and one Latino served on the board. John observes that "the United Way has a kind of catch-22. They've told us we need a better [ethnic] representation on our board, but 32 percent of our membership's black, 32 percent Hispanic, and 32 percent Anglo, ... and the blacks and Hispanics in the community that have the ability [to give the $2,500 per year assumed by board membership] are already serving on three or four different boards. We don't need people on the board who can just show up to meetings but not contribute."

As a Latino, John found himself a novelty among agency leaders in the city. However, he was lucky in his timing. He was preparing to change Big Valley's funding structures just as the funders themselves were beginning to recognize the need to reevaluate their traditional conceptions of youth and to reassess objectives for youth programming. John's primary strategy became to ensure that the insights of youth, voices from the streets and from the clubs, were heard in the ensuing discussions among the youth policy community and among Big Valley Boys and Girls Clubs planners. It was a grass-roots approach to program and policy development that was in keeping with John's personal mission to alter and redefine not only Boys and Girls Clubs but also youth support structures throughout the community.

In general John Peña finds that the Big Valley United Way has made great strides towards redefining and opening up their traditional funding structures: "They're listening. . . . [And] I shoot straight with people telling them what I think and what we're doing and what works and what doesn't work. A lot of other agencies have not wanted to talk about what doesn't work because they're afraid of losing funding." The result of the United Ways' listening and John's and others' talking is a priority-setting system that targets at-risk populations for expanded funding while it cuts back on funding to traditionally middle-class and upper-middle-class organizations such as the Boy Scouts or the YMCA. According to John this shift in philosophy has created "some extremely tough pressure from the community that somewhat dictated to [the United Way] how some of the funding should be [allocated]. . . . Volunteers and leaders in these agencies, businessmen who want more [United Way] money for their old boys network, [are producing this pressure.]"

In another catch-22 situation, while John's mission to serve disadvantaged youth means his clubs attract the at-risk populations that are now the United Way's top priority, his mission to expand club programs to serve these youth better has resulted in a percentage decrease in the amount of United Way funding each program receives. Between the need to find extra program money and the demands of his new capital campaign, John devotes over 80 percent of his time to marketing and networking. He has not taken on any substantive collaboration with other organizations because he feels that others are "looking to improve their organization and their image as opposed to what's best for the kids. And everybody has a different objective for whatever collaboration they're looking for." Instead he prefers to network by serving on school and community task forces and youth issues committees, using them as springboards for reaching other players in the funding community.

From John Peña's point of view, "shooting straight" with the potential funders he meets through networking means that youth must be major participants in discussions and events with funders and policymakers, marketing both themselves and the Big Valley Boys and Girls Clubs. For example, while serving on a task force charged with developing a strategy to respond to a recent escalation of gang violence, John was appalled that the majority of the panel knew nothing about youth's life on the streets:

I said, "I think some of you don't understand the real problem with gangs in Big Valley and what these kids go through. The next meeting I will have three gang members here. If you want to learn about gang members and why they do the things that they do, be here." The rule was no media. And as these kids started to talk, I said, "You can ask them anything you want." You could have heard a pin drop. It changed the whole process of how to address the gang problem. 'Cuz now [the task force members are] more sensitive to the youth and why they're involved and how they got involved and how difficult it is to get out.

John's task force contributions helped show the director of a major Big Valley foundation that prevention combined with inter-vention was the best approach to curtailing gang involvement and violence. The foundation had sponsored a communitywide effort for a few years, then discontinued the funds. When the director lamented a resurgence in gang activity, John quickly reminded him of the foundation's actions, saying, "Now see what happened? The kids have nothin' to do, and it was much easier for gangs to recruit them. If you want a short-term fix for a problem, then give it short-term funding. (Funders) put too much money into inter-vention and treatment, way too much. If you did [more] on the other end you wouldn't have those problems." John's assessment apparently caught the funder by surprise. He responded, "You know, nobody's ever put it that way before. And you're right." Such personal networking is John's primary opportunity to be an advocate on his youth's behalf.

Another example of John's method of helping youth market themselves and their Boys and Girls Clubs is the annual Steak and Burger Dinner, the clubs' largest fundraiser. The dinner pairs youth from the clubs with adults from the business community who pay $50 a plate to eat a hamburger while their young dinner compan-ion enjoys steak. John sees this as both a fundraiser and a great way for the business people to see that "these are not bad kids." The TeenTalk program has taken this marketing of youth a step further. Not only are they star programs used by the United Way in fundraising efforts but they open doors for individual youth in all the places the programs are performed, from corporate luncheons to schools to community centers.

In order to be successful John Peña has made it his mission to give subordinated populations a voice in public funding policy, to give his youngsters a wide-ranging program that meets their true needs, and to change the community's view of disadvantaged youth.

Luanna Williams: Use What You Have Got

In many ways Luanna and the Arroyo Community Center sit firmly outside the Big Valley funding establishment ably negotiated by John Peña. Because the center is part of the human services arm of the city government, Luanna faces numerous restrictions on her activities. She is the only director of a city multipurpose center who grew up in the neighborhood he or she serves, and she has often been warned by her supervisors that she is "too involved" with Arroyo and that she should attempt to "divorce" herself from the community. But for Luanna, Arroyo's youth and the community come first. Whether she is taking the lead in community organizing because she knows "there's a problem and somebody has to speak out," or personally driving kids to a school function when the buses fail to arrive, even though "it's totally against policy to transport kids," Luanna often finds herself pushing the limits of city regulations. "When you know it's things that are going to benefit kids," she explains, "you have to bend."

Like recessions elsewhere in the nation, Big Valley's financial downturn in the early 1990s resulted in severe city budget cuts. Even though such services as youth programs were even more crucial during this time, the city was forced to cut 10 percent of the program budget for three consecutive years. By the summer of 1992, Luanna was left with a budget of $3,000 for an entire year of programs, including all supplies and equipment. City limitations on the ways Luanna can raise funds outside the structure of the city government have taught her to stretch this money and other resources to their fullest and to take full advantage of the methods she is allowed to use. These methods often result in small sums, so she has to seek many donors, not only of money, but of other gifts and of opportunities for her youth, in keeping with her goal of opening doors for youth.

Luanna cannot directly solicit funds from Big Valley foundations or the United Way. Moreover, she says, "Having the city funding almost works against us. There is a sense that because we have the multipurpose center here we don't need anything else in the community. And the city won't let us go out and work for funds. As a city facility and a city employee, I can't solicit. I can't go to foundations, I can't go to anyone really big and say, 'Hey, give us this.' I can go to the Neighborhood Action Group meetings or the little guy... but that's it."

Arroyo is one of Big Valley's most economically depressed neighborhoods, with one of the city's highest percentages of children, and the Arroyo Community Center with its many functions is the neighborhood's only service agency. It was also the first such center established in Big Valley (in 1973), and its space compared to other sites is quite limited. The city's misperception that the center is sufficient for Arroyo youth is compounded by a belief that the neighborhood churches are providing a bevy of youth programs. However, the churches' impact has changed according to Luanna, and most of Arroyo's twenty-plus churches now work only with the youth who have grown up "within their walls." Even the youth who have grown up in the churches are increasingly giving up the church programs because, according to Luanna, the older churchgoers "don't think the kids should do anything but study the Bible and do just churchy-churchy stuff. Whereas kids want to expand, do a few more things."

Not only has the traditional impact of the Arroyo churches been reduced, but Arroyo is also increasingly finding itself without an active group of young and middle-aged community leaders. Since its inception as a settlement for freed slaves Arroyo has been a highly insular community, priding itself on its self-sufficiency. In recent years, however, with the encroachment of new shopping districts, many businesses in the community have closed down. The remaining grocery and liquor stores, the youth point out, are owned by new arrivals from the Middle East. Also, young adults who would once have stayed in the community are increasingly choosing to leave in search of an upscale life-style. Luanna sees Arroyo's population "evolving into an older group, a very younger group, and then just a few in the middle range." She says, "It's the ones in the middle range that we really need. The ones that are out there making the money and can bring the money into the community. We don't have them."

Given the lack of programs and funds available for Arroyo youth, confinement to city funds has become increasingly painful. On her $3,000 budget, Luanna allows each program $50 during the school year, saving the rest of the money for summer. These programs include Black History Month, day care, and the Girl Scouts Valentine's Day dinner. City support comes to less than $1 for each program participant. Staff positions have also been drastically cut. In 1992 Luanna lost two support staff positions out of six and a half, including her only male staffer, who was transferred to another center.

Monies funneled through city coffers can be capricious. For example, federal Job Training and Placement Act (JTPA) funds for summer jobs were restricted in the summer of 1991, leaving Luanna with less than half of the fourteen summer staffers she usually relies upon to work alongside her Girl Scout volunteers in the summer day camp. With over three hundred and fifty children and youth in the camp, care and attention became less personal and attendance tapered off sharply by summer's end, a rare occurrence during Luanna's tenure at the center. Early in 1992 the uncertainty of JTPA funding combined with the center's crowded facilities led Luanna to limit summer enrollment for the first time. However, she did receive all fourteen of her JTPA positions. Then came the Los Angeles inner-city riots over a jury's failure to convict four policemen in the beating of African American Rodney King. Two weeks later, Luanna says, "the federal funding suddenly jumped sky high! [The city] called us, everybody, and said, 'How many more kids can you take? We've got $2.5 million for this program!' So we still have kids coming in." Luanna, like other recipients of this youth funding boom, welcomed the additional money but noted that the short lead time allowed for little planning, left many teenagers out of job-training processes, and was, sadly, not linked to long-term efforts.

Luanna stretches to the fullest any monies available. For example, a main draw of the summer program is its field trips, and she has a "trade secret ... to enable all of the kids to go on at least two or three field trips." She hikes up the price of each trip by at least twenty-five cents. "For instance, if we go roller-skating, it's $2.00. I charge 'em $2.25. It's usually eighty-something of 'em that go. So there's enough to cover all those other kids [who can't pay]."

Luanna has relied primarily upon the human resources of her core group of volunteers and dedicated community members and her own creative negotiation of the system. "I learn[ed] to work around the system. What I've done is locate a few key people that I know positively are on my side, and I speak [to the establishment] through them. It took me many years and many sleepless nights and many scared times when I thought I was going to lose my job before I learned that you had to do some things in order to get what you need." Although ten years of working in the system have taught Luanna to negotiate effectively, she also has a special resource that other nonmainstream and poor neighborhoods lack: Arroyo's relative political sophistication, cohesion, and experience. This resource is a product of the contacts and political clout of Arroyo's Neighborhood Action Group, one of the neighborhood action councils that was formed in Big Valley in the early 1980s when the city received federal block grants for neighborhood renewal.

Luanna has also had the guidance and support of Arroyo matriarch Millicent Quarry. This community leader, who is now in her seventies, has helped Luanna tap many in-kind contributions that make the youth program work. Through Millicent's contacts an owner of the Countrytime Barbecue donates briskets for the Black History Month dinner and a state senator donates money for Easter baskets or a catered Christmas party for the kids. Luanna recalls one time that the senator "spent $800 on the caterer for food. I mean these kids had lavish finger foods! And each kid got a bag full of toys and goodies."

Luanna has also learned to use the Arroyo Youth Promoting Pride organization (AYPP), a group she helped found, as a conduit for small donations. These funds have proved crucial to keeping the center's programs appealing to youth. From the $200 offered by a local bank for Halloween candy to $750 donated by an arts organization, small increments make a big difference to Luanna's shoestring program. Nickel and diming her way to program parity, she sees such contributions of $750 as godsends. AYPP, which grew out of collaboration with the police force and has grown into a voice for Arroyo youth, is a promising cornerstone in Luanna's drive to secure more money for her center programs: AYPP can "just put [the donated money] in this little fund, and they're really open to anything that the kids need, and they're open to Luanna. So all I have to do is funnel them the money, and then, when I need something, I don't have to go through an act of Congress [in dealing with the city] to get it." Many of Luanna's core group of young adult volunteers, whom she fondly refers to as "my young people," are on AYPP's board. They have proven instrumental in opening further opportunities for Arroyo youth, and she says, "I'm beginning now to get them to understand that we have to go out there and look for some funding."

Luanna also steps outside her neighborhood to uncover more opportunities for her youth. Unlike the many African American activists who confine their work to their own communities, Luanna spans political, institutional, and social boundaries. Rather than develop a new power structure, she chooses to pry open the doors to the established power structure. Her strategy is keyed to the realities of Big Valley. Historically, community organizations that have worked outside of the establishment have had little success in finding funding and surviving in United Way–dominated Big Valley. Moreover, the African American community has lacked the economic base to develop alternative forms of funding, the African American churches appear insular, and until recently, Arroyo was not threatened by the urban redevelopment that has galvanized so many other African American communities into political action. In the face of these realities Luanna chooses the route she perceives will lead to her goals. She says, "While all the community center people are minority people, in outside things... the more I get involved on high-up boards, [I] can see that the way they think of minorities hasn't changed that much. We still have to prove that we can do as much as everyone else. So it's a challenge to me." By opening the doors of the establishment she not only brings resources to her center but also enables her youth to cross institutional boundaries. After almost fifteen years of volunteering with Girl Scouts, Luanna was elected to the Scouts' city board as Vice President of Council Diversity. Even in her work with the Girl Scouts, an organization for which she is a strong advocate, she has found some surprise expressed at her abilities, and she acknowledges that "it's the fact that the Girl Scout organization has basically been an all-white organization. There are now some blacks that are beginning to move onto some management boards. . . . But [the organization] still feels, 'We've just got them on here just to show them that we're diverse.'"

Providing leadership also means managing resources or "gifts" from agencies that fail to understand the daily realities of Arroyo youth. For example, the local Campfire council wanted to offer their outreach program at the center, but they required that center volunteers or staff participate in program activities, under the direction of Campfire leaders. Luanna simply could not supply more volunteers, but she says, "Campfire finally got the message this year that if they wanted to do a program at my center they had to come out and bring their [own] staff and volunteers. [Otherwise] there's nothin' to be done."

Another collaboration that had a difficult time initially was a basketball league. The downtown YMCA, with money from the United Way to work with so-called disadvantaged youth, approached Luanna with an offer to provide the facilities, T-shirts, and several of the teams if she would provide some of the center's youth. The YMCA had no other access to disadvantaged youth and Luanna had more youngsters than she could handle. But during the first season the YMCA demanded that Arroyo team members produce birth certificates, after several mainstream parents protested that many of the taller and more highly skilled African American Arroyo youth could not possibly be under thirteen, the league age limit. Initially only the Arroyo youth were asked for birth certificates, but Luanna insisted that the European American youth should also have to produce them. The YMCA agreed, but staff continued to make distinctions in how they treated the different teams. For example, Luanna's boys were not allowed to play until they produced the certificates, yet Luanna discovered that a suburban team was permitted to play even though their coach had forgotten their certificates. The next year Luanna and the basketball players experienced "a season of silence," during which the YMCA made no attempt to contact them about the league. However, the following season, the YMCA director visited Luanna personally to ask for a team from the center since the YMCA was at risk of losing its priority funding. Since that relatively inauspicious beginning the center has developed a strong relationship with the YMCA. Luanna currently serves on the YMCA's board of directors, and center youth participate in all the YMCA team sports activities for youth and use the YMCA swimming pool twice a week in the summer.

For Luanna, the crucial resource battle has been the one to gain access to the power structures and resources, both experiential and financial, available to young people of the Big Valley establishment, while working within the restrictions of her city role and funding, "a dilemma of working within the system, trying to create change in an institution that cuts your check." Although they frame their tasks differently, both John Peña and Luanna Williams have adopted a similar broad strategy of working within the system in which they find themselves, to change its assumptions and strategies and to expand its perceptions beyond "them and us" to embrace the diversity of the Big Valley community.

The Ties That Bind in River City: Negotiating Support Within the Cooper House Family

Until recently, youth services in River City could build upon a rich ethnic and philanthropic heritage. Steve Patterson finds that Cooper House is rich not only because of the sizable endowment left to it by the founders of the Cooper Factory, but also because it is steeped in that ethnic and philanthropic history. As Eastern and Southern European workers came to work in River City's factories from the mid-1800s on, factory managers divided the work and housing assigned to laborers along ethnic and linguistic lines as one method of discouraging labor unions from gaining a foothold. The resulting ethnic solidarity showed itself in churches and fraternal organizations that became the heart of each small ethnic community and provided social services to their respective communities.

While Cooper House was established by a wealthy industrialist who wanted to honor his wife and her lifelong interest in community service, it too became an important part of its close-knit community. Since its founding in 1901, it has been affiliated with the Boys Clubs but has always included girls. It has flourished within that framework also, because of what Steve Patterson calls the national organization's "very autonomous governing form" and the fact that the house's generous endowment has allowed it to set its own agenda and rules. Serving generations of youth from a tight-knit community, Cooper House developed a culture that reflected that community and a strong base of local support, as its numbers of dedicated alumni show.

When Steve came to Cooper House in 1988, he found that the endowment allowed the house to focus on working with youth when many other community service agencies either did not have funding or were redirecting their efforts, offering services to contend with the high adult unemployment rate. Cooper House's endowment produced $265,000 in operating funds for 1989, and Steve says that the house has been rare for him in that "you can actually do your job because you're not concentrating on money, you're concentrating on doing your job." Given the endowment, the inward-looking community, and the weight of Cooper House tradition, the resources issue that Steve has faced is not so much acquiring funds as it has been how and for whom the resources will be used.

When the bottom dropped out of River City's industrial base in the late 1970s, the city's prosperity ended and its social stabil-

ity began to decline. Over 130,000 people, primarily young workers, left River City by 1980, leaving behind a disproportionate
number of the very young, the old, and welfare recipients. A
shrinkage in city, state, and federal funds for youth has been met
with a concurrent decline of interest in youth services on the part
of River City fraternal organizations as well as philanthropic
groups. One of Steve's greatest challenges during his first year was
convincing the house's board members and the tradition-bound
alumni that, in response to changing economic times, the house
needed to reevaluate its mission, cease its isolation from other
youth organizations, and expand its conception of neighborhood
youth in order to pick up the slack that had developed as a result
of general economic decline.

Cooper House needed to redefine the way it thought of neighborhood youth for three reasons. First, its population base was
shrinking, and the construction of a superhighway only fifteen
yards from the house effectively cut it off from part of its neighborhood. By the late 1980s, Cooper House, long assured of an
active pool of youth due to the loyalty of former Housers and the
house's strong recognition in the immediate community, was no
longer drawing a full complement of youth.

Second, neighborhood youth were growing up in different
kinds of families. Two-parent families were being increasingly
replaced by single-parent families. Heightened drug and alcohol
abuse among unemployed, disillusioned adults were also taking
their toll on youth. Yet these sons and daughters of the traditional
European American working class, whom Steve calls the "new at-
risk," were falling outside the funding loop.

Third, in the area surrounding Cooper House, many welfare
recipients were receiving subsidized housing from the city's stock
of foreclosed properties, and neighborhood youngsters were
increasingly African American and poor. As other youth organizations lost their funding, more youth in traditionally African
American neighborhoods close to Cooper House had time on
their hands and nowhere to go.

Assessing these changes Steve Patterson decided that Cooper
House had "the money, but we need to learn how to use it to the

benefit of all." He began a campaign to change Cooper House's image in both the eyes of the new neighborhood youth and the eyes of the alumni, volunteers, and board members, as well as other youth agencies.

As far as the neighborhood youth were concerned he had to tackle the view that Cooper House was expensive, even though membership is $3.50 a year. The "unspoken rule" that "if you can't pay, you can't play" had had an effect among youth like Buddy. "Even though almost [every inner-city youth organization] has a policy that states they turn no one away because of financial burdens," Steve explains, "no one really promotes [the policy] either. Consequently very few know or take advantage of this opportunity at Cooper House."

Steve has found attracting African American youth to be a large hurdle. In spite of recruitment efforts through the schools, African American youth are hesitant to participate in Cooper House activities. The house had set itself off-limits to them in the past, and with interracial tensions increasing in the schools, they are suspicious about the reception they will find.

The changes Steve Patterson is instituting have led to some resistance on the part of staff, volunteers, and alumni who are accustomed to the organization as it "has always been." His operating resources are secure, but his support among personnel, particularly volunteers, is in danger of weakening. However, his relationship with his board of directors, extremely active partners in house activities, is positive. Steve regards this relationship as both personal and professional, and is pleased with the board's response to his program changes. The board, in turn, has prompted Steve to seek additional funding from outside sources to support some of his new programs, particularly those focused on education.

The education programs are becoming especially important for both youth and the larger community. As factory jobs are lost, youth who would once have filled those jobs after high school need opportunities to pursue the diverse options that college allows. Throughout the 1980s, even before Steve came to Cooper House, the house had been steadily increasing its scholarship funds through alumni fund drives and community fundraisers and by reallocating operating budget monies. Under Steve's guidance the house has also implemented additional tutoring and educational programs to supplement its traditional skills-based and leadership activities. Seeking further outside funding will be a challenge for this particular wizard, however. Youth are not high on River City's service agenda, and his organization is known to be relatively rich. But Steve will not divert operating funds from a number of the traditional programs to educational programs because it would weaken core, ongoing programs.

Because Cooper House has been highly independent and in many ways unique it has also been institutionally isolated. However, collaborations with other youth organizations are now high on Steve's priority list as he looks for ways of making his material resources available to more youth. He faces the challenge of finding partners who are committed to youth and not looking to Cooper House primarily as a source of funding for a failing program. Steve is also trying to end Cooper House's isolation by opening the organization's doors to adults with adult education and worker-retraining programs. He sees adult programming as a way of strengthening the community and, as a result, the environment for youth. However, he continues to put youth first. When the board wanted to offer additional classes to factory employees, Steve convinced them that he should contract this service out to local community college staff to avoid reducing the time his staff had with the youngsters. He also convinced them that afternoon classes should be moved out of Cooper House. He says, "Fortunately, they were understanding about that.... But I think you need that kind of commitment if you're in this work, that the kids will always come first."

Steve and other youth leaders in River City want youth to come first when city resources are allocated. There are signs that the city has a sense of youth as its future in city officials' commitment to rebuilding the city's workforce and economic strength, even though youth are not exclusively the focus of this retraining and education effort. City officials also believe they have time to stop the city from becoming a place ruled by gangs and drugs. As one community organizer says, "We have the money and the expertise, all we need is the plan and the commitment to carry it out, before it becomes too late." The warning signs have hit home in River City and the city is mobilizing to improve its future. Steve Patterson is part of this effort, and he sees the need to continually refocus the city's attention on its youth as his personal mission.

Chapter Ten

Sustaining Places of Hope:
How Three Programs Negotiate
Support in One City

Although such dimensions of the Lakeside environment as budget cutbacks following severe economic downturns, segregated neighborhoods, and a strong labor union history and philanthropic tradition affect all the city's youth organizations in much the same way, the realities that Roberto Colon, Reggie Jones, and Michael Carroll confront when they seek out organizational resources differ in important ways. The strategy of each leader is different. Roberto Colon's strategy is shaped by the presence of machine politics and street gangs and by the conceptions of innercity youth held by the civic elite. Reggie Jones works the corporate and political system to support his grass-roots organization. Although as engaged in the African American community at the program level as Reggie, Michael Carroll uses more traditional resources and mainstream attitudes to enhance his organization.

We look at each of these three wizards as they develop their resource strategies, and we conclude this chapter with a discussion of the commonalities we found in all six leaders in their search for funds and opportunities for inner-city youth.

Roberto Colon: Latino Youth and the Political Machine

To seek public and private resources for his programs and for Latino youth generally, Roberto Colon has learned to understand and negotiate a complex maze of patronage politics and traditional funding in a city where ethnic group empowerment has long played a major role in the battle for resources. But unlike John

Peña and Luanna Williams, who could work effectively to change the system from the inside in Big Valley, Roberto finds he can best affect the entrenched machine of Lakeside politics and the public programs and dollars associated with it from the outside, through back-channel political activities.

As Lakeside's neighborhoods took shape on the sprawling plains of the Midwest, they were most often defined by bankers, real estate agents, and municipal zoning officers whose largely unwritten housing policies firmly maintained racial and ethnic segregation until the mid–twentieth century. A political system that traded political appointments, contracts, and delivery of services in exchange for large neighborhood, and therefore ethnic, voting blocks has reinforced the politicization of ethnicity in Lakeside and kept it largely segregated to this day.

Lakeside's gangs also have a long history. By the time large waves of Puerto Rican immigrants, including Roberto Colon's parents, began to arrive in the neighborhood of Porter Crossing, it was already marked by overcrowding, gangs, and clear ethnic rivalries resulting largely from competition for jobs and services. For many newcomers membership in a gang was a means of survival; therefore Roberto's view of the gangs is historically tempered. He says, "Gangs have been here since the beginning. In Lakeside, when the Italians came and the Irish came, these new immigrants came, gangs were formed. It's a cycle. It's history."

Although neighborhood lines blurred in the 1970s and 1980s, the tradition of political influence continued to affect delivery of youth services. Roberto's dilemma with municipal resources is exemplified by his experiences with Lakeside's park districts. YMCAs and cities' parks departments sometimes share resources. However, Lakeside's parks department agendas have been politically determined for decades, and a prized payoff for political supporters has been an appointment to head a community recreation program. Roberto acknowledges some change since a new mayoral administration was elected in the mid-1980s, but he also feels that the practice of hiring program heads who were "not social workers or recreational leaders" but had ability to deliver votes has resulted in a leadership vacuum in the community parks and recreation centers intended to serve youth. Roberto asserts that the centers in the established middle-class and suburban communities that contribute generously to political campaigns are becoming "country clubs" while inner-city, less politically consequential communities are given little. "The only public facility in our neighborhood," quipped another Latino activist, "is the county jail." Roberto is outraged at the inequities:

In the inner city, the parks are dilapidated, and resources are limited, and there's still patronage. You look at the park district budget . . . your eyes come right out, and you say, "Where's all this money goin'? Where are all those tax dollars?" They got [only] thirty kids in their day camp! When I looked at the program budget for the year [for the inner-city park advisory council I am on], it was $500 for programs for the whole year. I said, "How are you going to run programs with $500?" "That's what they gave me" [replied the park director]. [Yet] they built a $1.5 million facility [in a wealthier neighborhood]. You know who's using it? The YMCA is running adult basketball! We're running adult basketball out of this $1.5 million facility!

Roberto does work with a park program in Porter Crossing because he is "personal friends" with the director: "We grew up together, so he opens the door." But apart from that he is rarely willing to work with the city parks programs, considering such city collaborations as unreliable, impractical, and demanding too much compromise. "I will not deal," he says.

To find resources beyond the YMCA for his youth, Roberto has moved outside the Lakeside establishment, forming networks built of friendships and working relationships. Of all the many boards and committees he has served on, the one which is perhaps closest to his work and heart is the Latino Youth Services Network (LYSN), an organization of agency representatives that is the state's largest Latino youth network. LYSN began as a gang intervention coalition with a mission to save lives. Many of the Latino youth agency leaders in Porter Crossing and neighboring Puerto Rican communities grew up together. Now in their mid- to late thirties, these second-generation Puerto Rican "yuppies," as one agency leader characterizes them, say they are "looking at what our fore-parents couldn't do." Many of them are directors of the agencies that helped them survive their own teenage years. Luis Gonzales, the director of the Porter Crossing Boys and Girls Clubs, for example, began attending the club faithfully after his seventeen-year-old brother was killed in a 1979 gangland shootout. That same summer of violence gave birth to LYSN. Roberto says that what brought the youth leaders who founded LYSN together was, "We were tired of going to funerals." The response of neighbor-hood youth organizations acting independently was clearly not sufficient to curb the violence and stop the deaths. Roberto recalls that the agencies realized that each of them was "working in vac-uum," not knowing what the others were doing. They needed to share resources to be effective.

The LYSN network quickly grew from its youth organization base, adding directors of hospitals, schools, health services, and universities to the coalition. During the initial years of the net-work, communication about youth needs and resources increased, but members continued to struggle over how to deal with the increasing gang violence. The prosperous city that had proven such a draw for immigrants had become a city increasingly marked by limited resources, decaying infrastructure, and a burgeoning lower-income and nonmainstream population. With a declin-ing tax base services began to suffer, most notably the city's schools. The teachers' union mounted twenty-five strikes within a twelve-year period. Compounded by increased gang activity in the schools, dropout rates soared. With increased numbers of youth on the streets, gang activity and violence escalated. The streets became the "equal opportunity employer" of necessity for many inner-city youth. Roberto describes how the gangs' charac-ter is changing dramatically as drugs become big business for the gangs:

[A few] years ago you had the city divided into two major gang factions. That has broken down now. It no longer is [a] "Who can we count on to help us keep our turf?" issue. The issue now is, "How are we going to keep control of our local drug sales?" So you got all the gangs that were together under one flag fighting each other.... Now it's a whole different animal, because you're talking about an underground economy that hasn't been in existence before. But now it's grown. It's an accepted career option for our kids. It's survival for them. Here's an irony—they want to stay in school now so they can get the skills to succeed in the drug business.

In addition to his efforts to provide more and better out-of-school programs for youth, Roberto has worked hard to promote school reform in Lakeside. Part of this work has been simply making accurate figures available. Roberto and LYSN discovered that school dropout rates were being compiled on a yearly basis, resulting in a low figure of 17 percent. LYSN pushed for a four-year analysis that would document how many incoming freshman actually graduated. Calculated on this basis, the dropout rate jumped to over 75 percent at some inner-city secondary schools. To help create momentum for the school reform movement, Roberto and other LYSN leaders have involved youth in the advocacy efforts. For example, young people organized a funeral march of over one thousand people in front of the local high school, with candles and a casket representing the death of Lakeside's inner-city youth. Roberto sees this march and other LYSN efforts as maintaining crucial pressure on Lakeside's school reform effort.

Increasingly LYSN has taken on an advocacy role for its members. Roberto, who served as LYSN president for three years, refers to the relationship between the YMCA and LYSN as a "partnership in advocacy." The network has "become a catalyst. It opens doors." Some of the doors give access to funds. According to LYSN leaders, although Lakeside's African American community has long had political power, the Latino community has only begun to realize its political clout.

LYSN's advocacy arm continues to be its most successful element, possibly because LYSN activists have maintained a focus on a small set of integrally linked youth issues: school dropouts, intertwined causes and effects of gang participation, and teenage pregnancy. In addition, perhaps because the network was generated by the agency leaders themselves rather than some funding group or government agency, participation in the network is seen as meaningful, not "just one more thing to do" in these leaders' already overcrowded schedules.

What is perhaps Roberto's greatest current resource challenge has less to do with the priority the establishment assigns to non-mainstream youth than with the establishment's "youth problem" definitions and potential solutions. Like John Peña, Roberto Colon understands that these definitions drive public and private youth policies. In Lakeside intervention is out and prevention is in as a response to gangs. From the perspective of many in Lakeside, inner-city youth are to be feared, and youth policies must be devised to control and punish these feared youth. In this view the most important youth service initiative is not service *for* youth but protection *from* them. Enforcement, the province of the police and the court system, has shown little rehabilitative promise. Meanwhile, prevention programs are typically focused on younger children, "catching kids before they get into trouble," and programs such as Head Start that have proven effective with young children get increased funding. As a result Roberto and other leaders working primarily with teenagers find themselves witnessing the creation of a "lost generation" of youth, without the services and guidance that could lead them into productive adult lives.

Ironies abound. Just as civic leaders are recognizing that increased support services must be available to young parents to ensure the success of early childhood programs, the funding of programs for teenage youth, who are not just the young parents of the future but often the young parents of today, is increasingly cut back. The school reform advocated by Roberto and LYSN as one answer to gang violence actually undercut initiatives for direct intervention in the lives of active gang members when the Lakeside Intervention Network (LIN), the street intervention plan co-chaired by Roberto that put sixty caseworkers including Cruz Sanchez on the streets, was sacrificed to direct more funds toward the schools in response to the cries for reform. By 1989 most of the street workers had been pulled off the corners, midnight basketball outreach programs were phased out, and LIN's staff and funds were shifted towards school and after-school time. Although Roberto asserts that at the height of LIN's street work violence was down, in 1990 he found himself being given a going-away plaque. He says, "As I see it, all the emphasis in Lakeside now has been put into the schools. But I think there's still a whole population out in the streets, youth that are not getting any attention and services."

The Porter Crossing YMCA is rare in its attempt to offer the resources of both prevention and intervention programs, balancing traditional prevention activities during the day with active intervention alternatives at night. The immediate genesis of the Porter Crossing Gang Intervention and Alternatives program was LIN's demise. Roberto Colon was seeking to bring his street intervention efforts closer to home, with resources under more immediate control. He says, "[I was attempting] to start dealing with a population that I feel has been totally neglected by the social service field because it is one of the most difficult to work with. It is one that the foundations, the corporations, don't realize is a viable program to fund. I feel that the city and community have basically given up on gangs, so we started this little program to do interventions out in the community." Because he did not "know of any foundation that has street gangs in [its] eligibility for funding requirements," he decided to turn to his more traditional base of support, the YMCA central office.

Roberto had previously found an extremely supportive environment for his activism and cutting-edge programs in his relationship with the YMCA's downtown Lakeside and national offices, and he was to find it again. If he had felt "constrained" by them he says, he "probably wouldn't be a part of [the YMCA]." His ability to maintain a certain autonomy within the YMCA culture has been extremely important in allowing him to carry out his mission for his own local community, in allowing him to be a wizard. He says that, although YMCA "decisions are still made at the top," they "at least include me in the [decision] process.... And they do it well." In this case, to get his funding he spearheaded a return to an earlier YMCA policy of making localized responses to neighborhoods. The downtown Lakeside office approved initial grants of $50,000, which were used by neighborhood YMCAs in a variety of ways. Roberto used his grant as seed money for GAIN.

As described earlier, to establish GAIN as a resource for youth, Roberto also had to win over his board members and negotiate the sanction of the gangs themselves. He finds that his diverse board, with large numbers of Latinos and women, and members "from the preacher's wife to the detective to the guy from Pepsi-Cola," has been extremely supportive in both time and money. He points to high attendance at noon-time board meetings in mid-August and a willingness to write $10,000 checks as testaments to board members' support, but when it came to bringing gang members into the YMCA, many on the board were hesitant. They were worried that the gang members would corrupt the "good kids." They also recalled other youth organizations' attempts to work with gangs in the early 1970s, and how those attempts had been painful failures, degenerating into covers for illegal operations and sites of gang retaliations. Roberto won them over with assurances about his personal gangland knowledge and guarantees that gang members would not mix with the other youth at the YMCA.

Roberto finds that the YMCA affiliation is a resource that not only gives him a solid and supportive base of operations but also relieves him of many tasks and responsibilities that would divert time and energy: "The Y gives me the organizational backing that I need, with all the structures in place, to run the organization. I don't worry about payroll, and I don't worry about business, paying bills, the IRS. We have that structure [and] the attorneys [in place]." He is also grateful for the YMCA resources that he called on to keep Manny out of jail when he was wrongly arrested.

The YMCA affiliation gives Roberto's programs, including GAIN, legitimacy with all elements of the community: parents, board members, and gang leaders. It also opens doors to funders.

For example, the graffiti removal that keeps Tito and other GAIN members employed is paid for through the Mayor's Summer Jobs Program, one of the largest employers of Lakeside youth during the summer months (and a testament to the contract system of providing services in Lakeside). Roberto's access to these funds is greatly helped by the Y name and also by his LYSN affiliation.

Through the downtown YMCA, Roberto also has access to United Way funding. While he lauds the United Way as "very generous" and points to "real valuable things" they've done, he thinks they have "become very limited. They pick their niche and they stick with it ... depending on what the trend is.... The Ph.D. from the university... says, 'The latest thing is single moms with four kids. We need to do something about it.' And that's where those decisions are done. I don't mean to [sound] critical now. I'm not a very negative person, [and] United Way is great. In Lakeside last year, they raised $103 million, which is why [the Y] got $3 million out of that. But as far as the inner city [goes], I think what they've been funding are specialized programs, meaning that kids are already perceived and diagnosed with problems."

The labeling of youth in order to match them up with specific funding categories is one of the greatest funding dilemmas for inner-city youth organizations. Some youth leaders call funders' changing fashions and fads "flavor of the month" or "flav." Roberto Colon, like other youth agency leaders, is often forced to seek funding while an issue or label is "hot." In 1990, for example, he felt he and others needed to quickly localize the national attention being paid to drugs and substance abuse and backed by President Bush. Agency heads throughout Lakeside acknowledge the practice of window-dressing established programs to make them appear as though they address the latest hot topics in the local funding community made up of the United Way, local foundations, and the city government.

In all his efforts to find resources, Roberto stays tightly focused on the youth issues that are his passion and his mission, and this seems connected to his success. For example, during a working conference of major Lakeside funders to discuss recommendations for funding to combat youth violence, Roberto says that no one was mentioning gangs:

As usual, we [were] a reactionary government. As a result of the [1992 inner-city] riots in L.A., [the] United Way here in Lakeside, all the major foundations, said, "We need to come together because we gotta deal with the potential violence." Like we didn't have violence every summer for the last ten summers? But [they were thinking] of what happened in L.A. So they brought everybody together. They brought the head of schools, head of parks, the mayor's office, all the major foundations, the presidents of the Y, the Boys Club, Lakeside Youth Centers; everybody came and said, "What are we gonna do?" And the issue was, "Let's do something to prevent the violence." So they talked and they said, "Here's what we gotta do. We gotta have a jobs task force. We gotta have a task force for sports and recreation, one for the arts, long-term planning, financial development..." But not one word came out about gangs. And fortunately I think for us, my president [had] invited me to this meeting. And I said, "Excuse me, I thought we were here to deal with the issue of violence.... I haven't heard one word about dealing with the main problem in this city, and that's the problem of gangs." Silence in the room. No wants to deal with it. They feel that [it's a] prevention [issue]. It's a law enforcement issue. Our mentality of gangs in the U.S.A. is that we're at war with these guys! We have to eliminate them. They are the enemy. I'm saying, "That's not the way to deal with it."

The result of Roberto's sticking to his mission was that some of the $2.5 million the foundations raised for the summer programs did indeed go to a gang intervention task force.

Michael Carroll and Reggie Jones: Working the System for Grass-roots Organizations

Across town, in Francis Homes, Michael Carroll and Reggie Jones face largely different conditions as they seek resources for BEST and the Gymnasts. In contrast to Roberto Colon who works within the nationally based YMCA, Reggie directly accesses the business community and Michael enlists more traditional funding sources. The programs that appear to appeal most to Francis

Homes's African American residents are such highly local efforts as a teenagers' theater group organized by members of a professional theater, an advocacy and job placement program formed by one-time residents of the neighborhood, a sports-oriented intervention group run by a former YMCA employee, an after-school club for unwed mothers and fathers sponsored by the local health clinic, Reggie's high-profile gymnastics team, and Michael Carroll's multifaceted scholarship programs. Only two of the ten highest-profile youth organizations in Francis Homes claim a regional or national affiliation. The city-based Lakeside Youth Centers outpost has its own building in the middle of the housing development and is heavily used by children and youth in one of the three Francis Homes gang territories. A YMCA, perched on the dividing line between the greater Francis Homes neighborhood and gentrified yuppie neighborhoods to the north and east, struggles not entirely with success to serve its diverse population. Except for sports tournaments and special events Francis Homes youth say they rarely use YMCA facilities because of the cost of membership and the danger in crossing rival gang territories. In addition Francis Homes residents tend to be suspicious and cynical about mainstream organizations' commitment and ability to meet their needs. "The man," many residents believe, fails to understand the neighborhood's needs and preferences, and worse, is likely to exploit the African American, low-income residents of Francis Homes or treat them disrespectfully. A friend of Reggie's, who founded and runs an extremely popular sports league for Francis Homes youth, puts it bluntly:

I'm not trusting them corporate types because ... to be very honest, I just don't trust white males.... I just don't have the confidence that I would have if it was a black male out there [coaching one of my teams]. I don't think [white males] really have the commitment [to black kids] at heart. Maybe there's one or two, but of the total thirty-five or forty that I have out there [volunteering in the sports program], there are not all that many you can trust in. They don't know what it takes.... They are not familiar with this inner-city structure, with [our community or our culture].

Also unlike Roberto Colon, both Reggie Jones and Michael Carroll are willing to use the existing political system to serve their organization's needs and interests.

Reggie Jones and Networks of Funders

As an elected official, Reggie Jones understands and uses the political system and influence networks to their fullest to support his mission for youth. He sits on practically every youth agency board in Francis Homes. The ultimate networker, he has not only guided fledgling Francis Homes programs through filing for nonprofit status and setting up the structure needed to run their youth agencies but also is helping individuals in other cities establish programs similar to the Reggie Jones Gymnasts.

Reggie also successfully exploits private-sector interests and has secured funding from a bevy of corporate sponsors, a network he has nurtured over his thirty-plus years of working with the Gymnasts. Reggie donates his time, but an additional $150,000 is now needed each year to cover uniforms, transportation expenses such as vans and gas, and salaries of support staff. As the team grew in prestige and Reggie's own networking skills developed, he secured performance fees as well as donations of money, equipment, and facilities from business contacts. Reggie's marketing process also includes his careful monitoring of both performance quality and team members' deportment.

Exceptional among youth organization leaders in his ability to tap into mainline corporate America, Reggie has increased the team's level of corporate sponsorship over the past decade, adding such names as Amoco, United Airlines, Syntex Laboratories, and Bell Telephone to the list of supporters. The sponsorship jewels in Reggie's corporate crown are McDonald's and Coca-Cola, but he points out that at $25,000 a year each, the big names can scare off other donors without fully supporting the program themselves. However, at each performance, Reggie distributes the team business card, not only to market his players but also to provide a public relations return to the nearly thirty corporate sponsors and contributors of in-kind donations that keep the team running and who are listed on the back of the card.

Reggie Jones estimates that he receives about $150,000 per year in in-kind donations. Sports stores donate traveling bags, warm-up suits, and uniforms; a car dealership gives the team a good deal on vans; an insurance company donates the coverage for the vehicles; a chiropractor takes care of injuries; a restaurant feeds the entire team for free any time they stop; an airline company gives them good rates for team travel. But in spite of all the funds and donations Reggie receives from outside sources, he usually finds his personal commitment to the team eating into his own pocket. In midsummer of 1992 he told us, "I'm $9,000 into this organization already this year. Last year it was $14,000." He often ends up supplying 10 percent of the program budget himself, an expense he is reluctant to write off as a tax deduction because, he says, when you're a politician, "you're always looking over your shoulder."

Reggie limits his reliance on traditional youth services funding sources such as foundations and the government. Only three foundations have given to the team in its thirty-three years. At one point Reggie devoted a great deal of his time to seeking foundation support, even going so far as to pay $1,500 to a company to solicit foundation monies, an effort that proved unsuccessful. He greatly prefers the personal touch of the telephone call to the grind of paper work, and although he has written a few grant proposals, corporate deal making and marketing is much more his style. He has also never sought funds from the United Way (indeed, the infrastructure of his one-man show probably would not meet United Way requirements), but he flourishes through alternative funding sources.

Reggie uses his public-sector contacts to support salaried positions for the older team members as coaches and teachers at a local community center. Thirty-two thousand dollars a year comes from the state employment and training office and some funds also come from the Lakeside Board of Education for the Gymnasts working as staff in after-school programs. Through his political work and his position with the school district Reggie knows the various pots of state and local government money for which his youth are eligible. Perhaps even more important to the Gymnasts as individuals, he uses his contacts and knowledge of the public sector to locate jobs and college scholarship funds for team members. Throughout all his efforts he has maintained the local character of a grass-roots organization for his team while successfully soliciting a wide range of mainstream sources for funding and other resources.

Michael Carroll and Funding to Maintain Independence

Down the street at Building Educational Strategies for Teens, Michael Carroll takes an entirely different approach to developing his grass-roots base. Unlike Reggie Jones, who grew up in the Francis Homes community and returned to it as something of a neighborhood hero, Michael Carroll's initial base came from a church known for its largely European American, older congregation. In many ways Carroll personifies just the kind of outsider Francis Homes holds most suspect—a European American well-educated middle-class do-gooder and "fixer" of African American youth.

When Michael first came to Grove Street Church in 1977, the tutoring program in the church's basement taught only a handful of youth and was completely supported by the church. However, the church's Young Life-Francis Homes outreach program had a ready pool of teenagers and strongly influenced Michael Carroll's philosophy of how to work with youth. Young Life emphasized listening to youth and valuing their input on program direction. Heeding this concept, Michael adapted his fledgling tutoring program and designed a strategy for slowly building trust and acceptance for him and his program in Francis Homes. As BEST's participation grew, Michael encouraged church board members to make the decision that moved the program site into the heart of the projects.

Unlike Reggie, who had a ready-made network of community contacts, Michael had to move cautiously in establishing alliances in the community. Conscious that well-meaning outsiders did not usually last in the projects, he concentrated on program quality as well as youth input, slowly building BEST's reputation in the local community and in the larger Lakeside funding realm. He has been successful with Lakeside funders because of the high regard in which he and BEST are held, but nonetheless, he struggles with many of the same issues as Roberto Colon, attempting to reconcile the demands of downtown funders and agencies with his own understanding of the program's needs and goals. At a time when collaboration and networking are considered the sine qua non of youth policy, for example, Michael Carroll resists or circumvents requirements for interagency collaboration, finding it impractical on a program level. He recalls one disastrous experience from his first year at BEST when he arranged for his students to swim once a week at another youth agency: "We'd come over there and they [would have] just fired this guy or he didn't show up or the pool was locked. Here I was, I made this commitment to these kids that they'd go swimming. If I said we're gonna do something, we're gonna do it. It was like, now what in the hell do I do? I became so frustrated and angry being dependent upon another institution." Michael's strategy for BEST has been to fulfill promises of consistency and quality, and he cannot do that if other agencies let his young people down.

BEST does have longstanding relationships with two other youth agencies in Francis Homes, but it has also maintained its general autonomy in order to keep the desired focus on educational issues and to build a program that is "as credible as possible." It has to be credible for Michael, "for the kids in the community, the funding community, the potential volunteer pool, and the church." The "bottom line" for Michael is that "the program will sell itself."

Through ensuring the quality of his program, Michael has been able to attract and sustain a broad base of funding. During his first year at BEST, the church provided meeting space and the budget of $25,000, $10,000 of which went toward Michael's salary while the rest was consumed by van maintenance and supplies. In that first year, he ran the program himself with about ten hours a week of staff assistance from a church intern. After two years he realized that in order for the program to expand with the growing interest of the neighborhood youth he would have to seek outside financial support. His first grant was serendipitous. A tutoring volunteer from a local college brought his father to visit one day. The father, who happened to be on the board of a local foundation, was so impressed that a $5,000 check arrived in the mail the next week. Michael recalls just sitting back in his chair and "whooping."

Over the next two years a funding officer at the foundation saw to it that BEST continued to receive funds. With only a couple of pages of program description and a few conversations with the grant officer, the monies kept coming in. However, Michael was learning that the normal process was much more sophisticated, even at times unmanageable, because the funding life of a new program is essentially two years. Funds can easily be acquired for the first year. The program then often has to be "recast" during the second year in order to get additional funds. In the third year the program typically has to be funded by the agency's own discretionary funds because grant monies become much more difficult to receive from foundations and corporations interested in the latest approach to an issue rather than long-term, sustainable solutions.

Scholarship programs are one way Michael has attempted to secure the long-term commitments necessary for providing stable, quality programs. BEST's first scholarship program was developed with the family owners of a local factory. Michael prefers the more reliable funds from sources with a vested interest in BEST's success, like this factory, to "flavor of the month" support from philanthropies or social agencies. BEST's other scholarship programs rely upon both corporate and individual commitments, modeled upon the I Have a Dream program paradigm, in which a core group of students receive personal attention from support staff throughout high school and receive college scholarships upon graduation.[1]

As a more holistic approach to community educational needs has developed in Lakeside and the United States generally, Michael Carroll has secured government funding for summer jobs, adult education, and child-care programs. But, like foundation funding, government funding has proven erratic, dependent upon the latest public policy trends. Michael began BEST's junior staff program with four youth and Comprehensive Education and Training Act (CETA) funds in 1979. In 1980 BEST had eight high schoolers working as junior staff, but then CETA disappeared with the Reagan administration and the New Federalism. However, by that time, Michael had seen that the "work-study type of focus, or educational focus combined with the work experience, [was] an extremely powerful model to use." He recalls that "After CETA went away, we realized how central these kids were going to be to our organization and our future [so] we just incorporated [the school-year program] into our general operating budget." However, BEST does receive funds from the Mayor's Summer Jobs Program to cover junior staff salaries in the summertime. The pressure the junior staff program puts on the core budget has been further compounded by rising program costs. In 1979 each junior staffer received about $1,000 per year. Today the annual salaries have increased to between $4,000 and $4,500. During the 1991–92 fiscal year Michael was forced to cut the junior staff by almost half because funds were not available to maintain the forty junior workers BEST was then using.

Michael estimates that 65 percent to 70 percent of the monies BEST receives are restricted, including funds for adult education, the Future Teachers Program, scholarship programs, and the funds for summer junior staff. Nevertheless, while many agencies' programs suffer from shifting government and foundation demands and priorities—having to change or go without funding—the diverse base of corporate, foundation, individual, and government monies and the long-term nature of the funding Michael Carroll is acquiring for BEST's special projects help to assure the independence required to maintain the organization's strong focus on education.

Yet stable support for the infrastructure that plans, implements, and provides the base for BEST's eighteen different programs remains tenuous and an ongoing challenge. Multiple sources of funding mean that Michael Carroll faces multiple accountability requirements. Perhaps the most onerous are for the Title XX after-school programs and government-funded adult education classes. Under the new single-audit act, both demand accounting of categorical spending, threatening to double BEST's accounting costs. BEST's support staff had already increased during the early 1990s, and Michael laments that he has not been more successful in demanding that program monies be accompanied by funds for related infrastructure costs. "For years if they gave me the money to run the program I would do it," he says. "Now my board is telling me that I have to pay more attention to balance sheets and budget lines."

Like the leaders of many other youth agencies, for years Michael Carroll and his board of directors hesitated to seek United Way support, pointing to the strictures the United Way would place on the organization and the agency's tendency to fund only large, well-established institutions. But the United Way in Lakeside has been reaching out, making its funds more accessible to the city's successful grass-roots organizations. Accepting provisional membership for BEST in 1990, Michael has found many benefits—and detriments—to being a part of the United Way. The strongest benefit of United Way affiliation, says Michael, is that "it is a consistent source of funding month after month . . . like clockwork." This is a help in Michael's struggle to meet the costs of the support staff and procedures for his burgeoning agency. He also finds that "the compliance issues with United Way have not turned out to be as stringent as we originally anticipated . . . at least here in Lakeside they have tried to respond to those types of concerns." Accountability has been limited to "quarterly financial reports and annual statistical reports [service], which are probably only about four or five pages," while the independent breakout required by United Way for each program increased accounting costs by about 25 percent (to a total of $6,000 to $7,000 per year).

Michael Carroll's primary worry about United Way membership was that BEST would lose some established donors. Just as Reggie Jones worried that McDonald's and Coca-Cola's sponsorship would cost the Gymnasts other potential contributors, Michael Carroll was "concerned about the impact of certain corporations who put themselves on the restricted list. [If] they've given through the United Way... then they are not open to giving to any... United Way member." But he now finds that, except for one grant, being a United Way affiliate "hasn't really affected us [in the other funds we receive]." Given his need to develop a better organizational infrastructure, Michael also appreciates some of the obligations BEST's provisional United Way membership carries: "There's this whole checklist of items you have to get through to substantiate your organizational strength, [for example,] that the board reflects [the] ethnic balance of the youth. They pushed us to get those things done. I still have concerns about United Way—that they're arrogant in their attitude.... Their way is the only way.... But overall they've been helpful."

Like John Peña in Big Valley, Michael Carroll has now made developing the strength and balance of BEST's board of directors a top priority, but he too faces the challenge that the people who bring ethnic diversity to the board often cannot make substantial financial contributions. Michael says, "With the reality that we have a $1.5 million budget to raise, we've been in a very intentional recruitment process for people that can give substantially to us... or [who can give substantial amounts] through corporate donations or friend and family donations." For example, one recent recruit to the board is a thirty-five-year-old founder of a national video store chain. He and his brother gave over $100,000 toward BEST's general program expenses in 1992, while their father, also the owner of his own company, donated $150,000 toward the capital campaign.

However, with the recruitment of more movers and shakers, the board's ties to the Francis Homes neighborhood and the Lakeside African American community have weakened. African Americans now represent only one-third of board membership. Although Michael Carroll is concerned with maintaining an ethnic balance on the board consistent with BEST's youth, he also considers the diversity of the board as one of its strengths. The common denominator for all board members, he says, should be that they are "true supporters of BEST" and "highly committed" to the lives and futures of Francis Home youth. Through his many networking efforts to obtain corporate sponsorships, support from mainstream foundations such as United Way, and now through the composition of his board, Michael Carroll has moved BEST squarely into the establishment and has been largely successful in using establishment resources to further the interests of Francis Homes youth. His success as a spanner of community boundaries and his acceptance by established Lakeside interests stems largely from the fact that Michael is part and parcel of the establishment's systems. Thus for mainstream Lakeside individuals and agencies who wish to contribute in some way to Francis Homes beleaguered youth, BEST is the most comfortable bet in town. Reggie Jones was elected to the establishment; Michael Carroll was born to it. They both use it successfully, albeit in somewhat different ways, to create places of hope in Francis Homes.

Wizards' Search for Resources:
Spanning Boundaries and Negotiating Place

The secure and nurturing organizations that embrace some inner-city youth are fragile, vulnerable, and dependent organizations. Their leaders must continually work with outsiders to negotiate support, acceptance, and place. It is a job never completed, and defined by constantly changing challenges. Shifts in a city's economic base, demographics, and philanthropic dollars and tastes, alterations in the salience and character of other organizations' demands for attention and support occur regularly and in often unpredictable ways. Who could have foretold, for example, the sudden influx of funds following the 1992 Los Angeles riots? Yet the continuity and character of inner-city places of hope for youth ultimately depend on leaders' skill in negotiating support in these difficult local settings.

From one perspective, each of the six successful youth leaders faces different challenges and constraints and has different opportunities. Because the interaction between a youth organization and its immediate outside world is shaped by such factors as organizational purpose, institutional affiliations, neighborhood culture, and member characteristics each set of challenges, constraints, and opportunities is unique. Roberto Colon's gang members would be unlikely to appeal to corporate sponsors the way that Reggie Jones's elite performance Gymnasts do, while John Peña would find it very difficult to emulate Roberto's successful back-channel political activities through a Latino network because the Big Valley Latino community currently lacks the organization and political sophistication of Lakeside's Latinos. John Peña and Steve Patterson lead very different Boys and Girls Clubs and work with qualitatively different resource bases—Peña constantly underfunded, Patterson secure in his club's endowment. Michael Carroll and Luanna Williams move in different worlds— Luanna working lifelong neighborhood contacts, Michael trading on establishment ties and credentials.

Yet all of these leaders face a similar key problem as they work to garner program resources. They have proved their understanding of the inner city and its youth by the success of their organizations with those youth; however, the movers and shakers in the policy and social networks outside these leaders' organizations often misunderstand the realities of the inner cities and the young people who live there. The lack of fit between the interests of the well-intentioned community elite and the needs of inner-city youth and their organizations results in a substantial shortfall between needs and available dollars and threatens organizational survival and growth for most successful leaders.

As we have illustrated, often the "suits" responsible for allocating public and private resources and for framing policies and programs for youth focus on "youth problems" to be managed or fixed. Youth who most need help to acquire a positive view of themselves are offered instead programs that implicitly or explicitly label them as problems, as failures, as deviant. Thus Lakeside public dollars support enhanced recreational opportunities in parks in wealthy neighborhoods and simultaneously fund increased Special Weapons and Tactics (SWAT) teams for Porter Park. In Big Valley civic energy can be mobilized around controlling the gang problem or school dropouts, but not around efforts to identify the needs of inner-city youth. In dusty, hot Arroyo, for example, the public pool sits cracked and empty.

In many communities, apparently good ideas for community programs misfire because no one has considered what inner-city youth's lives are like. Often youth simply do not know about programs. Inner-city youth are not part of mainstream institutions, nor do they read the newspapers in which opportunities for them are announced. Their natural networks of peers and grass-roots organizations usually have no connections with establishment's channels for announcing youth opportunities. Even if they know about the programs, they may still be unable to use them because they cannot cross gang boundaries. Civic leaders in Lakeside were infuriated when Porter Crossing youth failed to show up for downtown job interviews they had arranged with effort. What they didn't realize was the way these youth can be hemmed into four blocks of gang turf, unable to read bus schedules and with no experience of any other neighborhood. Policymakers also sometimes fail to appreciate the stark poverty of the inner city and the dire financial straits its youth. Even seemingly modest camp fees, membership dues, or other costs of participation are often too high for youth to manage.

Institutional realities also look different from inner-city streets than from the top of the system. Civic leaders in Big Valley, in an effort to create a broader sense of community and to coordinate responses to social needs, have devised a countywide collaborative of youth agencies. The rationales for the Big Valley Youth Collaborative are sound: coordinate scarce resources, reduce redundancies, and create efficiencies of service. However, the organizations most attuned to inner-city families and youth are often unable to meet the criteria for funding and inclusion in the collaborative. Luanna Williams could not meet Campfire's demands for volunteer staff. Fee structures preclude John Peña's youth from participating in city sports leagues. A required collaboration between the parks and recreation department and Big Valley public schools fell apart because planners misunderstood the lines of authority and school personnel's concerns about facilities use. In contrast, Roberto Colon's LYSN, built by Latino heads of agencies out of proven personal relationships, achieved goals similar to those that were developed for the Big Valley Youth Collaborative but were met unevenly because organizational connections failed.

In Lakeside, requests for proposals from a major community philanthropic concern went unanswered by Porter Crossing youth agencies because proposal guidelines specified organizational collaborations impossible in the complex topology of Porter Crossing gang territories. In River City, Cooper House's independence from local United Way and other collaborative efforts reflects Steve Patterson's judgment that the house could not meet application requirements without seriously compromising its mission and operation. A large endowment permits this autonomy, but Patterson and his board's response isolates Cooper House from the larger River City youth services arena.

Wizards seeking resources struggle with the fact that they know one set of rules of the game—how to create organizations that inner-city youth will join and from which they will reap long-term benefits—while another set of rules is defined by institutions and individuals outside the everyday context in which the wizards and the hopefuls move. Both insiders and outsiders continue to try to educate the funders and policymakers about the true needs of inner-city youth and about strategies that can create the places that create hopefuls. Ironically many of the aspects of organizational life that are standards of legitimacy in the world outside successful inner-city youth organizations are threatening to the flexible, youth-driven programming so important to producing hopefuls. Tightly specified accounting and evaluation procedures and revision of goals to reflect prevailing interpretations of problems and strategies should be tools, not the ends in themselves they are sometimes made to appear.

To overcome the barriers thrown up by the conflicts between the two sets of rules, wizards make aggressive use of personal networks to get the resources they need without sacrificing the characteristics that make their programs work. Luanna exploits her community connections to procure volunteers for the center, trades on her ties to such establishment organizations as the Girl Scouts, and builds interagency relationships, such as her membership on the Big Valley YMCA board, with her mission foremost in mind. John Peña endures countless dinner meetings and ceremonial events in order to advocate for inner-city youth, and seeks and accepts invitations to speak to diverse groups of people about the Boys and Girls Clubs and the needs of youth. He has infiltrated Big Valley establishment channels even more than Luanna, chairing high-profile community task forces on school outcomes and on gangs, among others.

Reggie Jones uses his political contacts to open doors with corporate sponsors for the Gymnasts and to identify scholarship and employment opportunities. Michael Carroll trades on his establishment identity and strong church ties to build support for BEST. Roberto Colon harnesses the energy and frustration of Lakeside's Latino community to strengthen existing networks and build new political coalitions. Our six wizards put as much time into trying to supplement the weak support of checkbook charity with strong donor ties to the organization and concrete donor appreciation of youth's everyday world as they do into creating an attractive, positive place for youth to be. Managing the complex setting outside the youth organization is a never-finished and often frustrating task. But it is this energy invested in the larger community that ultimately enables the wizards to implement their own proven missions and to moderate organizational isolation. As important as dollars are to the inner-city youth organization, wizards recognize that political support and a broadened community concern for inner-city youth are equally critical.

Chapter Eleven

Keeping Hope Alive: An Appeal for Action

The conclusions we draw from our research are simultaneously encouraging and discouraging. They are optimistic because the youth, youth leaders, staff, and volunteers who spoke to us showed us that the "answer" to the "youth problem" is not difficult to grasp. As the wizards have said to us on more than one occasion, they "know what to do." These successful leaders and the places of hope they have created for inner-city youth disprove others' disheartening conclusion that these youth are a lost cause, a perspective that inhibits policymakers and the public from imagining and supporting the activities and environments that could nurture inner-city youth, make them feel welcome, and fit their needs.

Our conclusions are discouraging because they also bear witness to the restricted realities within which hopeful inner-city youth and supportive adults attempt to create safe and caring environments. Outrage and frustration that nobody seems to care whether people in the inner-cities hope or despair, live or die, pervades the lives of inner-city youth. These feelings often manifest themselves as masks of defiance—masks that dare anyone to get close. "I don't got friends," said one embittered, proud youth from Francis Homes. "You can't trust nobody but yourself."

The youth and adults we met and introduced here struggle daily with the affront and lack of trust conveyed to them by society's general repudiation of their lives and their futures. And these burdens are largely inconceivable to those who live elsewhere. The virtual absence of worthwhile activities to occupy their hours and hours of free time, of someone to care for and about them, exacerbates the heavy responsibilities borne by most youth of the inner city and feeds the desperation of their everyday lives. A gang member turned youthworker describes this "typical" family environment in his Francis Homes high rise:

Some kids . . . they be really wantin' to go do school. . . . But their parents are hooked on drugs and that be bothering them when they be in school. They mind don't be focused on books. And they'll stop going like that too. Worrying about they parents: "What I'm gonna do if one day I come home from school and my mom is laying there dead? OD'd on drugs? Or my pop's laying there dead? Or they find him in a bar somewhere shot up? In an alley or something?" These kids got nobody to do all this [school or sports with]; they's mind full of worries, so they jus' think why try.

When this is youth's reality, they see few alternatives to it, and the bitterness and disappointments of their daily lives are reinforced by the negative expectations that rain upon them from the community, school, and the media. They hear and see themselves depicted as animals, derelicts, no-good bad ass kids who want only to rip off society. Tito says, "Some people don't even consider us regular people. . . . All of us want to be somebody. Nobody wants to be out there [on the street] doin' that shit. We're ready to go [given the opportunity]." The streets and their gangs inevitably become hazardous sanctuaries for youth who can bear no longer the hurt of neglect and their invisibility in schools or the labor market. Much policy for inner-city youth reflects conceptions of them born from fear, and this policy rushes to control, creating an environment that Roberto Colon likens to a war between a community and its youth. Yet, as Roberto also says, these are "*our* kids."

Myths About Inner-City Youth

What "everybody knows" about inner-city youth and their ambitions, interests, and capacities is largely off the mark. The experiences and achievements of the young hopefuls we met and of their youth organizations challenge the following myths.

Myth: *Some Youth Are Beyond Hope*

This myth[1] and its corollary, which states that it's too late to intervene once youth hit adolescence, support policies that focus scarce resources on young children only or fund programs for teenagers that take a get-tough stance. The hopefuls defy these myths. To be sure, there are youth in the inner-city who are, as one street worker says, "the cranks—the [sociopathic] kid who will shoot someone in the face point blank and then sit down to dinner like nothin' happened." But "cranks" are the minority and by no means found only in the inner city. The youth described in this book, and the adults who support them demonstrate that the futility of assistance perceived by outsiders results not from qualities inherent in the youth but from either the character of the assistance intended to help them or from the absence of any assistance. By our rough estimate at least three-quarters of the youth growing up in the caldron of the inner city are potential hopefuls, but only a small portion of these young people find their way to organizations that effectively give them hope.

Once they have joined an organization like any one of the six we have described here, inner-city youth continually demonstrate that they are not the marginal human beings many in society suppose. The young people we met show that teenagers can stop their destructive behaviors. Our hopefuls were not, for the most part, lucky kids who had some particular advantage, nor as we pointed out earlier, were they the "invulnerable children" whose internal resolve enables them to overcome obstacles destroying the lives of their peers. In Big Valley, both Keisha and Rosa pointed to their neighborhood youth organization as crucial in helping them meet challenges they confronted as young women. A majority of the youth we met in Lakeside had some kind of gang association prior to finding their way to the Reggie Jones Gymnasts, BEST, or GAIN. Buddy and several of his friends at Cooper House admit to numerous brushes with the law, action on the margins of the illegal drug business, and theft prior to membership in the house. Cooper House provided an alternative, engaged them, and, they say, "kept us on the good path."

Given a chance, given trust and responsibility, these "bad kids" grabbed the chance to be worthy of trust and to earn respect. They care for and protect expensive sound equipment, supervise and maintain athletic equipment, oversee the use and security of computers and audiovisual materials. They are entrusted with vans, facilities, and with the well-being and care of the most precious resource of all, younger children. Outsiders who judge inner-city youth as beyond redemption treat young persons with destructive behaviors as individual pathologies, not the products of failed institutions, violence on the street, and lack of care. The hopefuls and the youth leaders who judge them by what they become when given security, responsibility, and care testify that nothing matters more to most inner-city youth than establishing their worth by finding a purpose, protection, and love.

Myth: Inner-City Youth Are Lazy

The hopefuls want to have fun and enjoy hanging with their friends, but they also work long and hard at their tasks. Rosa and her colleagues in TeenTalk write and perform a number of scripts, learning all there is to learn about the issues the scenes take up. Tyrone and the other Gymnasts practice and perform six and sometimes seven days a week in the high-pressure atmosphere of an elite athletic team. Buddy and his friends at Cooper House arrive on time everyday for their job and club responsibilities. Teri and Keisha take responsibility for the education and enjoyment of their young charges; Tito spends hours replacing gang graffiti with fresh paint and murals that brighten the neighborhood and the soul. Successful youth leaders expect much of the hopefuls, and much is returned. The youth we met also demand much of themselves and of each other, and their successes are the source of enormous pride and self-esteem.

These youth, so often held to have little positive to contribute to the community, prove they have much to give. Luanna's Girl Scouts spend hours volunteering at the community center, senior citizens' homes, and the local hospital. The Gymnasts give free performances all over greater Lakeside, to the great pleasure of children's groups, hospitals, and other organizations unable to pay for the show. Roberto's GAIN staff and members are effectively on call twenty-four hours a day, seven days a week, to provide counsel, protection, a bed, or a meal to Porter Crossing youth. Steve Patterson's Cooper Housers work as volunteers in River City wherever they can be useful: in nursing homes, with the homeless, in hospitals, and in schools. BEST's participants, too, see service to their Francis Homes community as part of their covenant with BEST, lending helping hands and hearts to many of their neighbors. The joy of the hopefuls is evident in their capacity to give, their belief that they have something of worth to share with others and that they can play a legitimate role in society. Hopefuls want fun, but they also want to engage in real work and in activities valued by the neighborhood community.

Myth: Teenagers Do Not Want Any Discipline

All the organizations where hopefuls gathered provided clear and firm discipline, and authority based in a minimal number of rules with maximal impact. We saw youth move eagerly from the chaos of their everyday environment into a group's secure circle of known rules, certain discipline, and strong behavioral norms. These youngsters dispel the belief that adolescents, especially those from the inner cities, reject any attempts to guide their behavior. They accepted group rules that stressed responsibility to the group as well as to oneself, commitment, and integrity. They sought the concern and security conveyed by strong discipline as long as they perceived the discipline as fair. The swift and certain discipline that followed infractions strengthened the group by reinforcing norms that the members agreed were important. The rules also increased the value of membership. Many Cooper Housers and Gymnasts claimed proudly that an important appeal was that "not just anybody can belong."

Myth: *Teenagers Do Not Want to Join Organizations*

Proposals for youth programs often are rejected on the belief that youth are uninterested in organized activities led by adults. This myth is disproved by the organizations we studied. The Reggie Jones Gymnasts have a waiting list of several thousand youth from all over Lakeside who want the prestige, safety, and "ticket outta here" team membership provides. BEST's rolls are full to capacity. Roberto Colon cannot meet the demand of gangbangers who want to get off the streets and into GAIN. "What we need are one hundred Robertos," says Tito, who counts himself lucky to have a space in the program. River City teenagers not only join Cooper House, they are "down the house" on average more than twenty hours each week, essentially all of their free time. Luanna Williams's vital Arroyo Girl Scout troop, as she says, disproves the conclusion that "teenage girls, especially African Americans, won't get involved in scouting." Membership in John Peña's TeenTalk drama group is a sought-after prize for which teenagers from all over Big Valley compete. Organizations that are successful in giving hope to despairing inner-city youth are oversubscribed, in continuing demand, and utilized to their fullest. As Roberto Colon told us, "These guys, they are so proud. They want so bad to connect with something they are in control of, that they can be part of."

It is true that adolescents do not want to join organizations that punish them, that label them as misfits or bad or behind other youth, or that treat them as social problems. Adolescents do not stick with organizations that offer impersonal herd programming, provide no sense of belonging, no sense of place, and no sense of sustained identity and purpose. Organizations that let youth drop in find that these youth also drop out and acquire little loyalty to the group or its mission. Such organizations and activities, while well intentioned, are disappointments to youth and their sponsors. They fail because they provide a *space* for youth to be in, not a *place for youth to be*. They supply lockers, membership cards, a spot to hang jackets, and a game room or a ball court but not personal attention, a sense of mission for themselves and the youth, and a family.

It is important that inner-city youth have somewhere to go and something to do and crucial that those places and actions be positive. The young people we met came to the wizards' organizations in the first place because the places and activities looked like fun; they stayed because the organizations supplied a group and a purpose that meant something *to the youth*. They told us: "We know we're accepted here." "People care." "There's always someone to listen." "We're learning stuff for life." The loneliness and suspicion of outsiders that the inner-city environment breeds into its youth also drives them to a place where they can belong. If that place is not a positive youth organization, it will be a gang.[2] In fact effective youth organizations look very much like gangs in the kinds of supports and recognition they provide to their members, but the outcomes of the two groups could not be more dissimilar. The gangs lead to violence, crime, and quite possibly death; the effective youth organizations enable youth "to take a different road" that leads to life and a productive future.

Realities Faced by Inner-City Youth

While we did find successful inner-city organizations, the sad fact is that few effective resources are available to inner-city youth and the kinds of organizations and environments that produce hopefuls are scarce. Instead existing resources are often inadequate, misdirected, or inappropriate.

Helping institutions do not help consistently. Schools, too often below par by any measure, are experienced as hostile and demeaning environments where neither youth nor their interests are heard or taken seriously. Police are experienced as enemies, a rival gang, or indifferent adults; social service agencies as unconcerned and punitive. All these institutions appear to act in accordance with the myths we identified rather than with youth's realities. Youth agencies and programs also often instantiate the inner-city myths. When asked what would make a difference for inner-city youth, one of Luanna Williams's Girl Scouts spoke for most youth we met when she said, "I would change people's attitudes, 'cuz some adults, when they look at you, they think, 'She's never gonna do anything because she's already gotten pregnant or she got in trouble.' Instead of helpin' [kids], they're jus' puttin' them down. Why, I don't understand. You can change a person."

The hopefuls believe inner-city youth can change the prevailing mythology if members of the establishment "just give us a chance, give us a place to learn, to try." But few inner-city youth are able to find such chances and places. Instead they find programs that are either inhospitable, irrelevant, or physically or financially inaccessible. Ironically the developmental programs that could benefit inner-city youth exist primarily in cities' suburbs or wealthier enclaves where these efforts are just one resource among many for advantaged youth. Even when such programs are brought to the youth of the inner city who have no resources, the programs generally do not accept youth already in trouble and most in need of a caring hand if they are to find "good paths" and a responsible future. Instead, these "problem" young people are consigned to be "fixed" rather than enabled.

Nevertheless, the leaders of all youth organizations are typically caring and well intentioned. So how do the constraints arise that result in ineffective or simply nonexistent programs? We found, and our wizards believe, that the logic of design underlying youth organizations' directions and methods is a product of beliefs held by powerful agents in the larger environment. Ironically, when policies for inner-city youth are formed, the insiders— the youth and their immediate leaders—are treated as outsiders while the true outsiders—the broader community and its civic agents—make the choices that shape the number and kinds of programs inner-city youth will receive. One of the reasons we call the successful leaders wizards is that they are highly skilled in navigating around or changing this inappropriate and ineffective policymaking process in order to let youth's voice be heard and to get support for the program approaches they understand youth to need.

In addition to establishment attitudes, low levels of support constrain inner-city organizational effectiveness. We found low levels of support provided for inner-city programs relative to other youth initiatives and low levels of support for youth generally relative to other social groups. When policymakers debate the ultimate benefits of social programs, question reasonable social investments, and compare demands for budget or other resources, adolescents generally, and inner-city teenagers in particular, lose mightily in these policy conversations. The tragic reality is that those who need the most in terms of services and resources typically get the least, and what they do get often misses the target.

"No-man's-land," "combat zone," "occupied territory"—these metaphors sometimes casually employed by media and the public describe real streets, real homes, real threats to youth's lives day after day in the inner city. They are true descriptions of the bleak maps of inner cities, places where no one can safely move—not grandmothers, mothers, fathers, young children, or adolescents. More than a quarter of this nation's young people grow up in such pitiless places, uncertain about tomorrow, unable to imagine a hopeful future: "Dead or in jail, that's our future." "Lyin' by, gettin' high. . . . The future be dead." "Get 'em off the streets," advises a shot caller (main drug dealer) for a Francis Homes high rise. "[Give them] somethin' else to do. . . . If you ain't' got nothin' to do, you ain't got no money or nothin'. If you ain't doin' nothin', why not get out there and help sell drugs? Make some money. So you'll be able to go places. You know what I'm sayin'?" Wizards and hopefuls know what he is saying. Many in the establishment have yet to get the message.

Their faces tight with anger, inner-city youth speak of the realities of betrayal and racism, of a society that cares little for or about them, renders them invisible, and ignores their pain. Dollars invested in inner-city youth are often justified in terms of benefits to the larger society. These dollars are said to enhance global competitiveness, reduce violence, slash the welfare rolls, and increase tax revenues. But what of the youth themselves? Where is the morality in a position that sees inner-city youth only as problems to the larger society and cannot look at them as individuals who have their own needs and their own value? Where is the soul in a society that allows so many of its youth to be without hope? The despair expressed by youth of the U.S. inner cities bespeaks the collapse of this nation's social compact with its youth.

What the Hopefuls Seek

Adolescents everywhere look for a group as well as a personal identity. The empty gyms, undersubscribed sports teams, and other activities that attract and retain disappointing numbers of inner-city youth reflect these youths' judgment that these groups are not for them rather than a general disinclination to join groups. Our research found no specific programs or missions that made a difference in organizations' successes with inner-city youth. We did find that all of the places created by the extraordinary people we call wizards and wizards' assistants share these common features:

- They have family-like environments in which individuals are valued and rules of membership are clear.

- Their activities offer opportunities for active participation and present real challenges that result in accomplishments as defined by youth as well as by the larger society.

- They are youth driven and sensitive to youth's everyday realities, values, aspirations, and interests.

- They assume that youth are a resource to be developed, not a problem to be managed.

- They are sufficiently flexible and attuned to inner-city youth to respond to the unpredictable crises and demands that punctuate youth's lives. They recognize each youth's need to be treated as an adult while still sheltered as a child.

- They are tangibly local, operating within and through the neighborhoods, institutions, and social relationships that make up youth's everyday realities. As Cruz says, "to really get the respect, you have to understand the neighborhood [and not assume that youth with the] same ethnic background [will all be alike]."

- They enable youth through family-like challenging, prodding, nagging, teasing, loving, and providing of multiple opportunities for practice and experience.

- They reach out to inner-city teenagers with messages that they will hear even though many are alienated from mainstream institutions, resigned to dead-end lives, and suspicious of anything that purports to be good for them.

Policymakers and analysts assert that little is known about how youth make decisions to join an organization and to stick with it. The hopefuls we met supply this necessary knowledge.[3] The places wizards imagine and provide by listening to the hopefuls have many dimensions. They can be viewed as activities, peer groups, support systems, havens, microeconomies, or webs of interpersonal relationships. They can be Girl Scout troops, tutoring programs, street interventions, Boys and Girls Clubs, sports teams, or performance groups. But most of all, the youth organizations that change inner-city youth's lives are families and communities. The skills of wizards and their assistants are skills of community building, constructing places that engage adults and youth together in hopeful, concrete, productive purposes. These wizards are restoring the nation's social compact with it's youth, one at a time.

Leaders Who Know What to Do

To a person, all the effective leaders we met—both the ones described in this book and others—operate in whole or part outside conventional policy frames and must struggle to align the demands of the outside world with the rhythms, needs, and character of the place they have created for the hopefuls. These wizards are leaders of a different stripe than those described in administrative manuals and personnel handbooks. They are individuals who make the system work despite itself. They are not careerists in the conventional sense of that word but passionate advocates for youth. They are not bureaucrats guided by routines but lead and manage simultaneously guided by the needs, interests, and ever-changing realities that face their youth.

We found that the wizards recognize a fundamental contradiction between the needs of the vulnerable youth of the inner city and the institutions, programs, and policies typically developed to "help" (or control) them. They do not let their own focus on youth waver as they seek funding and deal with demands for "impact assessments," head counts, programmatic accounting, fluctuating definitions of the "youth problem," and trendy solutions. They try to connect policy and the broader community with real youth and programs that result in young men and women who want to be productive adults, and they try to dispel imagined realities and misplaced myths about "those kids." Wizards create programs out of their own enthusiasms and experiences with youth, without reliance on models or "proven" approaches. They agree that the central problem facing them is not what to do but how to fund and support what they know has to be done. "We know what to do," says John Peña. "We know what enables an inner-city kid to move from all the negatives of life to something better, something positive, but it's really hard to do within the present funding and policy contexts."

The "it" that wizards know how to do is not a model program, but a community created by the adults associated with the program that respects the interests, attitudes, and needs of the youth themselves. Impatient with the time-worn debate about who is at fault for the plight of the inner cities and with policies based on fictions, contemptuous of perspectives rooted in culture-of-poverty assumptions that ghetto youth need to be "rehabilitated,"[4] the wizards seek autonomy and trust from the larger community so they can get on with the job of providing youth with the opportunities they need to learn a new view of the future and then move into that future.

The wizards do not believe that sociology is destiny. Young people of the inner city want a better life and will reach for it given a real chance to learn the needed skills, attitudes, and values. The youth of U.S. inner cities need more realistic policies and funding from the establishment. And they need many more wizards to create places of hope. They need, and will require, many people who are willing to put their belief in youth into action, who are willing to take on the challenge of being loving family, trusting friend, and dedicated teacher to youth who now lack others' love, trust, and dedication. As Tito puts it, "Kids *can* walk around trouble, if there is some place to walk to, and someone to walk with."

Notes

Chapter One

Epigraph: Adrienne Rich (1987), *Unwinding the Vietnam War: From War into Peace*, ed. Reese Williams, Washington Project for the Arts (Seattle, WA: Real Comet Press).

1. In transcribing the speech of interviews and of the everyday activities of the youth centers, we have tried to retain the informality of the speech while also allowing for ease in reading. The "eye-dialect" of words such as "tryin'" and "gonna" represents all groups' informal speech. We have omitted pauses; fillers such as "um," "like," and "you know"; and extraneous interruptions. There is no intention to stigmatize the talk of any speaker, and the modified spellings are used in full awareness that all informal English speech differs from what standard spelling indicates. Brackets enclose information understood but unstated by the speakers. All quotations are drawn directly from transcriptions of interviews, meetings, and activities.

2. See, for example, the figures and analyses presented in N. Weber (1992), *Independent youth development organizations: An exploratory study* (New York: Carnegie Council on Adolescent Development); S. A. Hewlett (1991), *When the bough breaks* (New York: Basic Books); J. Dryfoos (1990), *Adolescents at risk* (New York: Oxford University Press); and L. Schorr (1988), *Within our reach* (New York: Doubleday). The terms authors apply to the young peo-

ple and families of U.S. inner cities are multiple, imprecise, and confusing. *At risk* or *disadvantaged*, for example, are categories typically applied to youth who come from families that are poor, dysfunctional, or depart in some fashion from the idealized two-parent, mother-at-home family of the past. However, almost everyone who has worked with or studied youth agrees that *at risk* crosses economic categories to apply as well to middle- and upper-class youngsters. Dryfoos, *Adolescents at risk*, argues that all children growing up in the United States today are at risk to some extent. Other labels confuse as well. *Minority*, typically meant to signal ethnic or racial identity other than European American, is a meaningless designation in most inner-city neighborhoods (and some states), because individuals of African American, Latino, or Asian origin make up the majority. However, these labels do connote unequal opportunity or lack of access to the resources and privileges enjoyed by Americans who grow up with adequate income, strong social institutions, or other supports to healthy development. In this book, we use the terms *mainstream* or *establishment* independently of ethnic or racial identity to describe those who possess a positive social position or access to it. We employ these terms to underscore the importance of economic status and to acknowledge that many minorities who have "made it" and moved away from the inner city and into the mainstream or establishment, have little more understanding of the realities of inner-city life than do European Americans who have never experienced it. We understand, however, that our usage too is problematic because it does not attend explicitly to the racism that also is a fact of life for African American, Latino, or Asian youth in the inner city.

3. For elaboration of the daily realities of youth growing up in U.S. inner cities see, for example, W. J. Wilson (1987), *The*

truly disadvantaged: The inner city, the underclass, and public policy (Chicago: University of Chicago Press); K. Auletta (1982), *The underclass* (New York: Random House); and The children of the shadows: Shaping young lives (1993, April 6, 8, 11, 13, 15, 18, 20, 22, 25), ten-part series, *The New York Times*, Section A.

4. For further discussion of invulnerable children, see B. Lefkowitz (1987), *Tough change* (New York: Doubleday); and E. J. Anthony & B. J. Cohler (eds.), (1987), *The invulnerable child* (New York: Guilford Press).

5. L. Videka-Sherman (1992), New-style settlement houses, *Rockefeller Institute Bulletin*, 41–44, identifies these four characteristics as distinguishing settlement houses from other social service agencies.

6. See, for example, Dryfoos, *Adolescents at risk*, and Schorr, *Within our reach*. F.A.J. Ianni (1989), *The search for structure* (New York: Free Press), is an exception, but his analysis does not extend beyond the immediate context or event to consider the social and historical roots of a young person's embedded context and perceived realities.

7. See, for example, R. H. Price, M. Cioci, W. Penner, & B. Trautlein (1990), *School and community support programs that enhance adolescent health and education* (New York: Carnegie Council on Adolescent Development); M. B. Styles & K. V. Morrow (1992), *Understanding how youth and elders form relationships: A study of four linking lifetimes programs* (Philadelphia, PA: Public/Private Ventures); and Weber, *Independent youth development organizations.*

8. Carnegie Council on Adolescent Development (1992), *A matter of time: Risk and opportunity in the nonschool hours*, Report of the Task Force on Youth Development and Community Programs (New York: Carnegie Corporation); E. Medrich (1991), *Young adolescents and discretionary time use: The nature of life outside school* (New York: Carnegie Council on Adolescent Development).

9. Dryfoos, *Adolescents at risk*, p. 25.

10. Carnegie Council on Adolescent Development, *A matter of time*.

11. L. Stern (1992), *Funding patterns of nonprofit organizations that provide youth development services: An exploratory study* (New York: Carnegie Council on Adolescent Development).

12. J. MacLeod (1987), *Ain't no makin' it* (Boulder, CO: Westview Press).

13. Weber, *Independent youth development organizations*, examines grass-roots organizations for youth in depth and finds that this type of organization is most likely to be aimed at adolescents.

Chapter Two

1. Children Now (1993), *California: The state of our children* (Oakland, CA: Author).

2. K. Zinsmeister (1990), Growing up scared, *Atlantic Monthly*, 265 (6), 49–66.

3. Statistics on child abuse are overwhelming, and professionals in the field acknowledge that the incidence of physical and sexual abuse is much greater than reported or suspected. See T. Bear, S. Schenk, & L. Buckner (1992/1993), Supporting victims of child abuse, *Educational Leadership*, 50(4), 42–47; D. Besharov (1990), *Recognizing child abuse* (New York: Free Press); E. Blume (1990), *Secret survivors* (New York: Free Press); S. Butler (1978), *Conspiracy of silence* (San Francisco: New Glide Publications); and J. Crewdson (1988), *By silence abused* (New York: HarperCollins). Experts also agree that child abuse ignores social class, race, or ethnicity. One-third of college students responding to a questionnaire indicated they had been sexually abused; incest in affluent families occurs to a much greater extent than reported; and sexual abuse was one of

three reasons youth gave for running away from home (Butler, *Conspiracy of silence*).

4. J. M. Simons, B. Finlay, & A. Yang (1992), *The adolescent and young adult fact book* (Washington, DC: Children's Defense Fund), report that every day ten teenagers and thirteen young adults are killed by firearms (p. 2). Children Now (1993), *California: The state of our children* (Oakland, CA: Author) notes that in California youth homicides increased 59 percent between 1988 and 1991; the equivalent of more than twenty-five classrooms of young people were murdered in the state in 1991.

5. Simons, Finlay, & Yang, *The adolescent and young adult fact book*.

6. Catalyst for School Change.

7. Simons, Finlay, & Yang, *The adolescent and young adult fact book*.

8. J. Gross, (1992, March 29), Collapse of inner-city families creates America's new orphans: Death, drugs and jail leave voids in childhood, *The New York Times*, Section A, pp. 1, 15.

Chapter Three

1. We borrow this term from Marty Beyer (1991, April), First, you find a wizard, *Corrections Today, 53*, 166–174. She uses it to describe the effective individuals she met in her work with juvenile justice programs. J. Dryfoos (1990), *Adolescents at risk* (New York: Oxford University Press), p. 239, also comments that most successful programs are associated with an individual, a "charismatic leader."

Chapter Five

1. We will look more closely at the thorny question of ethnicity in Chapter Six, where we discuss answers to our

questions in diverse settings and examine how much it matters that a leader is of the same ethnicity as the young people he or she aims to engage. We have also written extensively about issues of ethnicity in S. B. Heath & M. W. McLaughlin (eds.), (1993), *Identity and inner-city youth: Beyond ethnicity and gender* (New York: Teachers College Press).

2. See, for example, the classifications of "new morbidities" and programs for "at risk" youth elaborated in J. Dryfoos (1990), *Adolescents at risk* (New York: Oxford University Press).

3. Carnegie Council on Adolescent Development (1992), *A matter of time: Risk and opportunity in the nonschool hours*, Report of the Task Force on Youth Development and Community Programs (New York: Carnegie Corporation); N. Weber (1992), *Independent youth development organizations: An exploratory study* (New York: Carnegie Council on Adolescent Development); R. Halpern (1991), *The role of after-school programs in the lives of inner-city children: A study of the urban youth network after-school program*, Discussion Paper 044 (Chicago: Chapin Hall Center for Children, University of Chicago).

4. M. B. Styles & K. V. Morrow (1992), *Understanding how youth and elders form relationships: A study of four linking lifetimes programs* (Philadelphia, PA: Public/Private Ventures), discusses Public/Private Ventures' evaluation of its mentoring programs and highlights and elaborates this important point about the conditions under which inner-city youth accept adults. Adults need to be understanding of youth's silences, respectful of their privacy, and understanding of their need to feel in control of the relationship.

5. The context created by others is a central point in R. P. McDermott (1976), *Kids make sense* (Unpublished doctoral dissertation, Stanford University).

Chapter Eight

1. J. Galaskiewicz (1985), *Social organization of an urban grants economy* (New York: Academic Press), p. 46.

2. This phrase comes from R. M. Titmuss (1971), *The gift relationship* (New York: Pantheon Books), a work on altruism and social policy.

3. Both Titmuss, *The gift relationship*, and P. M. Blau (1964), *Exchange and power in social life* (New York: Wiley), examine exchange or gift relationships, and the role of "egoism" or altruism in social life. They find no support for altruism alone as a motive in exchange relationships, as is sometimes (ideally) assumed, and they identify a mix of reasons for entering into gift relationships such as those described here.

4. In their examination of relationships between youth and elders in four different mentoring programs, M. B. Styles & K. V. Morrow (1992), *Understanding how youth and elders form relationships: A study of four linking lifetimes programs* (Philadelphia, PA: Public/Private Ventures), report that major differences between effective and ineffective patterns of interaction, or "satisfied" and "dissatisfied" pairs, resulted from pair members' having different styles of interaction. Elders in satisfied relationships "allowed the relationships to be youth-driven in their content and timing" (p. iii) and understood youth's reluctance to trust, to reveal details of family or personal life, or to be dictated to in any aspect of the relationship.

Chapter Ten

1. The I Have a Dream Foundation, founded in the early 1980s by Eugene Lang, guarantees participating students college scholarships if they graduate from high school. Lang, a corporate executive, began the foundation in the belief that the extraordinarily high dropout or failure rates

found in inner-city schools would be reduced if students had support for a dream of college education, support that included financial assistance and mentoring through high school. BEST's program offers that same support and vision to its members.

Chapter Eleven

1. For example, K. Auletta (1982), *The underclass* (New York: Random House); M. B. Katz (1989), *The undeserving poor* (New York: Pantheon Books); and W. J. Wilson (1987), *The truly disadvantaged: The inner city, the underclass, and public policy* (Chicago: University of Chicago Press) elaborate and analyze conventional wisdom about poor minority youth, especially African American youngsters growing up in the nation's urban areas.

2. Experts on gangs that are differentiated by ethnic affiliation or by location, purpose, or makeup agree that young people's need for affiliation, belonging, status, and safety leads them to gangs and sustains their involvement with those gangs. For example, see A. Campbell (1991), *The girls in the gang*, 2nd ed. (Cambridge, MA: Basil Blackwell); J. Hagedorn (1988), *People and folks: Gangs, crime and the underclass in a rustbelt city* (Chicago: Lake View); J. Moore (1978), *Homeboys: Gangs, drugs and prison in the barrios of Los Angeles* (Philadelphia, PA: Temple University Press); J. Moore (1991), *Going down to the barrio: Homeboys and homegirls in change* (Philadelphia, PA: Temple University Press); J. D. Vigil (1988), *Barrio gangs: Street life and identity in Southern California* (Austin: University of Texas Press); and J. D. Vigil (1993), Gangs, social control, and ethnicity: Ways to redirect, in S. B. Heath & M. W. McLaughlin (eds.), *Identity and inner-city youth: Beyond ethnicity and gender*, pp. 94–119 (New York: Teachers College Press).

3. C. Higgins (1988), *Youth motivation: At-risk youth talk to program planners* (Philadelphia, PA: Public/Private Ventures), containing Public/Private Ventures' report on consumers' perspectives, makes much the same point and highlights similar organizational features as the reasons youth offer for staying in or leaving a program. The Institute for Education in Transformation (1992) echoes these themes in *Voices from inside: A report on schooling from inside the classroom* (Claremont, CA: Claremont Graduate School), a report of students' views on schooling.

4. Culture of poverty theorists explain many of the social ills associated with ghettos and those who live there in terms of the cultural and behavioral adaptations to poverty and to social policies that have created disincentives to work and self-sufficiency. The culture of poverty diagnosis and policy approach centers on incentives for individual change. For example, E. C. Banfield (1968), *The unheavenly city: The nature and nurture of our urban crisis* (Boston: Little Brown) is a classic culture of poverty analysis; C. A. Murray (1984), *Losing ground: American social policy 1950–1980* (New York: Basic Books) links continued poverty and violence to the liberal social policies of the 1970s.

Selected Readings

A project such as this one draws upon diverse sources—academic and conventional, fugitive and nontraditional. The readings list that follows is intended to indicate only those references we found especially useful and to suggest the diversity of the resources we used over the course of our research. It is by no means a complete project bibliography. We have listed, for example, only a few of the journal and newspaper articles and report series that we found relevant. In order to honor promises of confidentiality, we purposely omitted publications specific to the three cities where we did our research, although local histories, analyses, and records were, of course, essential background for this book.

Anderson, E. (1990). *Streetwise*. Chicago: The University of Chicago Press.

Anson, R. S. (1987). *Best intentions: The education and killing of Edmund Perry*. New York: Random House.

Anthony, E. J., & Cohler, B. J. (Eds.). (1987). *The invulnerable child*. New York: Guilford Press.

Augenbraum, H., & Stavans, I. (Eds.). (1993). *Growing up Latino: Memoirs and stories*. Boston: Houghton Mifflin.

Auletta, K. (1982). *The underclass*. New York: Random House.

Banfield, E. C. (1968). *The unheavenly city: The nature and nurture of our urban crisis*. Boston: Little Brown.

Bear, T., Schenk, S., & Buckner, L. (1992, December/1993, January). Supporting victims of child abuse. *Educational Leadership, 50*(4), 42–47.

Benard, B. (1990). *The case for peers*. Portland, OR: Northwest Regional Educational Laboratory.

Benson, P. L. (1990). *The troubled journey: A portrait of 6th–12th grade youth*. Milwaukee, WI: Lutheran Brotherhood.

Berkowitz, L. (Eds.). (1984). *Advances in experimental social psychology*. Orlando, FL: Academic Press.

Besharov, D. (1990). *Recognizing child abuse*. New York: Free Press.

Beyer, M. (1991, April). First, you find a wizard. *Corrections Today, 53*, 166–174.

Blau, P. M. (1964). *Exchange and power in social life*. New York: Wiley.

Blume, E. (1990). *Secret survivors*. New York: Free Press.

Boissevain, J. (1974). *Friends of friends: Networks, manipulators and coalitions*. New York: Basil Blackwell.

Bowman, P. J. (1991). Work life. In J. S. Jackson (Ed.), *Life in black America* (pp. 124–155). Newbury Park, CA: Sage.

Breton, R. (1991). *The governance of ethnic communities: Political structures and processes in Canada*. New York: Greenwood Press.

Butler, S. (1978). *Conspiracy of silence*. San Francisco: New Glide Publications.

Cahill, M. (1991). Community youth programs—Bridging gaps in personal, cultural, and public identity. Paper presented at the Ethnicity, Race and Gender in Youth Organizations Conference, Stanford, CA.

Campbell, A. (1991). *The girls in the gang* (2nd ed.). Cambridge, MA: Basil Blackwell.

Carnegie Council on Adolescent Development. (1989). *Turning points: Preparing American youth for the 21st century*. New York: Author.

Carnegie Council on Adolescent Development. (1992). *A matter of time: Risk and opportunity in the nonschool hours*. Report of the Task Force on Youth Development and Community Programs. New York: Carnegie Corporation of New York.

CBS News. (1992, August 6). *Street stories: Family secret*. Television program transcript. New York.

Checkoway, B., & Finn, J. (1992). *Young people as community builders*. Ann Arbor: Center for the Study of Youth Policy, School of Social Work, The University of Michigan.

Children Now (1993). *California: The state of our children*. Oakland, CA: Author.

The children of the shadows: Shaping young lives. (1993, April 6, 8, 11, 13, 15, 18, 20, 22, 25). Ten-part series. *The New York Times*, Section A.

Children's Defense Fund. (1990). *Children 1990*. Washington, DC: Author.

Children's Defense Fund. (1990). *The nation's investment in children*. Washington, DC: Author.

Cole, M., & Nicolopoulou, A. (1991). *Creating sustainable new forms of educational activity in afterschool settings*. Chicago: Spencer Foundation.

Coleman, J. S. (1990). *Foundations of social theory*. Cambridge, MA: Belknap Press.

Connell, J. P., & Wellborn, J. G. (1991). Competence, autonomy and relatedness: A motivational analysis of self-system processes. In M. Gunnar & L. A. Stroufe (Eds.), *Self processes and development: The Minnesota Symposia on Child Development* (Vol. 11, pp. 43–77). Hillsdale, NJ: Erlbaum.

Cooper, C. R. (Forthcoming). Cultural perspectives on continuity and change across the contexts of adolescents' relationships. In R. Montemary, G. R. Adams, & T. P. Gullotta (Eds.), *Personal relationships during adolescence* (Vol. 6). Newbury Park, CA: Sage.

Crewdson, J. (1988). *By silence abused*. New York: HarperCollins.

Csikszentmihalyi, M., & Larson, R. (1984). *Being adolescent: Conflict and growth in the teenage years*. New York: Basic Books.

Cummings, S., & Monti, D. J. (1993). *Gangs: The origins and impact of contemporary youth gangs in the United States*. Albany: State University of New York Press.

Dryfoos, J. (1990). *Adolescents at risk: Prevalence and Prevention*. New York: Oxford University Press.

Duranti, A., & Goodwin, C. (Eds.). (1992). *Rethinking context: Language as an interactive phenomenon*. Cambridge, England: Cambridge University Press.

Early, G. (Ed.). (1993). *Lure and loathing: Essays on race, identity, and the ambivalence of assimilation*. New York: Penguin Press.

Eckert, P. (1989). *Jocks and burnouts: Social categories and identity in the high school*. New York: Teachers College Press.

Edelman, M. W. (1987). *Families in peril: An agenda for social change*. Cambridge, MA: Harvard University Press.

Edleman, P., & Ladner, J. (Eds.). (1991). *Adolescence and poverty: Challenge for the 1990s*. Washington, DC: Center for National Policy Press.

Education and Human Services Consortium. (Multiple dates). *Series on collaboration*. Washington, DC: W. T. Grant Foundation.

Erickson, J. B. (1991). *1992–1993 Directory of American youth organizations: A guide to 500 clubs, groups, troops, teams, societies, lodges, and more for young people* (4th ed.). Minneapolis, MN: Free Spirit.

Feldman, S. S., & Elliott, G. R. (Eds.). (1990). *At the threshold: The developing adolescent*. Cambridge, MA: Harvard University Press.

Ferguson, R. F. (1990). *The case for community-based programs that inform and motivate black male youth*. Washington, DC: Urban Institute.

Ferguson, R. F. (1992). *Research on employment, schooling and community based initiatives, with an emphasis on young black males*. New York: Rockefeller Foundation.

Ferguson, R. F., & Jackson, M. S. (1992). *Black male youth and drugs: How racial prejudice, parents and peers affect vulnerability* (Working Paper No. H-92-9). Cambridge, MA: Malcolm Wiener Center for Social Policy, John F. Kennedy School of Government, Harvard University.

Freedman, M. (1993). *The kindness of strangers: Adult mentors, urban youth, and the new voluntarism*. San Francisco: Jossey-Bass.

Furano, K., Roal, P. A., Styles, M. B., & Branch, A. Y. (1993). *Big brothers/big sisters: A study of program practices*. Philadelphia, PA: Public/Private Ventures.

Galaskiewicz, J. (1985). *Social organization of an urban grants economy*. New York: Academic Press.

Gans, H. (1962). *The urban villagers: Group and class in the life of Italian-Americans*. New York: Free Press.

Garlington, J. A. (1991). *Helping dreams survive: The story of a project involving African-American families in the education of their children.* Washington, DC: National Committee for Citizens in Education.

Goffman, E. (1974). *Frame analysis: An essay on the organization of experience.* New York: HarperCollins.

Goodwin, C., & Duranti, A. (1992). Rethinking context: An introduction. In A. Duranti & C. Goodwin (Eds.), *Rethinking context: Language as an interactive phenomenon* (Vol. 11, pp. 1–42). Cambridge, England: Cambridge University Press.

Gross, J. (1992, March 29). Collapse of inner-city families creates America's new orphans: Death, drugs and jail leave voids in childhood. *The New York Times,* Section A, pp. 1, 15.

Grubb, W. N., & Lazerson, M. (1982). *Broken promises: How Americans fail their children.* New York: Basic Books.

Gusfield, J. R. (1981). *The culture of public problems: Drinking-driving and the symbolic order.* Chicago: University of Chicago Press.

Hacker, A. (1992). *Two nations: Black and white, separate, hostile, unequal.* New York: Ballantine Books.

Hagedorn, J. (1988). *People and folks: Gangs, crime and the underclass in a rustbelt city.* Chicago: Lake View.

Hagedorn, J. M. (1991). Gangs, neighborhoods, and public policy. *Social Problems, 38*(4), 529–542.

Hagedorn, J. M. (1992). *Homeboys, dope fiends, legits, and new jacks.* Milwaukee: Urban Research Center, University of Wisconsin.

Halpern, R. (1991). *The role of after-school programs in the lives of inner-city children: A study of the urban youth network after-school program* (Discussion Paper 044). Chicago: Chapin Hall Center for Children, University of Chicago.

Hamburg, D. A. (1992). *Today's children: Creating a future for a generation in crisis.* New York: Times Books, Random House.

Harrington, M. (1981). *The other America: Poverty in the United States.* New York: Viking Penguin.

Harrington, M. (1984). *The new American poverty.* New York: Holt, Rinehart & Winston.

Hausman, A. J., & Prothrow-Stith, D. (1992). Patterns of teen exposure to a community-based violence prevention project. *Journal of Adolescent Health, 13*(8), 668.

Heath, S. B., & McLaughlin, M. W. (Eds.). (1993). *Identity and inner-city youth: Beyond ethnicity and gender.* New York: Teachers College Press.

Hechinger, F. M. (1992). *Fateful choices: Healthy youth for the 21st century.* New York: Carnegie Council on Adolescent Development.

Hechter, M. (1987). *Principles of group solidarity.* Berkeley: University of California Press.

Hewlett, S. A. (1991). *When the bough breaks.* New York: Basic Books.

Higgins, C. (1988). *Youth motivation: At-risk youth talk to program planners.* Philadelphia, PA: Public/Private Ventures.

Hodgkinson, H. L. (1991). *Beyond the schools: How schools and communities must collaborate to solve the problems facing America's youth.* Arlington, VA: American Association of School Administrators National School Boards Association.

Huff, C. R. (1989). Youth gangs and public policy. *Crime and Delinquency, 35*(4), 524–537.

Huff, C. R. (1990). *Gangs in America.* Newbury Park, CA: Sage.

Ianni, F.A.J. (1989). *The search for structure.* New York: Free Press.

Institute for Education Transformation. (1992). *Voices from inside: A report on schooling from inside the classroom.* Claremont, CA: Claremont Graduate School.

Israel, B. (1988). *Grown-up fast.* New York: Poseidon Press.

Jackson, J. S. (Ed.). (1991). *Life in black America.* Newbury Park, CA: Sage.

James, F. J. (1988). Persistent urban poverty and the underclass: A perspective based on the Hispanic experience. Paper presented at the Conference on Persistent Poverty, Trinity University, San Antonio, TX.

Jankowski, M. (1991). *Islands in the street.* Berkeley: University of California Press.

Jencks, C., & Peterson, P. E. (Eds.). (1991). *The urban underclass.* Washington, DC: The Brookings Institution.

Johnson, C. M., Sum, A. M., & Weill, J. D. (1992). *Vanishing dreams: The economic plight of America's young families.* Washington, DC: Children's Defense Fund.

Jones, A. N. (1993). The female warrior: Are girls getting meaner? *YO! Youth Outlook, 1,* 2.

Kane, T. J. (1987). Giving back control: Long-term poverty and motivation. *Social Service Review, 61*(3), 405–419.

Katz, M. B. (1989). *The undeserving poor.* New York: Pantheon Books.

Kotlowitz, A. (1991). *There are no children here.* New York: Doubleday.

Kozol, J. (1991). *Savage inequalities: Children in America's schools.* New York: Crown.

Lacy, G. L. (1992). *Community-based organizations responding to the needs of African American and Latino youth.* Washington, DC: William T. Grant Foundation Commission on Youth and America's Future.

Lasley, J. R. (1992). Age, social context, and street gang membership: Are "youth" gangs becoming "adult" gangs. *Youth and Society, 23*(4), 434–451.

Lefkowitz, B. (1987). *Tough change.* New York: Doubleday.

Lemann, N. (1991). *The promised land.* New York: Knopf.

Littell, J., & Wynn, J. (1989). *The availability and use of community resources for young adolescents in an inner-city and a suburban community.* Chicago: Chapin Hall Center for Children, University of Chicago.

Littwin, S. (1986). *The postponed generation: Why American youth are growing up later.* New York: Morrow.

Lynn, L. E., Jr., & McGeary, M.G.H. (Eds.). (1990). *Inner-city poverty in the United States.* Washington, DC: National Academy Press.

MacLeod, J. (1987). *Ain't no makin' it.* Boulder, CO: Westview Press.

McLoyd, V. C. (1990). The impact of economic hardship on black families and children: Psychological distress, parenting, and socioemotional development. *Child Development, 61,* 311–346.

Medrich, E. (1991). *Young adolescents and discretionary time use: The nature of life outside school.* New York: Carnegie Council on Adolescent Development.

Milburn, N. G., & Bowman, P. J. (1991). Neighborhood life. In J. S. Jackson (Ed.), *Life in black America* (pp. 31–45). Newbury Park, CA: Sage.

Minow, M. (1990). *Making all the difference: Inclusion, exclusion, and American law.* Ithaca, NY: Cornell University Press.

MEE Productions (1992). *The MEE report: Reaching the hip-hop generation.* Philadelphia, PA: Robert Wood Johnson Foundation.

Moore, J. (1978). *Homeboys: Gangs, drugs and prison in the barrios of Los Angeles.* Philadelphia, PA: Temple University Press.

Moore, J. (1985). Isolation and stigmatization in the development of an underclass: The case of Chicano gangs in East Los Angeles. *Social Problems, 33*(1), 1–12.

Moore, J. (1988). *An assessment of Hispanic poverty: Is there an Hispanic underclass?* San Antonio, TX: Tomas Rivera Center, Trinity University.

Moore, J. (1991). *Going down to the barrio: Homeboys and homegirls in change.* Philadelphia, PA: Temple University Press.

Morris, S. W. & Company. (1992). *What young adolescents want and need from out-of-school programs.* New York: Carnegie Council on Adolescent Development.

Murray, C. A. (1984). *Losing ground: American social policy 1950–1980.* New York: Basic Books.

Murray, C. A., Bourque, B. B., & Mileff, S. J. (1981). *The national evaluation of the cities in schools program* (Vol. 4). (Final Report). Washington, DC: National Institute of Education, U.S. Department of Education.

Nelson, C., & Tienda, M. (1989). The structuring of Hispanic ethnicity: historical and contemporary perspectives. In R. D. Alba (Ed.), *Ethnicity and race in the U.S.A.* (pp. 49–74). New York: Routledge & Kegan Paul.

Nicholson, H. J. (1987). Operation SMART: From research to program—and back. *International Conference of Girls and Technology.* (ERIC No. ED 302 403)

Noddings, N. (1993). For all its children. *Education Theory, 43*(1), 15–22.

Novak, M. (1980). Pluralism in humanistic perspective. *Concepts of ethnicity* (pp. 27–56). Cambridge, MA: Belknap Press.

O'Brien, R., Pittman, K., & Cahill, M. (1992). *Building supportive communities for youth: Local approaches to enhancing youth development.* New York: Carnegie Council on Adolescent Development.

Packard Foundation. (1992). *The future of children: School linked services, 2*(1). Los Altos, CA: Center for the Future of Children, The David and Lucile Packard Foundation.

Padilla, F. (1992). *The gang as an American enterprise.* New Brunswick, NJ: Rutgers University Press.

Pittman, K. J. (1991). A framework for defining and promoting youth participation. *Future Choices, 3*(2), 85–91.

Pittman, K. J. (1991). A new vision: Promoting youth development. *Testimony Before the House Select Committee on Children, Youth and Families.* Washington, DC: Academy for Educational Development.

Pittman, K. J. (1992). *Defining the fourth R: Promoting youth development through building relationships.* Washington, DC: Academy for Educational Development.

Pittman, K. J., with Wright, M. (1991). *A rationale for enhancing the role of the non-school voluntary sector in youth development.* New York: Carnegie Council on Adolescent Development.

Price, R. (1992). *Clockers.* Boston: Houghton Mifflin.

Price, R. H., Cioci, M., Penner, W., & Trautlein, B. (1990). *School and community support programs that enhance adolescent health and education.* New York: Carnegie Council on Adolescent Development.

Prowthrow-Stith, D., & Weissman, M. (1991). *Deadly consequences: How violence is destroying our teenage population and a plan to begin solving the problem.* New York: HarperCollins.

Rankin, J. (1992, September/October). Youth employment: Why P/PV's STEP didn't work baffles researchers. *Youth Today,* pp. 6–8.

Rogoff, B., & Lave, J. (Eds.). (1984). *Everyday cognition: Its development in social context.* Cambridge, MA: Harvard University Press.

Rose, M. (1989). *Lives on the boundary: The struggles and achievements of America's underprepared.* New York: Free Press.

Rosenbaum, J. E. (1992). *Youth apprenticeship in America: Guidelines for building an effective system.* Washington, DC: William T. Grant Foundation Commission on Youth and America's Future.

Roth, J., & Hendrickson, J. M. (1991). Schools and youth organizations. *Phi Delta Kappan, 72*(8), 619–622.

Sampson, R. J. (1991). Linking the micro and macrolevel dimensions of community social organization. *Social Forces, 70,* 43–64.

Sampson, R. J. (1992). Family management and child development: Insights from social disorganization theory. In J. McCord (Ed.), *Facts, frame-*

works, and forecasts (Vol. 3, pp. 63–93.). New Brunswick, NJ: Transaction Books.

Sander, J. (1991). *Before their time: Four generations of teenage mothers.* New York: Harcourt Brace Jovanovich.

Schoem, D. (Eds.). (1991). *Inside separate worlds.* Ann Arbor: The University of Michigan Press.

Schorr, L. (1988). *Within our reach.* New York: Doubleday.

Schwartz, G. (1987). *Beyond conformity or rebellion.* Chicago: University of Chicago Press.

Seidman, E. (1991). Growing up the hard way: Pathways of urban adolescents. *American Journal of Community Psychology, 19*(2), 173–201.

Sherraden, M. (1992). *Community-based youth services in international perspective.* New York: Carnegie Council on Adolescent Development and William T. Grant Foundation Commission on Youth and America's Future.

Simons, J. M., Finlay, B., & Yang, A. (1992). *The adolescent and young adult fact book.* Washington, DC: Children's Defense Fund.

Small, S. A. (1990). *Preventive programs that support families with adolescents.* New York: Carnegie Council on Adolescent Development.

Sorin, G. (1990). *The nurturing neighborhood.* New York: New York University Press.

Spergel, I. A. (1986). The violent gang problem in Chicago: A local community approach. *Social Service Review, 60*(1), 94–131.

Spergel, I. A. (1992). Youth gangs: An essay review. *Social Service Review, 66*(1), 121–140.

Stern, L. (1992). *Funding patterns of nonprofit organizations that provide youth development services: An exploratory study.* New York: Carnegie Council on Adolescent Development.

Styles, M. B., & Morrow, K. V. (1992). *Understanding how youth and elders form relationships: A study of four linking lifetimes programs.* Philadelphia, PA: Public/Private Ventures.

Sullivan, M. L. (1989). *Getting paid: Youth crime and work in the inner city.* Ithaca, NY: Cornell University Press.

Sullivan, M. (1992). *The politics of social policy.* New York: Harvester Wheatsheaf.

Taylor, C. (1990). *Dangerous society.* East Lansing, MI: Michigan State University Press.

Terkel, S. (1992). *Race: How blacks and whites think and feel about the American obsession.* New York: New Press.

Thrasher, F. M. (1926). *The gang.* Chicago: University of Chicago Press.

Titmuss, R. M. (1971). *The gift relationship.* New York: Pantheon Books.

Torriero, E. A. (1993, May 17). Ex-cons turn teens away from gang life. *San Jose Mercury News,* pp. 1, 12.

Trolander, J. (1987). *Professionalization and social change: From the settlement house movement to neighborhood centers, 1886 to the present.* New York: Columbia University Press.

Turner, J. C. (1987). *Rediscovering the social group: A self-categorization theory.* New York: Basil Blackwell.

Videka-Sherman, L. (1992). New-style settlement houses. *Rockefeller Institute Bulletin,* pp. 41–44.

Vigil, J. D. (1988). *Barrio gangs: Street life and identity in Southern California.* Austin: University of Texas Press.

Vigil, J. D. (1993). Gangs, social control, and ethnicity: Ways to redirect. In S. B. Heath & M. W. McLaughlin (Eds.), *Identity and inner-city youth: Beyond ethnicity and gender* (pp. 94–119). New York: Teachers College Press.

Wacquant, L.J.D., & Wilson, J. W. (1991). The cost of racial and class exclusion in the inner city. In N. R. Yetman (Ed.), *Majority and minority: The dynamics of race and ethnicity in American life* (pp. 498–511). Boston: Allyn and Bacon.

Watson, B., & Jaffe, N. (1990). *The practitioner's view: New challenges in serving high-risk youth.* Philadelphia, PA: Public/Private Ventures.

Weber, N. (1992). *Independent youth development organizations: An exploratory study.* New York: Carnegie Council on Adolescent Development.

Weir, M., Orloff, A. S., & Skocpol, T. (Eds.). (1988). *The politics of social policy in the United States.* Princeton, NJ: Princeton University Press.

West, C. (1993). *Race matters.* Boston: Beacon Press.

Williams, T., & Kornblum, W. (1985). *Growing up poor.* Lexington, MA: D. C. Heath.

Wilson, W. J. (1987). *The truly disadvantaged: The inner city, the underclass, and public policy.* Chicago: University of Chicago Press.

Wistow, G. (1982). Collaboration between health and local authorities: Why is it necessary? *Social policy and administration, 16*(1), 44–62.

Yetman, N. R. (Eds.). (1991). *Majority and minority: The dynamics of race and ethnicity in American life* (5th ed.). Boston: Allyn and Bacon.

Zill, N., Sigal, H., & Brim, O. G. (1984). Development of childhood social indicators. In E. F. Zigler, S. L. Kagan, & E. Klugman (Eds.), *Children, families, and government: Perspectives on American social policy.* Cambridge, England: Cambridge University Press.

Zinsmeister, K. (1990). Growing up scared. *Atlantic Monthly, 265* (6), 49–66.

Index